Praise for Paul Cartledge and

THERMOPYLAE

"[Cartledge] has an easy, vivid style, a cool mastery of facts and theories, and a commonsensical imperviousness to flimflam of any sort."
—*The New Republic*

"Cartledge brings [the Spartans] to life again with verve and [style]."
—*Milwaukee Journal Sentinel*

"Our leading historian of Sparta, Cartledge is second to none in the ability to subject myth to the cold light of scholarship. He offers a lucid overview of the Greco-Persian relations at the start of the war, an elegant description of Sparta in a nutshell, and a prudent introduction to the work of Herodotus. There is also a witty and erudite tour of Thermopylae allusions through the ages." —*The New Criterion*

"What Cartledge does so well is explain the ancient world of Greeks and Persians." —*The Seattle Times/Post Intelligencer*

"A masterful account. . . . A class in Western Civilization that instructs and entertains. . . . Cartledge emerges as an eloquent apologist of the Spartan way." —*Kirkus Reviews* (starred)

"Paul Cartledge has done more than anyone to explore what Spartan society was really like and to comprehend its ideas and rituals. . . . [He] tells his story well—he is never afraid to leave scholarly analysis for good straightforward narrative—and there is much to enjoy in his account." —*History Today* (UK)

"Engaging, extensively researched, and eminently accessible."
—*Library Journal*

PAUL CARTLEDGE
THERMOPYLAE

Paul Cartledge, professor of Greek History at the University of Cambridge, is the author of *Alexander the Great*, *The Spartans*, and *The Greeks: Crucible of Civilization*.

PAUL CARTLEDGE

THERMOPYLAE

THE BATTLE THAT CHANGED THE WORLD

VINTAGE BOOKS

A DIVISION OF RANDOM HOUSE, INC.

NEW YORK

To the Assistant Staff of
The Faculty of Classics in the
University of Cambridge
and to the memory of
Behnaz Nazhand
(d. 7 July 2005)

FIRST VINTAGE BOOKS EDITION, NOVEMBER 2007

Copyright © 2006 by Paul Cartledge

Library of Congress Cataloging-in-Publication Data

Cartledge, Paul.
Thermopylae : the battle that changed the world / by Paul Cartledge.
p.   cm.
Includes bibliographical references and index.
ISBN 978-1-4000-7918-6
1. Thermopylae, Battle of, Greece, 480 B.C.   2. Greece—History—Persian Wars,
500–449 B.C.   3. Thermopylae (Greece)—History, Military.   I. Title.
DF225.5.C37   2007
938'.03—dc22   2007024272

Author photograph © Hans Herewith
Maps by ML Design

www.vintagebooks.com

Printed in the United States of America
10   9   8   7   6   5   4   3   2   1

Contents

Contents

Preface

> This is the setting-forth of the research [historiê] of Herodotus of
> Halicarnassus, done so that the achievements of men may not be
> lost to memory over time, and that the great and wondrous deeds
> of both Greeks and barbarians [non-Greeks] may not lack their
> due glory; and especially to show what was the cause why the
> two peoples fought against one another.
>
> Herodotus *Histories* 1.1

SHORTLY AFTER finishing my last book – on Alexander III 'the
Great' King of Macedon (and a great deal more besides) between
336 and 323 BC(E) – I paid a visit to Thermopylae in preparation for
writing this one. From plotting the world-changing course of Alexander
the Great over most of the known world to charting the history-
changing defence of a narrow pass by a Few. The task was similar in
many ways – the weighing of evidence, the estimation of consequence
and implication, the judgement of value – but here the subject, though
comparably massive, is concentrated in one act carried out in a little
space: a suicidally defining stand for 'freedom'.

The 'Hot Gates' – that is what 'Thermopylae' means in ancient
Greek – are a narrow pass in north-central mainland Greece. The
'gates' bit referred to the fact that this was the natural and obvious
route for any invading army coming from the north to defeat the forces
of central or southern Greece. They were called 'hot' because of the
presence nearby of natural healing sulphur springs still there today.
Here it was that in August 480 BCE an ancient Greek 'Few', represent-

ing a small and wavering grouping of Greek cities, made their heroic stand against the oncoming might of a massive Persian invasionary force. They were headed by an elite force from Sparta, the single most powerful Greek polis, or citizen-state.

It is disconcerting to find that today the 'National Road' linking Athens with Greece's second city, Thessaloniki in Macedonia, carves its way slap bang through this deeply historic site. Imaginative reconstruction of the ancient scene is not much helped, either, by the occurrence of key changes in the geomorphology of the region. Since the fifth century BCE there have been at least two major earthquakes, and besides those the River Spercheius has laid down alluvial deposits that have caused the sea to recede some five kilometres to the north. So that what was once a narrow (20–30 metres wide) mountain defile with the sea roaring close by on one side has become a road through a fairly broad coastal plateau, with the sound of the sea but a distantly gentle murmur (when, that is, the roar of the trucks and other motor traffic hurtling by does not drown it out).

The modern memorials to Leonidas and the other Greeks killed here in desperate battle in 480 BCE were first erected beside the National Road in the mid-1950s by the Greek government with the aid of American money. This was not all that long after a devastating civil war (1946–9) had left at least half a million Greeks dead. This intestine conflict in its turn had followed hotly on a period of deeply unpleasant foreign occupation by the Axis powers of first Italy and then Nazi Germany (1941–4), notwithstanding the heroic Greek resistance in late 1940 that prompted comparison precisely with their ancestors' derring-do of 480 BCE.

Clearly, the soothing balm of a memorial to men who had famously given their lives resisting a foreign invasion and an attempted conquest was then sorely needed. The monuments, which have been added to since the mid-1950s, are indeed still suitably powerful and evocative. But if you cross to the other side of the National Road, the rewards for the student of 480 BCE are even greater. Close by is what has been identified – almost certainly correctly – as the low hill on which the Spartan King Leonidas and his few Spartans mounted their heroic 'last stand' against Great King Xerxes's Persians. If you search among the scrub that overlies the site, you will come upon another modern memorial, this one set flat into the ground and decorated appropriately with green Laconian stone (*Lapis lacedaemonius*) from an area south of Sparta. This memorial is poetic in a literal as well as a metaphorical sense: inscribed upon it is a copy of the two-line epigram, an elegiac couplet, composed twenty-five centuries ago by the contemporary praise-singer Simonides son of Leoprepes from the island of Ceos. This reads, in its most usual English translation:

> Go tell the Spartans, passerby,
> That here, obedient to their laws, we lie.

Obedience and freedom, self-sacrificing suicide . . . Thermopylae is a place of witness, redolent of the Spartans' paradoxical cultural values that need explaining now as much as at the time, when Persian Great King Xerxes uncomprehendingly wondered at the report of these fearsome warriors combing their hair in preparation (though he did not know it) for a beautiful death.

In *Alexander the Great: The Hunt for a New Past* I considered the final act in one of the greatest dramas in Middle Eastern history: the conquest by Alexander of the once mighty Achaemenid Persian Empire, founded by Cyrus II, also 'the Great', in about 550. In this book I am going back a century and a half and looking at that empire when it was at or near its peak, in terms of expressible and visible power wielded from its historic centre in Iran. In 334 Alexander invaded the Asiatic Persian Empire from the European 'west', from northern Greece. In 480 Great King Xerxes of Persia invaded Europe – that is, Greece – at pretty much the same point but from the 'east'. In the very broadest historical perspective of all it is indeed the cultural 'East versus West' dimension of the conflict that obtrudes. This is as it should be. Herodotus, our first and best historian of what I shall call the Graeco-Persian Wars, saw things this way himself (see the epigraph on p. ix), and it is in his balanced footsteps that I seek very distantly to tread.

Moreover, this clash between the Spartans and other Greeks, on one side, and the Persian horde (including Greeks), on the other, was a clash between Freedom and Slavery, and was perceived as such by the Greeks both at the time and subsequently. In fact, the conflict has been plausibly described as the very axis of world history. 'The interest of the whole world's history hung trembling in the balance', so the world-historically minded nineteenth-century German theoretician Hegel powerfully put it. At stake were nothing less than early forms of monotheism, the notion of a global state, democracy and totalitarianism. The Battle of Thermopylae, in short, was a turning-point not only in the history of Classical Greece, but in all the world's history, eastern as well as western.

So we are dealing here with the earlier of the two gigantic clashes of cultures and civilizations that helped to define both the identity of Classical Greece and, as a consequence, the nature of our own cultural heritage. Scholars and other professionally interested parties still argue the toss as to whether Alexander's conquest of the Persian Empire was a Good Thing or a Bad Thing. There are fewer doubters as regards the (loyalist) Greeks' resistance to intended Persian conquest in 480–479. But even in this case there are some who say that conquest and incorporation of mainland Greece by Persia would not necessarily have been the total cultural disaster that old-fashioned 'orientalist', eurocentric historians like to pretend. We professional historians are at least all agreed that, as things appear to us looking back over the past two and a half millennia, Greece – Classical Greece – is one of the major taproots of our own Western civilization. This is not so much in the sense that there is an unbroken continuity of direct inheritance, but rather in the sense that there has been a series of conscious choices made – in the Byzantine era, in the mainly Italian Renaissance, in the age of Enlightenment and in the nineteenth-century age of imperialism

– to adopt the Classical Greeks as our 'ancestors' in key cultural respects.

However, the story I have to tell is not as uncomplicatedly black and white as the stereotypes of ideological polarization, both ancient and modern, would like to have it. Neither were the Greeks, all of them, as pure as the driven snow, nor probably were the hearts of the Persians as dastardly black as all that. 'Probably' – because, unfortunately, the Persians have not left us the same kind of reflexive, introspective, cross-culturally comparativist literature that the Greeks, famously, did. To put it in the form of an aphorism, there was no Persian Herodotus – nor, if my reading of Achaemenid Persian culture of the late sixth and early fifth centuries BCE is at all accurate, could there possibly have been one. On the other hand, there is more than enough evidence to show that the Persian Empire was far more than just a brutal oriental despotism.

There were indeed Greeks living perforce where they had been transported as a punishment for their or their ancestors' political intransigence, deep in the interior of Iran or on another, fatally alien shore – that of the Persian Gulf. But among the Persians' many thousands of subjects in their far-flung Asiatic empire were the significant number of Greeks who lived in their own long-settled communities along the Anatolian littoral, from Chalcedon in the north (on the opposite side of the Bosporus strait from Byzantium, modern Istanbul) to the shore opposite the northern coasts of Rhodes and Cyprus in the south. For the most part they were left alone, so long as they paid their imperial taxes and tribute. On the other hand, there were Greeks who, as more or less free agents perhaps, opted to serve the Persians for pay – whether as craftsmen or as mercenaries.

There were even a few ideologically pro-Persian Greeks right at the heart of the matter, admitted to the inner sanctum of the Great King's deliberations wherever he happened at any time to be based. This might be in Susa, the main administrative capital, or Persepolis (as the Greeks later called it) in the deep south-east of Iran (modern Fars), or further north in Iran at Ecbatana (Hamadan) in ancient Media; and even further north and west still, in one or other of the viceregal capitals of the provinces, or 'satrapies', into which the Empire was divided for administrative purposes – at Lydian Sardis, say, adjoining Greek Ionia, which had been brought into the Empire very early on, even before Babylon, or at Phrygian Dascyleum, close to the southern shore of the Black Sea. Many of these 'Asiatic' or 'eastern' Greeks found themselves, willingly or willy-nilly, on the Persian side during the West–East contest with which we shall be principally concerned. In fact, almost certainly more Greeks fought *for* or at any rate *with* Xerxes than *against* him in 480–479.

So far as the 'loyalist' Greeks are concerned, those few, that is, who were in a position – and who plucked up the courage to resist the Persian invasion of mainland Greece in 480, this book will concentrate most extensively on the decisive contributions made by the Spartans, on whose extraordinary society and civilization there has recently been a quite remarkable focus of academic and more popular interest. Three television series have been aired, one of them in over fifty countries on the History Channel, the other two on the United Kingdom's Channel 4; it was for one of the latter, devised and presented by Bettany Hughes, that I wrote the accompanying book, *The Spartans: An Epic History* (original edition, Pan Macmillan 2003, 2nd edn, 2004). There have been no fewer than six discussion panels at international scholarly conferences, one held in the States, others in Scotland, Italy and France; and two actually held in or near modern Sparta itself. One of these was organized by Greek scholars including, centrally, members of the Greek Archaeological Service who work there, the other jointly by the British School at Athens (which has been involved with Sparta and Laconia one way or another since 1904 and is currently seeking to establish a research centre in the city) and the local Byzantine and pre-historic/Classical superintendencies of the Greek Archaeological Service. What can there possibly be still to talk about that merits focusing all this media and other attention on ancient Sparta?

This book will seek to provide a resounding answer or set of answers to this question, paying attention not least to the theme of Sparta's promotion (or otherwise) of freedom, both at home and abroad. There is all to play for – and a great deal at stake – in any history of 'Thermopylae'. The events of '9/11' in New York City and now '7/7' in London have given this project a renewed urgency and importance within the wider framework of East–West cultural encounter. The history of Thermopylae that I am offering here, however, is one that I would have chosen to write anyway. It is simply too good a story not to retell, on a cultural theme that is too important not to revisit.

Acknowledgements

In my *Alexander* book I tried to cover all possible bases, to pay due tribute to all the many friends and colleagues, especially Greek, who had in any way contributed to my formation as a historian of Greece and the Middle East in the later fourth century. I shall not repeat those tributes here. But I must add the names of two friends. The first, Tom Holland, is not a colleague in the technical sense but a master-historian all the same, from whom I have derived much key inspiration over the past year or so, since we met at the *Alexander* launch-party in Daunt's wonderful bookshop in Marylebone High Street, London. Tom Holland's *Persian Fire*, too, has, I hope, ignited some latent sparks of inspiration in me, as well as in his many thousands of other avid readers. The other, Peter Green, is the nonpareil of ancient historians, formidable alike in his thematic range, his acuteness of judgement and his fluency of expression.

I must also repeat, with pleasure and pride, the debts I owe to my publishers on both sides of the Atlantic, Pan Macmillan and Overlook Press of New York City, in the personal shapes of George Morley, Kate Harvey and Rebecca Lewis (Macmillan) and Peter Mayer (Overlook). It is also a delight to acknowledge the expert job done on the paperback of *Alexander* by Andrew Miller of Vintage (NY), as, previously, on the paperback of my *Spartans* book. In the same hall of fame I include my agent and friend Julian Alexander, but for whom (almost) none of this would have been possible. On a more personal note, I must thank my Laconological collaboratrix and friend, the broadcaster Bettany Hughes, and Dr Janet Parker of the Open University, archaeologist, critic and classicist, who once again has proved the most ideal of ideal readers. For generous help towards understanding how a modern Iranian might view the pre-Islamic heritage of her country, I am indebted to Farah Nayeri of the Bloomberg Corporation.

I must also thank the Mayor and Council of the modern *demos* (municipality) of Sparta for bestowing on me the huge honour of honorary citizenship. It is a sobering thought that, if I were a citizen of ancient Sparta, I would still, just, be eligible for compulsory military service (not necessarily in the front line of battle, perhaps), but yet not alas old enough, quite, to be eligible for election to the Spartans' massively honorific governing body, the *Gerousia* (Senate, minimum age sixty, the twenty-eight ordinary members apart from the two kings being elected for life).

Further thanks are in order regarding the Epilogue, the original oral version of which was delivered on 6 February 2003 in the Great Hall of King's College London, as the Thirteenth [Sir Steven] Runciman Lecture. For the invitation to deliver the lecture and for the accompanying resplendent hospitality I am deeply grateful to Matti and Nicholas Egon, the very models of enlightened benefaction. For other services related to the lecture I must also thank most warmly my friends and colleagues Professor Judith Herrin, lately Director of the Centre for Hellenic Studies at King's, her successor Dr Karim Arafat and, not least, his and my former doctoral supervisor at Oxford, Professor Sir John Boardman, himself a noted expert on both Classical Greece and the Achaemenid Persian Empire. Likewise, Appendix 3 has its origins in an oral presentation: it was first delivered on 19 May 2005 at the Museum of the History of the University of Athens, which is situated in the Plaka immediately below the Acropolis. For the kind invitation to help launch on that memorable occasion the book of essays on Herodotus published under the aegis of the En Kuklôi group, I must thank the group's Director, Dr Mairi Yossi of the University of Athens.

The book is dedicated, finally, to the assistant staff of my Cambridge Faculty, the faculty administrative officer, the faculty clerk, the librarians, the computer officer, the assistant museum curator, the secretarial assistants, the faculty photographer, the assistant keeper of the photographic archive and, not least, to the memory of the latter's sister, who was murdered in the terrorist outrage in London on 7 July 2005.

Timeline

All dates are BCE unless otherwise stated; many are approximate, especially those pre-500.

700	Homer; settlement of New Troy (Ilium)
570	Birth of Cleisthenes of Athens
550	Cyrus II the Great founds Achaemenid Persian Empire
546	Cyrus conquers Croesus King of Lydia
540	Cyrus through Mazares and Harpagus incorporates Greeks of Asia into Empire
530(–522)	Reign of Cambyses
529	Death of Cyrus
525	Persian conquest of Egypt; death of Polycrates of Samos
522	Interregnum, usurpation(?) in Persia
522(–486)	Reign of Darius I of Persia
513	Scythian expedition of Darius
508	Democracy instituted at Athens

?505	Death of Cleisthenes
499(–494)	Ionian Revolt
?493	Birth of Pericles
490	Battle of Marathon; accession of Leonidas
486(–465)	Death of Darius I; accession of Xerxes of Persia, son of Darius I and Atossa (daughter of Cyrus the Great)
?484	Birth of Herodotus
481	'Hellenic League' alliance formed; oaths sworn at Isthmus of Corinth
480	Invasion of Xerxes

May – Persian troops cross Hellespont

June – Persians advance from Hellespont towards central Greece

August, third week – Greeks take up positions at Thermopylae and Artemisium

18 August – Full moon: Olympic Games celebrated; Spartans celebrate Carneia

end August – Battles of Thermopylae (death of Leonidas) and Artemisium

early September – Persians occupy central Greece (Phocis, Boeotia); Spartans and other Peloponnesians build Isthmus wall

end September – Persians sack Athenian Acropolis; Battle of Salamis (*c.* 25 Sept.); Xerxes withdraws to Asia

479	Battles of Plataea and Mycale

478/7   *winter* – Delian League formed by Athens (minus Sparta and her allies)

477   Debate in Sparta whether to continue active anti-Persian aggression: Sparta decides to withdraw officially from anti-Persian activity but Pausanias does not return from Black Sea approaches

472   Performance at Athens of Aeschylus's *Persians*

?470   Regent Pausanias, victor of Plataea, recalled from Byzantium, dies at Sparta through enforced suicide

469   Birth of Socrates

465   Murder of Xerxes, succession of Artaxerxes I

?464   Earthquake at Sparta prompts massive Helot (esp. Messenian) Revolt

462/1   Sparta appeals to Athens for aid versus Helot Revolt under terms of Hellenic League alliance (481); pro-Spartan Cimon, father of Lacedaemonius (the 'Spartan'), responds positively but Athenians dismissed by suspicious Spartans; followed at Athens by ostracism of Cimon, and democratic reforms of Ephialtes and Pericles

460(–445)   First Peloponnesian War between Athens and Sparta and their allies; Sparta wins Battle of Tanagra 458 or 457

?460   Birth of Thucydides

447(–432)   Building of the Parthenon

c. 440   Remains identified as those of Leonidas returned from Thermopylae to Sparta for reburial

440–439   Revolt of Samos from Athens; promised Spartan help does not materialize

431(–404)	Atheno-Peloponnesian War (uneasy peace 421–414)
431	Both Sparta and Athens appeal to Persia for financial aid
?425	Publication of Herodotus's *Histories*
424/3	Death of Artaxerxes I; accession of Darius II
421	Peace of Nicias
413	Sparta invades Attica, garrisons Decelea
412/11	Sparta makes formal treaty with Persia via satrap Tissaphernes, ceding sovereignty of Greeks of Asia to Persian paymaster
407	Cyrus the Younger, 16-year-old son of Darius II Great King of Persia, sent as generalissimo to western provinces of the Empire; establishes cordial relationship with Spartan commander Lysander
405	Lysander returns for second tour of duty in the Hellespont region; with massive Persian aid wins Battle of Aegospotami
405/4	Death of Darius II, succession of Artaxerxes II
404	*spring* – Unconditional surrender of Athens to Sparta; end of Athens's Aegean naval empire, beginning of Sparta's
404–403	Thirty Tyrants junta installed at Athens with support of Spartan military garrison
403	King Pausanias of Sparta oversees restoration of democracy at Athens; imposition of general amnesty (for all except the Thirty and their closest henchmen)
402	Sparta covertly supports Cyrus the Younger's failed bid to overthrow and succeed older brother Artaxerxes II

400   Sparta declares war on Persia in name of 'liberation of the Greeks' of Asia

396(–394)   King Agesilaus II of Sparta (r. *c.* 400–360) takes over anti-Persian comand, by both land and sea

395   Outbreak of Corinthian War (revolt against Spartan imperialism led by Athens, Argos, Boeotia and Corinth, financed by Persia)

394   Agesilaus recalled from Asia to Greece

388   Sparta persuades Persia to abandon Athens and finance another Spartan fleet

387   Sparta gains control of Hellespont

386   Persia and Sparta together enforce the King's Peace, also known as Peace of Antalcidas (after the chief Spartan negotiator, admiral as well as diplomat): Greeks of Asia once more – as before 480, and during 412–400 – formally tribute-paying subjects of Persian Empire

371   Sparta and allies utterly defeated at Leuctra by Thebes and its allies under Epaminondas

369   Epaminondas oversees liberation of Messenian Helots and refoundation of liberated Messene

368   Epaminondas oversees new foundation of Arcadian Megalopolis

?366   Sparta's Peloponnesian League ceases to function

359   Death of Artaxerxes II, succeeded by Artaxerxes III, then of Agesilaus II, succeeded by son Archidamus III; Philip II becomes de facto King of Macedon

352   Archidamus briefly occupies Thermopylae in vain attempt
        to keep Philip out of central Greece

346   Philip wins Third Sacred War, destroys Phocis, celebrates
        Pythian Games at Delphi

344   Artaxerxes III recovers Egypt (in revolt since 404)

338   Philip II of Macedon (r. 360–336) wins Battle of
        Chaeronea and gains control of most of mainland Greek
        world; declares at Corinth a 'crusade' against Persian
        Empire with 'panhellenic' forces and himself as supreme
        commander

336   Philip assassinated, succeeded by son (by Greek wife
        Olympias) Alexander, Alexander III, later 'the Great'

335   Alexander destroys Thebes after revolt, exploiting
        Thebes's 'medism' in Graeco-Persian Wars

334–323 Conquest of Achaemenid Persian Empire by Alexander in
        name of 'liberation of the Greeks' of Asia and revenge for
        Persian sacrilege under Xerxes, 480–479

331   Decisive defeat of Persian Great King Darius III at
        Gaugamela (northern Iraq); Alexander becomes 'King of
        Asia'

331 or 330   Decisive defeat at Megalopolis of rebellion against
        Macedon led by Spartan King Agis III – last gasp of
        Sparta as would-be independent military power

323   Death of Alexander at Babylon; contest opens for control
        of Alexander's empire by 'Successors', not finally settled
        till 281; most of old Persian Empire falls to Macedonian
        self-proclaimed 'King' Seleucus I Nicator ('Victor'), most
        of old Greece to the Antigonid house based in Macedon

Family Tree of the
Achaemenid Royal Family

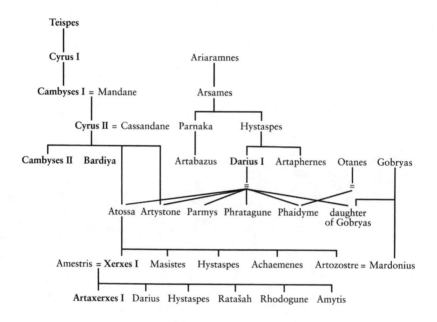

Maps

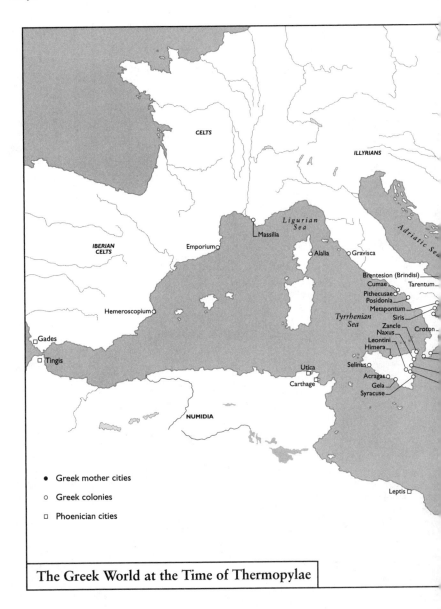

CELTS

ILLYRIANS

IBERIAN
CELTS

*Ligurian
Sea*

Massilia

Emporium

Alalia

Gravisca

Adriatic Sea

Brentesion (Brindisi)
Cumae   Tarentum
Pithecusae
Posidonia
Hemeroscopium   Metapontum
                                           Siris
                        Tyrrhenian
                            Sea   Zancle
Gades   Naxus   Croton
                                     Leontini
Tingis   Himera

                        Utica   Selinus
                    Carthage   Acragas
                                              Gela
                                           Syracuse

NUMIDIA

● Greek mother cities

○ Greek colonies

□ Phoenician cities

Leptis

The Greek World at the Time of Thermopylae

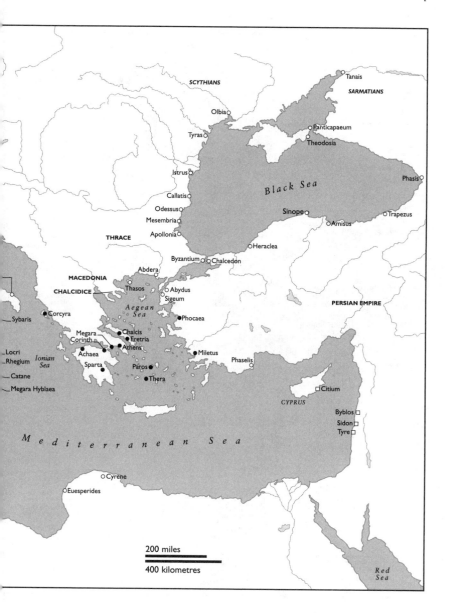

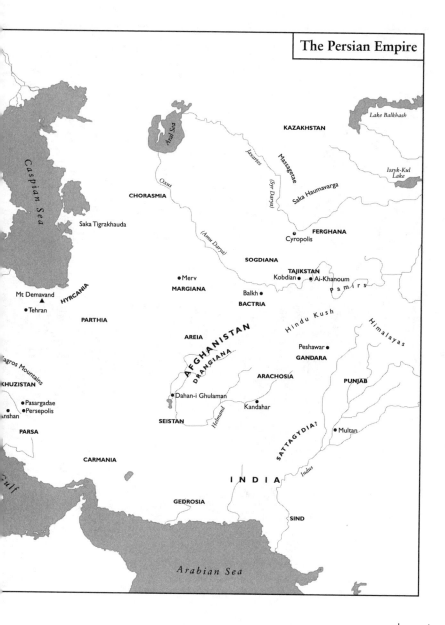

The Persian Empire

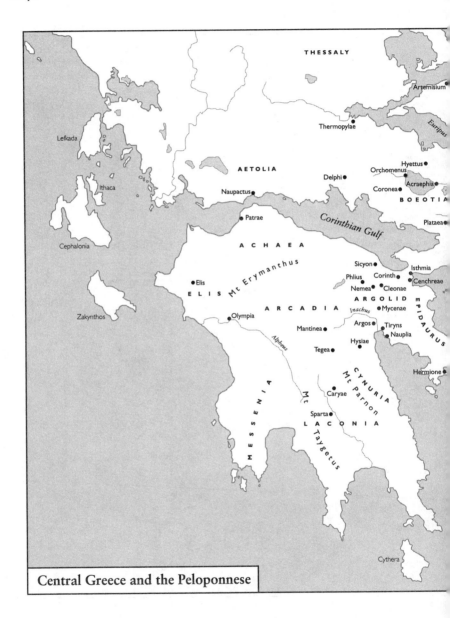

Central Greece and the Peloponnese

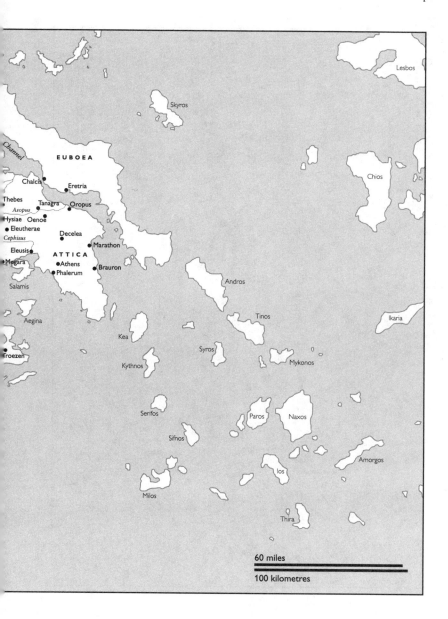

Lesbos

Skyros

EUBOEA

Chios

Chalcis

Eretria

Thebes
Tanagra Oropus
Asopus
Hysiae Oenoe
Eleutherae
Cephisus
Decelea
Eleusis Marathon
ATTICA
Megara Athens
Phalerum Brauron
Salamis

Andros

Aegina

Tinos

Ikaria

Kea

Troezen

Syros

Kythnos

Mykonos

Serifos

Paros Naxos

Sifnos

Amorgos

Ios

Milos

Thira

60 miles

100 kilometres

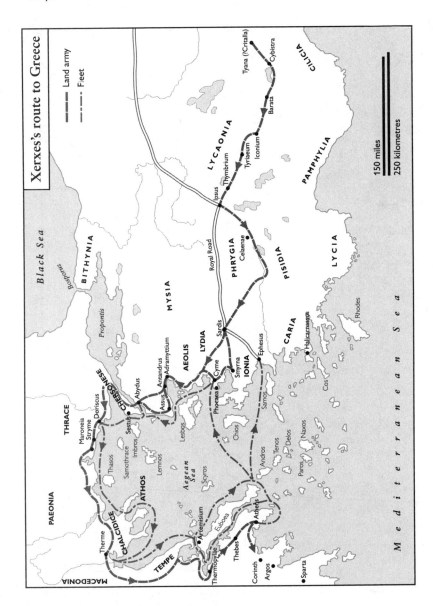

Xerxes's route to Greece

- - - - Land army
- · - · - Fleet

150 miles
250 kilometres

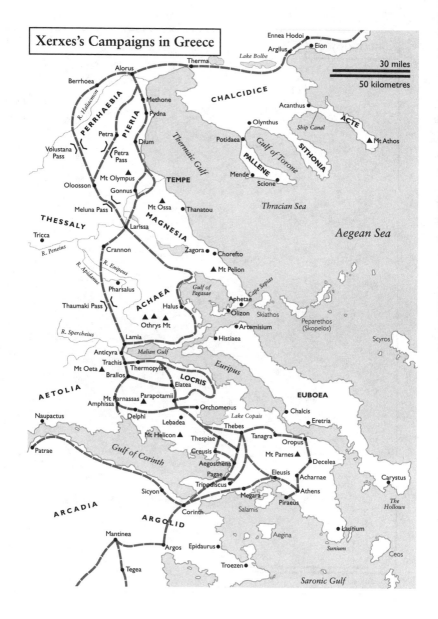

Xerxes's Campaigns in Greece

Ennea Hodoi
Argilus • Eion
Therma • Lake Bolbe

30 miles

50 kilometres

Alorus
Berrhoea

CHALCIDICE

Acanthus

ACTE

Methone
Pydna

Olynthus
Ship Canal

PERRHAEBIA
PIERIA
R. Haliacmon

Petra
Dium

Potidaea
Gulf of Torone
PALLENE
SITHONIA
Mt Athos

Voltustana
Pass
Petra
Pass

Mende
Scione

Mt Olympus
TEMPE

Oloosson
Gonnus

Mt Ossa • Thanatou

Thracian Sea

Meluna Pass
Larissa
MAGNESIA

THESSALY

Tricca
R. Peneius

Aegean Sea

Crannon
Zagora • Chorefto

R. Enipeus
R. Apidanus
Mt Pelion

Pharsalus
ACHAEA
Gulf of
Pagasae
Cape Sepias

Thaumaki Pass
Halus
Aphetae
Olizon
Skiathos

Othrys Mt
Artemisium
Peparethos
(Skopelos)

R. Spercheius
Lamia
Histiaea
Scyros

Anticyra
Malian Gulf
Trachis
Mt Oeta
Thermopylae
LOCRIS
Euripus

Brallos
Elatea

AETOLIA
Parapotamii
EUBOEA

Mt Parnassos
Orchomenus
Chalcis

Amphissa
Delphi
Lebadea
Lake Copais
Eretria

Naupactus

Mt Helicon
Thespiae
Thebes
Tanagra
Oropus

Patrae
Creusis
Mt Parnes
Decelea

Gulf of Corinth
Aegosthena
Eleusis
Acharnae
Carystus

Pagae
Tripodiscus
Eleusis
Athens

Sicyon
Megara
Piraeus
The
Hollows

ARCADIA
Corinth
Salamis

ARGOLID
Laurium

Mantinea
Aegina
Sunium
Ceos

Argos • Epidaurus

Tegea
Troezen

Saronic Gulf

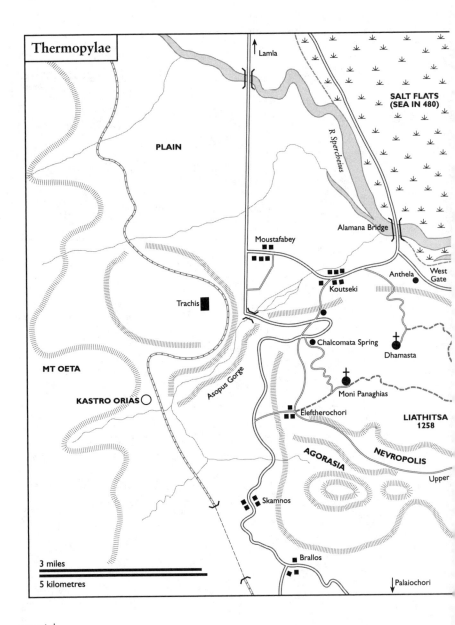

Thermopylae

↑ Lamla

PLAIN

R Spercheius

SALT FLATS (SEA IN 480)

Alamana Bridge

Moustafabey

West Gate

Koutseki

Anthela

Trachis

Chalcomata Spring

Dhamasta

MT OETA

Asopus Gorge

KASTRO ORIAS

Moni Panaghias

Eleftherochori

LIATHITSA 1258

AGORASIA

NEVROPOLIS

Upper

3 miles

5 kilometres

Skamnos

Brallos

↓ Palaiochori

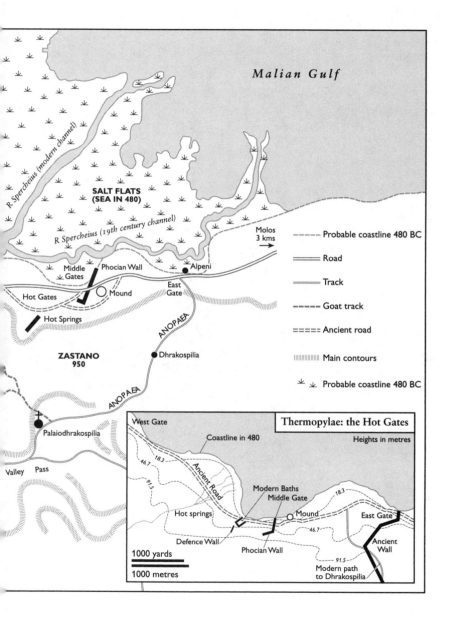

Malian Gulf

SALT FLATS
(SEA IN 480)

R Spercheius (modern channel)

R Spercheius (19th century channel)

Molos
3 kms

Middle Gates

Phocian Wall

Alpeni

Hot Gates

Mound

East Gate

Hot Springs

ANOPAEA

ZASTANO
950

Dhrakospilia

ANOPAEA

Palaiodhrakospilia

Valley   Pass

--------- Probable coastline 480 BC

========= Road

::::::::::: Track

- - - - Goat track

===== Ancient road

|||||||||| Main contours

⤬ ⤬ Probable coastline 480 BC

West Gate

Coastline in 480

Thermopylae: the Hot Gates

Heights in metres

46.7   18.3

91.5

Ancient Road

Modern Baths
Middle Gate

18.3

Hot springs

Mound

East Gate

Defence Wall

Phocian Wall

46.7

Ancient
Wall

1000 yards

91.5

1000 metres

Modern path
to Dhrakospilia

PROLOGUE

SETTING THE
AWFUL SCENE

*From Imagination to the Blank Page. A difficult crossing, the
waters dangerous. At first sight the distance seems small, yet what
a long voyage it is, and how injurious sometimes for the ships
that undertake it.*

C. P. Cavafy 'The Ships', prose poem 1895/6, trans. Edmund Keeley

EDWARD GIBBON described the process he chronicled in his Decline
and Fall of the Roman Empire (1776–88) as an 'awful revolution'.
He meant by that a radical process that changed the course of human
history in such a way and to so great a degree as to inspire awe. The
Graeco-Persian Wars of 480–479 BCE, preceded by the Battle of Marathon
in 490, occupied a much shorter timespan. Yet with the historian's
inestimable benefit of hindsight they can be seen to constitute precisely
such a shock- and awe-inspiring juncture in the affairs of mankind.

The Battle of Thermopylae was a cardinal component of those
Graeco-Persian Wars. In late August 480 BCE a smallish Greek force of
some seven thousand or so commanded by King Leonidas of Sparta
and headed by an elite force of specially picked Spartan champions
stood up to a vast imperial Persian army of invasion under the supreme
and personal command of Xerxes, Great King of Persia. The manner
of the Greeks' and especially the Spartans' (de)feat was absolutely
crucial at the time, in that it provided the relatively very few 'loyalist'
Greeks (as I shall call them) with the will and the example to continue

Mount Taygetus (summit: 2404 metres) towers over Sparta, casting it into shadow long before sunset, and dividing Laconia massively from Messenia. In the background to the right, late Byzantine Mistra (founded mid-thirteenth century) perches on a foothill of the Taygetus range.

to resist, and to go on, eventually, to throw the invaders back and out of Greece and the Aegean islands. Since then, Thermopylae has been a key ingredient in the Spartan myth, or legend. It has resonated indeed throughout the entire Western cultural tradition as a deed emblematic of the peculiar Greek and Spartan qualities of reasoned devotion to, and self-sacrifice in the name of, a higher collective cause, Freedom – or rather, a variety of definitions of Freedom.

But why, it may well be asked, in a book close to the heart of what Edgar Allan Poe called 'the Glory that was Greece', do we have to have a focus on war? There are two main reasons. War was and is the ultimately awful negative experience, humans killing other humans, often for the least altruistically admirable reasons and with the most atrocious brutality. The Greeks practised it with single-mindedness and gusto, to such an extent that it became a defining quality of their culture as a whole. To overlook the role of war in ancient Greece would therefore be to commit the historiographical sin of whitewashing the past. On the other hand, war also is or can be uniquely ennobling – giving expression to patriotic and comradely solidarity, including selfless self-sacrifice in such obviously 'good' causes as freedom, democracy and other lofty ideals. The Greeks were second to none in embracing that contradictory combination of the ghastly and the ennobling, which takes us straight back to the fount and origin of Western culture and 'civilization' – to Homer's *Iliad*, the first masterpiece of all Western literature; to Aeschylus's *Persians*, the first surviving masterpiece of Western drama; to the coruscating war epigrams of Simonides and, last but most relevantly of all, to Herodotus's *Histories*, the first masterpiece of Western historiography.

One of the most appalling of human creations, war has given rise to some of humanity's most sublime and influential literary creations. And not only literary: also to stunningly soaring visual monuments. Go to Delphi today – even the skeletal, ruined Delphi we perforce see, despite the best efforts of French and Greek excavators and conservators – and you will gain enough of an idea of the once astonishing superabundance of memorial building and sculpture. More precisely, of *war* memorial sculptures and buildings, structures such as the Treasury of the Athenians set at a visually striking angle of the Sacred Way. Or go to the Athenian Acropolis, and consider only the Parthenon: this uniquely beautiful and powerful temple was built in part *from* war booty and from the surplus of tribute from an Athenian-dominated anti-Persian military alliance, and it was built essentially *as* a war memorial. Truly, as Sophocles's Chorus put it in his tragic drama *Antigone*, 'awesome are the works of man' – for both good and evil. Or, as the Theban praisesinger Pindar, a contemporary of the Graeco-Persian Wars, sagely put it, 'War is sweet to those who have no experience of it. But the experienced man trembles exceedingly in his heart at its approach.'[1]

We in the Western world of the twentieth and twenty-first centuries, the centuries of total war, of the Flanders killing fields, of Stalingrad and Hiroshima, are surely well placed to appreciate this cardinal feature of ancient Greek culture, and in particular of fifth-century Spartan culture. Yet in another sense most of us are not in fact well placed at all. The summer of 2005, as I write, marks the sixtieth anniversary of the end of the Second World War, but that intervening period of three score years is one characterized by the total absence of a major international military conflict in either Europe or North America. Of course, there have been any number of serious wars: the Cold War, the Korean and Vietnam Wars, the Gulf War, the Iraq War, and the vicious civil wars in Bosnia and in Chechnya and in Rwanda, not to mention paramilitary terrorist atrocities in New York, Madrid, London, Omagh and elsewhere. But Americans and Western Europeans born in the years immediately after the Second World War have never – thank heavens – actually had to take up arms against a sea of foreign enemies and kill a fellow human being in the name of some patriotic or ideological cause. The President of the USA is also Commander-in-Chief of the US armed forces, but William Jefferson Clinton, notoriously, had not even undergone national service, let alone fought in the front line. It is said that during the US 'peacekeeping' operation in Somalia he was particularly shocked by the sight of the corpse of a US Ranger sergeant being dragged through the streets by a chanting mob. Listeners to Homer's *Iliad* in fifth-century BCE Sparta or Athens would presumably have felt quite differently, inured as they were to (all too) many similar sights, in ways that we just cannot begin to imagine, let alone empathize with.

Not, let me be clear, that the ancient Greeks thought war was in itself without qualification a Good Thing. On the contrary. Eirene, the goddess representing Peace, was a part of their common Greek mythology – a senior member of the pantheon from as early as the Boeotian poet Hesiod's authoritative verse genealogy of all the salient gods and goddesses, the *Theogony* (about 700 BCE). In 421 Aristophanes staged a comic play at Athens called *Peace*, named after the goddess; and it is made quite clear in the surviving text that it is only the arms manufacturers and dealers who make an unalloyedly positive 'killing' out of war. Some fifty years later, the Athenians officially instituted a religious festival of peace and commissioned from the father of the famous sculptor Praxiteles a moving statue group of the goddess cradling in her arms the infant Ploutos (Wealth, the title of another surviving play by Aristophanes, also named after the relevant deity, first performed in the early 380s).

So the Greeks in some sense valued and earnestly desired peace. Yet, despite these utopian yearnings, the harsh reality was that war was absolutely central to the Greeks' lifestyle and world view. The sacred 'Olympic truce', for example, which was declared by the state of Elis every four years (the span of an Olympiad), was technically an 'armistice', in other words a severely practical necessity in order to enable competitors and spectators to attend the Olympic Games in safety. It was not in any sense a pacifistic manifesto. A real, non-mythical world without war, in short, was for the ancient Greeks almost literally unthinkable. On the contrary: war was found by them to be exceptionally good for thinking with.

This is the second reason why any approach to the 'Glory that was Greece' cannot avoid taking the military route. For example, war was for the Greeks a crucial way of defining what they took to be the essential, unalterable difference between men and women. The Greek word for 'courage' or 'bravery', *andreia*, meant literally 'manliness', signifying that war was exclusively the business of men, because only men are by their essential nature brave, or brave in the right way. Only they, that is, can show the sort of courage required by war, 'the teacher of violence' (or 'harsh teacher'), as it is unflinchingly called by Thucydides, the great Athenian historian and not so great general of the Athenian–Spartan War of 431–404. You might be forgiven for thinking that that conflict must surely have been the war to end all wars – but very much not so, in harsh fact.

War, too, served, by extension, to define the citizenship of a Greek city: a Spartan or Athenian citizen in the full sense was by definition a warrior, a man of war. Women, excluded a priori by their 'nature', need not apply (though they were allowed to perform certain public citizenship roles, as priestesses). One of the principal functions of the public Assembly (*Ecclesia*) of citizens in Sparta or Athens was to decide questions of foreign policy, for which the English phrase of the ancient Greek equivalent was 'matters of war and peace'. On average, Athens in the fifth and fourth centuries was at war with some other state entity, Greek or non-Greek, for three years out of every four, and was never at peace for as long as a decade consecutively. Sparta lagged not all that far behind Athens's unenviable record. And war abroad spilled over into domestic politics and politicking. Indeed, one of the most conspicuous features of civic lawcourt justice in both Sparta and Athens was the political trials of unsuccessful – or questionably successful – generals and admirals, not excluding even Spartan kings.

The other major background factor is the mighty Achaemenid Persian Empire, the fastest-growing oriental empire before Genghis Khan's Mongol juggernaut. In the space of a generation, from its foundation about 550 BCE by Cyrus II the Great, it spread out from its Iranian heartland as far west as the Aegean and east Mediterranean seaboard (including Egypt, conquered by Cyrus's son, Cambyses) and as far east as Afghanistan, Pakistan and part of central Asia (where Cyrus himself died, still campaigning, in 529). A rash of revolts occurred on the death of Cambyses (522–521), but these were quelled by a distant relative who ascended the throne as Darius I. Darius had to cope with a further bout of revolt (499–494), this time actually led by his Greek subjects in western Asia, but he eventually effected a smooth repression. However, his attempt at reprisal and reparation on the other side of the Aegean came to grief at the Battle of Marathon in the territory of Athens in 490. This stinging defeat set the stage for an attempted conquest on a far grander scale undertaken, in the event of Darius's death (486), by his son and successor Xerxes (480–479).

The Greeks of the mainland were always deeply divided, both traditionally and systematically. When Herodotus at a climactic moment of his narrative invokes a definition of Greekness, the list of unifying factors that he cites signally does *not* include political co-operation, let alone union. Predictably, therefore, they were divided on the specific issue of how, or even whether, to resist Xerxes. Nevertheless, some few Greek cities and peoples, led by Sparta and Athens, did agree to. The members of this Hellenic League (a modern term) swore a binding religious oath at the Isthmus of Corinth, probably in autumn 481, jointly to resist a Persian invasion. Unfortunately, those sworn allies did not include the Greeks of Thessaly, the first Greeks outside his empire whom Xerxes would encounter after leaving Macedonia. Their aristocratic leaders took the path of least resistance, the one that led to Susa.

In Thessalian territory lay the first conceivable line of anti-Persian defence, the vale of Tempe between Mt Ossa and Mt Olympus. Once that had been abandoned by the coalition, the next and only feasible line of defence for the Greek loyalists was the pass of Thermopylae.

Even in this dire crisis of late summer 480, Sparta did not manage to send a full muster of its adult male citizen warriors to defend the pass, but instead dispatched only a token if elite force, commanded by one of its two kings, Leonidas. Sparta's coalition allies, too, if for different reasons, held back from sending their full fighting complements. The reasons they all gave at the time were religious, and undoubtedly religion in ancient Greece was always a genuinely powerful historical factor. But we may reasonably suspect that another, more mundane and less creditable but entirely understandable, motive was more potently at work here – namely, panic fear: fear that the Persians simply were too multitudinous to be resisted, either at Thermopylae or, possibly, anywhere else. After all, the vast majority of the several hundreds of other mainland Greek cities had already voted with their feet and decided willy-nilly to join or at least not oppose the Persians rather than try to beat them back.

So there were no Athenians at Thermopylae (though there were many thousands with the fleet at Artemisium) or Megarians, and, more controversially, only a few Boeotians, including a mere four hundred from the Boeotians' principal city of Thebes. Later, after Thermopylae, all the Boeotians except Thespiae (an enemy of Thebes) and Plataea (an ally of Athens) 'medized' – took the Persian side – so that the reputation of the Thebans especially was blackened when the Persians were eventually beaten back in 479. Apart from these, there were perhaps a thousand troops each from the two local Greek peoples most directly affected, the men of Phocis and the men of Opuntian Locris.

Against them were ranged the forces of the mighty Persian Empire. At its greatest extent, this empire encompassed some three million square kilometres of territory and a whole raft of languages, nationalities, religions and cultures including of course those of the Greeks permanently settled in what are now western Turkey and Cyprus.

The news was not always all bad. Though the Persians did levy tribute in cash and in kind, this was not generally felt to be grossly burdensome. And, like the Romans, the Persians did not govern all that much, or all that directly or obviously. They were on the whole pretty tolerant rulers, especially in matters of religion. The Empire's founder Cyrus famously liberated the Jews from their Babylonian exile and restored them to their Levantine homeland. That restoration had of course pragmatic motives and implications, but it was not undertaken solely because Cyrus was concerned about the strategic and political significance of his Jewish subjects as a major potential source of dissidence and disruption. The Jews for their part were obviously right to hail their Persian saviour as 'the Lord's anointed'.

On the other hand, some of the Empire's subjects, including Greeks as we have seen, did not consider forcible membership of an alien empire to be wholly and purely a blessing, and some of those did not merely contemplate the desirable prospect of liberation from it but actively sought to achieve that freedom by military means. Freedom too, in a variety of guises, was what was chiefly at stake in the Graeco-Persian Wars of 480–479. Persian Great King Xerxes, who was present in person at the Thermopylae and Salamis battles, is reported to have been astonished by the Spartans' conduct. He was labouring under a number of cultural misapprehensions. It had to be explained to him

At the West Door on the North Wall of Xerxes's Palace at Persepolis the Great King is depicted in relief, head and shoulders taller than his two attendants, one of whom carries the parasol that Greeks thought suitable only for women.

patiently that the Spartans behaved as they did because they were fighting for an ideal dearer than mere life itself: the ideal of freedom. Freedom – the freedom to develop their unique and uniquely influential civilization – is indeed what the Spartans and the other Greek loyalists eventually secured by defeating the Persians in 480 and repulsing them the following year, after further heroic struggles by both land and sea.

After Thermopylae (a defeat) and its linked naval battle at Artemisium (a draw) the next major encounter was the naval Battle of Salamis in late September 480, in which the Greek loyalists, led – brilliantly – by the maverick Athenian politician and general Themistocles (though technically the Spartan Eurybiadas was still Admiral of the Fleet), won a smashing victory. Some modern as well as ancient critics, including Herodotus, have judged this to be *the* decisive battle of the Wars. But actually that was the land Battle of Plataea, fought in

On this Athenian red-figure vase of the second quarter of the fifth century, the Athenians' patron goddess Athena holds an aphlaston (the curved stem from a Persian warship), a trophy to commemorate and celebrate one of the several Athenian naval victories over the Persians of this period, including above all the Battle of the River Eurymedon in Pamphylia (south-west Asia Minor).

Boeotia in the summer of 479 under the overall command of Spartan regent Pausanias and won, essentially, by the magnificent Spartan hoplites. Even Plataea was not, quite, the end. But the final battle of the quartet, an amphibious engagement at Mycale on the Asiatic coast opposite the Greek island of Samos, was more the beginning of the next phase of Graeco-Persian conflict than the end of the Graeco-Persian Wars of 480–479.

Mycale pointed forward to the formation of the Athens-based Delian League (478/7) that soon became an Athenian maritime empire and to the amphibious Battle of the River Eurymedon in Pamphylia in about 466. The Spartans, by contrast, predictably proved reluctant sailors. Formally, King Leotychidas had been in overall command at Mycale as Eurybiadas had been at Salamis, but he had had to be persuaded to abandon the safety and security of the Cyclades for a continent on which no Spartan king had yet set foot (and would not, in fact, until Agesilaus did in 396). He did not take part in the pursuit of the Persians to the Hellespont, let alone in the liberation of those Greeks in Macedonia and Thrace who were still under Persian control. Indeed, in a rather surprising anticipation of the Treaty of Lausanne (CE 1923) he proposed as a solution to the problem of the Greeks of Asia a compulsory exchange of populations: transplanting them to mainland Greece to take over the land occupied by the traitorous medizers, who should be 'cleansed' and forced to go to live in Asia where they spiritually belonged.

That, then, is the background of war and empire against which I am going to look again in detail at the role in 480 BCE of the Spartans, as acknowledged leaders of 'the Greeks' in resistance to the Persian invasion under Xerxes. I shall not disguise the brutality, the perfidy, the squalor of war – any war, all wars. But I shall also, and rather more, stress the positive outcomes of these particular Graeco-Persian wars, although they are outcomes in which the Spartans themselves for the most part chose not to be active participants. Both the rapid development of the world's first system of truly participatory direct democracy and the creation of enduringly inspirational works of literary and visual art were mainly achievements of the Athenians or of men crucially inspired by the culture of democratic Athens. On the other hand, even these Athenian achievements are not without their dark shadow. The Athenians' development of a maritime empire on the basis of continued resistance to Persia brought not entirely unfounded accusations of economic exploitation and brutal imperialist repression of supposedly free allies, and the famed Athenian silver that funded the fleet and so much else in the fifth century and later was extracted by the forced labour of slaves working in unimaginably torrid and often lethal conditions.

The dark side of Sparta's full moon is perhaps even more glaringly conspicuous. The Spartans' decision to base their entire *politeia* – their political and social regime and way of life – on exploitation of a native

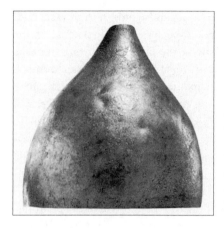

This bronze helmet of distinctive Assyrian type was worn by a Persian subject during one of the invasions of Greece, either in 490 or in 480/79; it was dedicated at Olympia as part of an official Athenian thank-offering of war-spoils with the following message inscribed upon it: 'The Athenians, to Zeus, having taken [it] from the Medes'.

Greek underclass, the Helots, must forever tarnish their halo. So obtrusive and potentially obstructive is the 'Helot issue' that some modern admirers of Sparta pretend either that the Spartans' rule over the Helots was not all that bad (if it had been, how could it have lasted for up to four centuries?) or that influential (Spartans – including two of the more prominent characters in our drama, King Leonidas and Regent Pausanias – were really all for liberating and enfranchising the Helots but unhappily were thwarted by their less farsighted and more reactionary fellow citizens). This, alas, is mere wishful thinking. Ancient admirers of Sparta, the 'laconizers' as they were called, were less squeamish and sentimental. They either celebrated the fact that economically speaking the Spartans were the freest of all the Greeks, thanks to the exploitation of the Helots, or claimed that the Spartan *politeia* was so admirable and ideally imitable that the unfreedom of the Helots was a tolerable – indeed a necessary – price to pay for it. My own considered and, I hope, balanced judgement is this: had the Spartan regime not been the way it was, warts and all, the Spartans could not have played the decisive role at Thermopylae and in other conflicts in 480–479 that they did in fact play. The Spartans thus have a paradoxically twofold or even contradictory role in the history of Western freedom both as a practice and as an idea(l).

Counterfactual 'What if?' history is of course a pleasing distraction for historians, but it can also be a highly useful way of exploring cause and effect. What if, for example, the resistance at Thermopylae either had not happened at all, or had been much less frighteningly determined and effective than, under the leadership of Leonidas and his Spartans, it actually was? What if the Persians in 480–479 had managed to absorb the Greeks of the mainland as well as those of the Aegean islands and the western Asiatic seaboard into their far-flung empire? So many questions. There is no question, however, but that, had the Persians won, Greek civilization of the ensuing Classical era would have been immeasurably different from what did in fact evolve in the fifth and fourth centuries under the impulse of self-liberation against seemingly overwhelming military odds.

Most would argue, too, that it would have been markedly inferior. For though the Persian Empire was notably pluralist and, by ancient standards, culturally tolerant, in somewhat the same manner as the Ottoman Empire in its later stages, it is doubtful in the extreme that it could or would have tolerated the Classical Greeks' patriotically inflected combination of democratic self-government and very particular and aggressive notions of freedom. That freedom in its turn was the condition of the cultural achievement that came to form the – or at least a crucial – basis of the Western cultural and political tradition, of which Sparta was and is a prime exemplar.

ONE

THE ANCIENT WORLD
IN 500 BCE: FROM INDIA
TO THE AEGEAN

In Lacedaimon are to be found those who are the most enslaved
[douloi] *and those who are the most free.*

Critias of Athens, *Spartan Society*

HERODOTUS BEGINS by placing his chosen subject of the Graeco-Persian Wars in the broadest framework of East versus West historical and (what we should call) myth-historical conflict. A major 'moment' in that chronic Greek–barbarian, West–East contest was the Trojan War sung by Homer in the *Iliad*. Like its companion epic the *Odyssey*, the *Iliad* was the culmination of a long bardic tradition of oral poetic composition and recitation stretching back to the Late Bronze Age or Mycenaean era. But if there was one Homer, that genius of a monumental poet who created the unified stories of Achilles and Odysseus, he would have lived somewhere in east Greece; that is, along the west Anatolian littoral or on one of its offshore Greek islands such as Chios, at around 700 BCE.

This was also, and not coincidentally, when Ilium or New Troy was founded on what was taken to be the site of Homer's Troy by Greeks coming out from central mainland Greece to settle permanently in north-west Asia Minor. Ilium was just one of a whole host of such new Greek foundations established during the age of Greek 'coloniza-tion' which occupied the two centuries from about 700–500.* This great movement of people was prompted by a variety of motives and factors including land hunger, political faction-fighting and sheer adventurism. By the end of it, Greeks were to be found perched (as Plato later put it) like frogs or ants around a pond – or rather two ponds, the Mediterranean and the Black Sea.

The resulting Greek world in the year 500 was not a political unit but rather a series of individual, independent, often mutually hostile political communities that mostly called themselves *poleis*, or cities. We would call them republics, though there were a number of monarchies among them too – and a unique 'dyarchy', or double kingship, Sparta. There were well over one thousand such independent units all told, scattered around much of the Mediterranean and Black Sea coasts – from, as the Greeks themselves said, the Pillars of Heracles (Straits of Gibraltar) to Phasis (in modern Georgia at the far eastern end of the Black Sea).

Most lived in Europe, extending from Byzantium (modern Istanbul) in the east to the southern coast of Spain in the far west, and taking in most of coastal Sicily and southern Italy and part of the French Riviera. There were some Greeks settled in Africa too, along the Mediterranean coasts of today's Libya and Egypt, most notably at Cyrene and at Naucratis in the Nile delta. But there were many more Greeks living in Asia than in Africa, and it was in Asia that settlement out of the Greek mainland had first begun, well before the 'colonization' movement proper. Miletus, for exam-ple, in Ionia was founded already in the eleventh century BCE, at the begin-ning of an era known to scholars as the Greek Dark Age (*c.* 1100–800). It was the Greeks of Asia and the major offshore islands (Lesbos, Chios and Samos) who first felt the lash of the Persian whip.

By 500 the Persian Empire, founded just half a century earlier, was established as the fastest-growing empire in the entire history of the

---

* The term 'colonization' is conventional, but strictly it is inaccurate, since most of these new foundations were independent settlements from the start, not colonial out-posts of a metropolitan power.

ancient East. It stretched from the Indian subcontinent to the eastern shore of the Aegean, and it encompassed the ancient territories of Egypt and Babylonia besides its Iranian heartland. The two cultures, the Greek and the Persian, overlapped, intermingled or clashed first at the western, Mediterranean margins of the Persian Empire. Some Greek cities located at the western fringe of Asia had even been forcibly incorporated into the Empire in the 540s. This situation provoked mixed reactions among the conquered Greeks themselves and among their cultural and ethnic kinspeople yet further to the west. In 499 a number of these eastern Greeks raised the flag of revolt, aided and abetted by the newly democratic city of Athens. The seeds of the Graeco-Persian Wars of 490 and 480–479 had been sown. The encounter at Thermopylae was only a matter of time.

The Graeco-Persian conflict must first be situated within its broadest geopolitical limits. The account that follows will move from East to West and look at the world through mainly Persian eyes. It begins in the Far East, with what the Greeks rather hopefully called 'India', though they meant only what is now Pakistan and Kashmir and but a relatively tiny part of the modern state of India.* The Persians were the first power with any claim whatsoever to a 'European' identity – via their membership of the 'Indo-European' language family – to establish a physical and political toehold on the subcontinent, during the reign of Darius I (about 522–486).

This tentative occupation involved passage over the Hindu Kush mountain range, what the Greeks called the Paropamisus, and passage, most easily, through the Khyber Pass. Hardly surprisingly, though, the

---

* Thanks to Alexander's conquest of 'India' in the 320s, the Greeks would gain some idea of the southward extension of the Indian subcontinent, but the mass of the subcontinent remained out of bounds to them. By the time of the great Indian Emperor Ashoka in the early third century BCE the Indians knew quite a lot about Greeks; enough, at any rate, for Ashoka explicitly to renounce the sort of empire-building for which Alexander the Great was famous – or notorious – and to embrace a new form of governance based on Buddhist principles of tolerance and compassion.

Besides Pasargadae and Persepolis, the third major palace in southern Iran was located at Susa in Elam; here in 1972 a massive headless statue of its builder, Darius I, was excavated beside his eponymous Gateway. But it had been made to be displayed in Egypt (conquered in 525 by Cyrus's son Cambyses) – hence the use of Egyptian hieroglyphic writing as well as Persian cuneiform on the statue itself, and the depiction round the base of Nilotic gods.

Persians' reach soon exceeded their grasp. The conquest of their version of 'India' proved just a brief moment within the two-hundred-year span of the Achaemenid imperial monarchy as a whole. From the Indians the Persian Empire demanded tribute, as it did from all its subjects. Herodotus tells us that India's contribution amounted to the fantastic, indeed fabulous, sum of 360 talents of gold-dust, in an era when gold was reckoned fourteen times more valuable, weight for weight, than silver.

But if the Persian Empire's Far East could be more or less willingly relinquished after Darius without threatening its integrity, that was not at all the case with the Empire's north-east frontier: the steppelands of Sogdiana, and Bactria, today's central Asia and northern Afghanistan. It was here that the Empire's great founder, Cyrus II, had met a gory end, fighting the Massagetae tribespeople of central Asia led by their fierce queen Tomyris (as the Greeks transcribed her name). And Darius's propagandistic relief sculpture at Bisitun in Media (not far from Ecbatana, modern Hamadan in northern Iran) was suitably rounded off by an image of Skunkha (who, by any other name, would presumably have smelled sweeter): he was King of the Skudra (Scythians) living east of the Caspian Sea.

Moving westwards through the Empire we come next to its Iranian heartland. In the deep south of Iran the region known as Fars preserves the speaking trace of its original Persian occupants. The Greeks gave two names to the major capital located down here. The earlier was 'Persai' - literally 'the Persians'. Later, when Iran had become part of the post-Alexander hellenized Middle East, it became Persepolis, 'City of the Persians'. This is the name that has stuck, though in its suggestion that Persepolis was a polis (citizen-state) in anything like the same sense as Athens, Thebes or Sparta it can be grossly misleading.

In Achaemenid times Persai/Persepolis functioned as, among other things, the Empire's chief ceremonial capital. It was the site of the great New Year festival and the place where tokens of imperial tribute were ceremonially borne in procession by representatives of the many sub-

At Darius's palace in Susa relief sculpture in stone was often replaced by friezes of colourful glazed brick made from sintered quartz; this (restored) example is said to have come from the north-east corner of the palace's central courtyard. The two opposed winged lions have human heads wearing the horned crown of divinity, with the royal symbol above.

ject peoples, as lavishly depicted on the walls of the Apadana, or great regal Audience Hall. It was near here too, at Naqsh-i-Rustam, that the Persians' kings were buried – or at least commemorated – in handsome rock-cut tombs. Almost as important to the Persians themselves was another capital further to the north and west in Iran – Susa in Elam, which served mainly as the principal administrative centre of government. Also important as a capital city was Ecbatana in Media. The Persian kings seem to have evolved a regular schedule of movement from one palatial capital to another depending on the time of year; upland Ecbatana, for example, was the royal residence in high summer. Apart from its sheer practicality and symbolic value, this royal nomadism may ultimately reflect the Persians' origins as transhumant pastoralists.

Next towards the West is Mesopotamia, the 'Between-the-Rivers Land' of modern Iraq, between the Tigris and the Euphrates. In 539 Cyrus secured the key citadel of Babylon on the Euphrates. This fabled city of great antiquity and of the wondrous 'hanging gardens' of Nebuchadnezzar was where another great conqueror, Alexander the Great, was to die two centuries later, and where, arguably, he intended to place the centre of his own new empire. The wealth of Babylonia was legendary, in both mineral resources and in arable crops.*

West again of Mesopotamia the Persians entered Anatolia, modern Turkey. It is very striking indeed that Cyrus should have thought to extend his empire as far as the Aegean, and therefore to embrace all Anatolia including certain Greek cities, in the 540s, before making sure of Babylonia next door. Immediately before Cyrus's reign the great power of Anatolia was the kingdom of Lydia, the inland region just to the east of Greek Ionia with its capital at heavily fortified – and heavily hellenized – Sardis. Ruled, in the mid-sixth century, by the proverbially wealthy Croesus, it was this kingdom that provided the political and cultural link between Anatolia and the Greeks of the mainland and Aegean islands.

Herodotus tells his story of Croesus's dealings with various Greeks with his usual lively aplomb. To start on the negative side of the ledger, Croesus was the first historical oriental king permanently to subjugate Greeks. At first he confined his attention to those of the Asiatic mainland (of Aeolis, Ionia and Caria, going from north to south), but he is said to have seriously contemplated adding to his domain the main adjacent Aegean islands, Lesbos, Chios and Samos, until it was pointedly borne in upon him that he was a land-based power and lacking any sort of suitable navy. On the other, positive side, the imperial rule

---

* There was plenty of scope here too for the business activities of a shrewd banking house, the Murashu of Nippur, whose instructive records have in part come down to us in decipherable cuneiform writing on baked clay tablets.

The practice of stamping gold, electrum (a natural gold-silver mix) and silver coins with distinctive decoration on front (obverse) and back (reverse) goes back to the Lydians in the early 6th century. Here in about 485 the Greeks of Cyprus, in a typical show of cultural miscegenation, have borrowed the Lydian lion for the obverse design of a silver coin and coupled it on the reverse with an octopus symbol borrowed from Greek Eretria on the island of Euboea (destroyed by the Persians in 490). The letter at below left of the reverse side is a Cypriot ka replacing Eretrian E.

of Croesus over the Greeks of Asia does not appear to have been massively burdensome. Herodotus tells a jolly moral tale of the reforming lawmaker Solon (appointed troubleshooter at Athens in 594) taking time out from his domestic business to visit Croesus in Sardis and deliver to him a homily on the true nature of happiness for a human being. The implication is that Croesus, though an absolute ruler, was no terrifyingly deadly oriental despot.

Herodotus's tale of their meeting must on chronological grounds be sheer fiction (since Solon was almost certainly dead well before Croesus came to the throne of Lydia about 560), but it is not fiction that Croesus engaged in sympathetic dealings with Greeks. Herodotus refers to his gifts to the oracle of Apollo at Delphi, and the extraordinarily well made group of chryselephantine statues (gold and ivory on a wooden core) discovered here, probably representing Leto and her two children Apollo and Artemis and done in an eastern Greek style, may well be a token or reflection of that generosity. Proof of this is still visible at Ephesus on the Ionian coast of Anatolia: here Croesus paid for elaborately beautiful architectural enhancements to the temple of Ephesian Artemis – St Paul's 'Diana of the Ephesians' – which in a later incarnation was ranked one of the Seven Wonders of the ancient world.

What of the Persians' interest in the Levant and in Africa, especially Egypt? Cyrus II's designated successor was his eldest son Cambyses. Like father, grossly unlike son. Whereas Cyrus was fêted even by his conquered subjects (the restored Jews went so far as to call him 'Messiah'), Cambyses suffered from a hostile press, both from his own Persian side and from the side of the Greeks. However, precisely, Cambyses died – it may have been by suicide or by murder – it was in unfortunate circumstances. His brief and relatively inglorious reign was followed by an interregnum, if not some sort of usurpation. But he had at least achieved one major feat: the conquest of Egypt. Greek sources tended to imagine that Cambyses was unhinged by his success, and that in his delirium he killed Apis, the Egyptians' sacred bull, at the old capital of Memphis. The sober records of the Apis priests themselves survive – and tell a different story. Cyrus's was a hard act for Cambyses to follow – as Darius's was to be for his son and successor Xerxes. But Cambyses should be given the credit for the incorporation of Egypt into the Empire, along with the Phoenicians of the Levant and Cyprus, who thereafter provided the bulk of the Empire's Mediterranean navy.

Our survey of the Persian Empire's development up to the year 500 concludes with Darius's expedition of 513 to 'the lands beyond the sea'; that is, to European Thrace beyond the Black Sea across the Bosporus strait dividing Asia from Europe. Today there is a permanent Bosporus bridge. Darius had to commission a temporary one, a pontoon bridge of many boats – likewise, the bridge whereby he crossed the Ister (Danube) later on in the same campaign. The Greeks liked to make out that this 'Scythian' campaign was a fiasco, but it presumably achieved what it set out to do. A new Persian province of European Thrace was thereafter firmly in place to guard Darius's north-west frontier, and a stepping-stone had been laid down for further European expansion in due course if and when that was felt desirable or necessary. By 500 Macedonia, on Thrace's western border, was also a Persian vassal state, and the Persians' tax-demanding writ extended to the borders of Greek Thessaly.

What of the other Greeks of the mainland? It was to them (if Herodotus is to be believed) that Croesus of Lydia's thoughts had turned in the 540s when he learned of the threatening rise of Cyrus to his east. Nor was it just these Greeks' military force that he hoped to exploit, but also the numinous power of their oracular gods. Croesus supposedly tested the alleged infallibility of a number of Greek oracular shrines. In the event, only Apollo's oracle at Delphi in central Greece, the 'navel of the universe', was able to solve his riddle. Croesus then formally consulted the Pythia, Apollo's prophetic priestess who with the aid of male priests issued measurably correct but sometimes fatally ambiguous pronouncements, on how he should react to Cyrus. The Delphic response solemnly informed him that if he crossed the River Halys, the eastern frontier of his kingdom, he would destroy a great empire. He did, and he did, but the empire he destroyed was, alas, his own, not Cyrus's. As things turned out, he was unable to derive any support at all from the mainland Greek city to which he had allied himself on the grounds that it was the most powerful military state in Greece. That state was Sparta.

Sparta in about 550, as Herodotus tells the tale, had recently undergone some sort of serious upset, but now it was flourishing both in its domestic political stability, guaranteed by the wise laws of Lycurgus, and in all its external wars. Herodotus was indeed persuaded that the Peloponnese as a whole was already 'subjugated' by Sparta. But there was one notable exception. The city of Argos never accepted Sparta's hegemony of the Peloponnese, let alone of any wider tract of Hellas. In about 545 Argos challenged Sparta to some kind of knockout test of supremacy: a battle between three hundred picked champions on either side. Sparta apparently lost initially, in so far as two Argives were left alive to Sparta's lone survivor, Othryades. But whereas the two Argives rushed off home to Argos to tell their fellow citizens the good news, Othryades did what a good Spartan hoplite (heavy-armed phalanx infantryman) had been trained from an early age to do. He remained 'in post' (*en taxei*) on the battlefield. This enabled the Spartans to claim, rather speciously, that it was they who had 'really' won the Battle of the Champions.

However much truth may, or may not, lie behind this improving parable, in gritty reality the Spartans and Argives did at about this time fight a full-scale pitched hoplite battle, and this the Spartans undoubtedly and unsurprisingly won. That demonstrated Sparta's pre-eminent military prowess sufficiently for Croesus. An eulogizing epigram on the victory, of uncertain date, captures an essential part of what we might call the Spartans' 'Thermopylae spirit': 'for Sparta, it is not dying but fleeing that is death'.*

The Spartans' writ now ran up the east coast of the Peloponnese as far north as Cynuria, also known as Thyreatis, uncomfortably close to Argos's own home territory. But notwithstanding Sparta's relative power at home, and despite Croesus's blandishments,† the Spartans honoured their pact of friendship and alliance in only a verbal and token way. On behalf of Croesus they sent as a herald, or diplomatic envoy, to Cyrus himself, a no doubt distinguished and experienced citizen called Lacrines, to warn him solemnly to keep his hands off Lydia. But Cyrus, already in Sardis, answered Lacrines contemptuously:

> Never yet have I been afraid of men who set aside a special meeting-place [agora] in the centre of their cities where they make and break oaths and cheat each other. If I have anything to do with it, it's troubles in their own backyard and not in Ionia that they will have to chatter about.[1]

The passage is remarkable for a number of reasons. Cyrus in 545 was apparently totally ignorant, not only of the Spartans' numbers (itself a very salient issue, as we shall see), but even of their very existence. Perhaps this is just a Herodotean dramatic device, but it may

---

*   *Palatine Anthology* 7.431. It would be good to know exactly when the epigram was composed, whether before or after Thermopylae.

†   For example, he made a valuable donation of gold leaf to coat a venerated and presumably wooden statue of Apollo at Thornax near Sparta (Herodotus 1.69).

also be an accurate reflection of reality – and a salutary warning against adopting too hellenocentric a perspective on Graeco-Persian affairs. Cyrus is hardly likely to have said the same, let alone said it honestly, about the Babylonians, for example.

The word *agora* in Greek could mean a political meeting-place as well as a commercial marketplace; in fact, it bore the former meaning before it acquired the latter. But Herodotus took Cyrus to be making a general reference to the existence and central importance of market exchange in the Greek world generally, since he added that the Persians have not a single such *agora* of their own anywhere. In a sense, Herodotus was technically correct about the Persians, because the royal command economy operated a centrally controlled redistributive system rather than a private-enterprise marketing system for the exchange of goods and services. But it was a very odd thing to make Cyrus say to the Spartans, of all peoples, since they were known to be the least commercially minded and oriented of all the Greeks. That, though, may have been part of Herodotus's subtle point, another way of underlining the Persian Great King's ignorance of the opponents who would, at the end of his story, play the leading role in confounding Cyrus's prediction of a Persian walkover against any Greek opposition – whether in Asia or, as he hints, in Europe.

Sparta, then, did not engage in any hostilities with Persia in the 540s – nor would it encounter the Persians directly in battle for another sixty years. Yet, despite Cyrus's rolling over of Croesus and his Asiatic Greek subjects, the Spartans felt so secure in their own backyard and so confident of their ability to throw their weight about abroad that in the last quarter of the sixth century they actually launched two naval expeditions. The former of these came as close to Asia as was possible without actually setting foot on the mainland, the furthest east that Sparta ventured militarily until the Atheno-Peloponnesian War. It was directed, in about 525, against the island of Samos and its tyrant ruler Polycrates. The antics of this piratical figure with his powerful navy had aroused the anxiety of Persia as well as of the local Samian aristo-

In the early fifth century, Persian scenes were understandably in vogue for decorating Athenian fine 'red-figure' painted pottery; on the main side of this amphora Myson has depicted a defeated King Croesus of Lydia atop his pyre (shortly to be miraculously quenched by Apollo), on the reverse Athens's founder-hero King Theseus together with his best buddy Peirithous in the act of carrying off the quintessentially oriental Amazon queen Antiope.

crats and oligarchs, whom he either suppressed or exiled. Sparta undertook this naval operation jointly with its Peloponnesian ally Corinth, a city with a longstanding naval tradition and of vital geopolitical significance, lying as it did athwart the isthmus separating the Peloponnese from central Greece.

The attempt to unseat Polycrates was a failure – it was left to the Persians and their Phoenician naval forces to finish that job off properly and keep their Aegean frontier secure. Nevertheless, in about 512, Sparta again sent out a naval expedition, but this time against a much nearer Greek power, Athens. At stake here for Sparta was pre-eminence not just in the Peloponnese but in southern mainland Greece more generally. Croesus had been given to understand that already in the 540s Athens was Sparta's nearest rival in military power. This was still the case thirty-plus years later, but during that period the political situation at Athens was transformed, introducing a further, ideological dimension to the conflict between them. Since about 545 Athens had been ruled by the family tyranny, or dynasty, of Peisistratus and his sons, and tyranny was coming to be identified with the denial of the Greeks' birthright of political freedom.

Once more, a Spartan naval campaign met with no success. But an expedition sent more conventionally, by land, two years later in 510 was a different story altogether. The energetic, expansionist and interventionist Spartan king Cleomenes I overthrew Peisistratus's eldest son and main successor Hippias. A more or less direct consequence of Sparta's termination of the Peisistratid family tyranny was the birth at Athens of the world's first democracy – though a democracy of the ancient Greek type, very different from any modern democracy. This was achieved through the reforms in 508/7 attributed to the leading aristocrat Cleisthenes; and it was hardly the result the Spartans had expected or desired. Instead of a pro-Spartan oligarchy they now had to deal with an anti-Spartan democracy.

This was the starting-point of an ideological polarity – Spartan oligarchy against Athenian democracy – that played itself out over the next hundred years, culminating in the disastrous Atheno-Peloponnesian War of 431–404.* Moreover, ex-tyrant Hippias had departed promptly for the more hospitable climes of Asia. He went over, that is, to the Persian sphere and dedicated himself as a vassal of the Persian Great King. The key linkage of Greek freedom and Persian tyrannical despotism was thereby forged.

---

* The Spartans eventually won that war, but (another paradox) did so thanks only to Persian money. The Athenians with their naval power and desire to liberate the Greeks of Asia presented a greater threat to Persian interests than did Sparta. So on the principle that 'my enemy's enemy is my friend', first the two westernmost Persian satraps and then a son of Great King Darius II channelled enormous amounts of money the Spartans' way to enable them to build a fleet that could eventually defeat the Athenians and rob them of their control of the Aegean, and especially its link to the Black Sea via the Hellespont.

TWO

THE DYNAMICS OF
EMPIRE: PERSIA OF THE
ACHAEMENIDS, 485

Among these countries there was a place where previously demons had been worshipped. Afterwards . . . there I worshipped Ahura Mazda in accordance with Truth reverently.

from Xerxes's '*Daiva*-Inscription'

THE PERSIAN EMPIRE was not only enormous in scale, it was also extremely heterogeneous and complex. Cyrus II 'the Great' (*c.* 559–530) and his son Cambyses (530–522), scions of the Achaemenid royal house, had carved out their vast empire by military conquest. But it was left to Darius I (522–486), a distant relative who shrewdly married Cyrus's daughter Atossa, to establish it permanently on secure foundations of tribute collection and bureaucratic administration. His son and successor Xerxes (486–465) attempted to emulate his great father in expanding the Empire, by conquering and incorporating the Greeks of the mainland, but he failed dismally, thanks to the Spartans above all, and died by an assassin's hand.

In our evidence for the mighty Persian empire and its dealings with Greeks lies an incurable paradox. We can read some of the Persians' own official records, several of which I shall quote extensively, and we can more

Of Mesopotamian derivation, these two colossal winged-bull effigies flank the East Door of the Gate of Xerxes at Persepolis and dwarf any human figures that dare pass through them.

or less accurately decipher the formalized language of the monuments of the Achaemenids' official art in their several palace centres. But for a contextualizing ancient narrative and an overarching explanation of Perso-Greek relations between 550 and 479 we cannot do without Herodotus. This is despite his undoubted shortcomings as a 'scientific' historian of the best modern type.* For example, although he did somehow gain access indirectly to some key Persian documents, he never learned Persian – or indeed knew any other language than his native Doric dialect of spoken Greek and the literary Ionic dialect in which he composed his *Histories*. One little token of his monoglottalism is his deeply erroneous, ethnocentric belief that all Persian proper names ended in 's'.

On the other hand, before we get too carried away by Herodotus's

---

* See Appendix 1.

deficiencies as an observer, reporter, recorder and historian of Persia, we have to remind ourselves that even in the Greek world there was no Herodotus before Herodotus. Even more to the point, the inegalitarian, hierarchical, top-down Persian world of absolute monarchy and strict court protocol never produced a Herodotus at all. Achaemenid Persia had scribes, many of them, but not one historian. Scribes, paradoxically, made any less restricted form of literacy unnecessary as well as, probably, unwelcome. But bureacracy and a passion for counting have their advantages for the modern historian of ancient Persia. Now that we can read many official Persian documents, thanks largely to Henry Rawlinson who in the nineteenth century deciphered Persian cuneiform script, we can at least get an intimate feel for how the administration worked at the centre and for the immense ethnic diversity of this huge realm, the first truly world empire.

Consider, for example, the light thrown by the quite recently published Fortification Tablets from Persepolis on the career of a high official whose name in Persian was Parnaka but whom Herodotus transliterated as 'Pharnaces' (note that 's'). Thanks to Herodotus, we already knew quite a lot about his important son Artabazus. Here, for instance, are a few words from a context following the Battle of Salamis in 480 BCE:[1]

> Artabazus the son of Pharnaces was already a famous man in the Persian army and was further to increase his reputation as a result of the battle of Plataea [in 479].

This Artabazus, as readers had already been informed,[2]* was the commander of the land troops of Parthians and Chorasmians who fought in Bactrian war-gear. He receives several commendatory mentions in his own right from Herodotus. In stark contrast, his father Pharnaces appears merely as that – as the father of his (admittedly famous) son. Yet we now know – and this is one of the more spectac-

---

* See Appendix 2.

ular discoveries made as a result of the decipherment of the Persians' own official bureaucratic records – that Pharnaces had been no less distinguished than his son; in fact, in his way even more so.

For in the years around 500 BCE he had been the very highest royal official at the main ceremonial capital of the Empire, Persepolis (Parsa in Persian). We also know from his official seal that Parnaka was a son of Irsama (Arsames). Now, that Irsama/Arsames was a grandfather of none other than Great King Darius I. Parnaka/Pharnaces, therefore, was a brother of Darius's father Hystaspes and the Great King's paternal uncle. We already knew from Greek sources that Darius had made a clever dynastic marriage to Atossa. Now we see too how he exploited blood-relations to grease the wheels of the highest imperial administration. This is the sort of extraordinarily illuminating insight to be gained from the primary Persian documents available now to us – but never to Herodotus – directly in raw form.

As for the Empire's ethnic diversity, there is no better means of direct access than via Darius's boastful text recording his construction of a palace at Susa in Elam, the Empire's principal administrative centre. Here is an extract from that long foundation charter:

> This palace which I built at Susa: its materials were brought from afar
> . . . The cedar timber was brought from a mountain called Lebanon.
> The Assyrian people [of northern Iraq today] brought it to Babylon
> [southern Iraq]. From Babylon the Carians [from south-west Anatolia]
> and Ionians [Greeks of central west Anatolia] brought it to Susa. The
> sissoo-timber was brought from Gandara [Afghanistan–Pakistan bor-
> der] and from Carmania [southern Iran]. The gold which was worked
> here was brought from Sardis [capital of the satrapy of Lydia, central
> west Anatolia] and from Bactria [northern Afghanistan]. The precious
> stone lapis lazuli and carnelian which was worked here was brought
> from Sogdiana [northern Afghanistan]. The precious stone turquoise . . .
> was brought from Chorasmia [central Asia]. The silver and the ebony
> were brought from Egypt. The ornamentation with which the wall was

adorned was brought from Ionia. The ivory which was worked here was brought from Ethiopia, and from India and from Arachosia [southern Afghanistan]. The stone columns which were worked here were brought from . . . Elam. The stone-cutters who worked the stone were Ionians and Sardians. The goldsmiths who worked the gold were Medes and Egyptians. The men who worked the wood were Sardians and Egyptians. The men who worked the baked brick were Babylonians. The men who adorned the wall were Medes and Egyptians.

Darius sums up:

Darius the king says: 'At Susa a very excellent work was ordered, a very excellent work was brought to completion. May Ahura Mazda protect me, and Hystaspes my father and my country.'

The great capitals located in the south of what is now Iran – Pasargadae (the original, built by Cyrus), Susa and Persepolis ('a vast over-egged pudding of an archaeological site', as one journalist has irreverently called it) – were complemented by a fourth at Ecbatana in Media, further to the north. That their public artwork was composed of materials from all four corners of the Empire we might have predicted; and likewise, if on a rather smaller scale, the sources of recruitment of the skilled workforce, including Ionians (Greeks) as in the Susa foundation charter quoted above. What is more extraordinary, however, is that out of this melange of disparate peoples and places each with their own distinctive cultural traditions was created a unified style, unique to the Achaemenids. Some would give Darius himself the credit for this, because it seems to presuppose a single controlling intellect, and this was an art focused on kingship (and without pretensions to global reach). But that may be to give him too much credit. Perhaps we should look rather for an anonymous Persian Imhotep* as the mastermind of genius behind the centrally linked building projects.

---

* 'Egypt's Leonardo', as he has been called: Ray 2001.

Achaemenid public art and architecture were also interestingly secular, in that no major religious monuments, of Egyptian or Babylonian type, for instance, were created. Their style was eclectic but coherent. For example, the Gate of Xerxes on the terrace platform at Persepolis, known also as the Gate of All Lands, was decorated, like the gatehouse at Pasargadae, with winged human-headed bulls. These were ultimately of Assyrian origin, whereas the distinctive Persepolitan column was derived from Egyptian and Greek models but arguably can be said to have surpassed both. However, the most stunning single building at Persepolis, still so today even in its ruined state, was the Audience Hall, the Apadana, closely parallel in its plan to that at Susa: a square columned hall with towers at the four corners and porticoes on three sides, the columns supporting double-bull capitals. What distinguishes the Apadana at Persepolis is the stone platform on which it is built. On the north and east sides this is decorated with staircases crammed with friezes of relief sculpture, each side a mirror image of the other. Repetition of motifs and forms – in this case showing the Persian Great King enthroned at the centre as processions of tribute-bearing subjects dressed in national costume from no fewer than twenty-three different peoples move towards him – was seen as a virtue by the Achaemenid rulers, since repetition conveyed the desired impression of power and inevitability. This Persian style was indeed the very reverse of an individualizing art form, such as that of the contemporary Greeks, though some of the masons at Susa did leave recognizable hieroglyph 'signatures' and some of the craftsmen there and presumably elsewhere were, as we have seen, Greeks. Another striking point is that, in sharp contrast to their Assyrian imperial predecessors, for example, scenes of warfare or hunting are absent from the walls of the Achaemenid palaces.

The Persians were related to the Medes and had succeeded them as imperial masters. They were not, however, more or less identical to each other, as the Greeks often fondly thought – they could even refer to the Persians as 'the Mede' in the singular. The Persians were the master people, as it were. There are no Persian tributaries in the pro-

Originally this double bull-headed capital in grey marble topped one of the forest of columns supporting the roof of the Apadana at Susa.

cession scenes depicted on the Persepolis Apadana, but there are Medes: dressed in the distinctive Median garb of knee-length tunic (different from the usual Persian long, pleated dress) or long-sleeved coat (*kandys*), tight trousers (much scorned by the Greeks) and a cap with neck covering and ear-flaps; and bearing as tribute clothes, a short sword (*akinakês*), bracelets and vessels.

This ethnic difference in the Iranian heartland was a microcosm of the heterogeneity of the Empire at large. Many different ethnic groups, many diverse creeds, many different languages jostled for living space under the Achaemenids' imperial umbrella. What unified them administratively was that the central court and government insisted on a mini-

In the Apadana (audience hall of the Palace) at what the Greeks called Persepolis (or Persae; Parsa in Persian) the Great King would receive annually, during the spring festival, tokens of submission and tribute from the subjects of his far-flung multicultural empire. Persepolis, founded by Darius I and further embellished by various successors, including his son Xerxes, was the empire's main ceremonial capital, lying not far from where the kings were buried at Naqsh-i-Rustam tomb at Naqsh-i-Rustam.

Alongside the steps of the grand staircase leading up to the Apadana (*see above*) members of the royal guard and officers of the court process in high carved relief.

mum annual contribution of tax and tribute in cash or kind, together with such military obligations as might from time to time be imposed either globally from the centre or at provincial level. The common linguistic currency of imperial administration and communication was Aramaic (the Semitic language spoken four to five centuries later by one Jesus of Galilee). But Darius also introduced a common monetary currency, the silver and gold coins known in his honour as 'darics'. Darius was indeed the first living ruler to have his image – always represented as an archer with bow and quiver in a vigorous 'running' pose – placed on his coinage (the idea and practice of coinage were themselves only about a century old when he came to the throne). Plutarch, among his *Laconian Apophthegms* (*Sayings of Spartans*), preserves this anecdote:

> *Since Persian coinage was stamped with the image of an archer [Darius], Agesilaus said as he broke camp [in 394] that he was being driven out of Asia by the King [Artaxerxes II] with the aid of thirty thousand bowmen [gold darics].*

The Achaemenid Persian empire's founder was Cyrus II the Great (r. 559–529), and this is his simply designed but imposingly large tomb at Pasargadae, his home town and the empire's original capital. Almost exactly two centuries after Cyrus's death and burial, Alexander the Great of Macedon, the new King of Asia, learned that the tomb had been broken into and looted and ordered its immediate restoration.

For tax and military purposes, the empire was carved up in all into between twenty and thirty provinces, or 'satrapies' (apparently a Median word in origin), each governed by a satrap or viceroy; most satraps were drawn from the extended and extensive royal household (which practised the harem system). In Book 3[3] Herodotus provides a remarkable 'catalogue' of the Empire's satrapies – twenty according to his reckoning – together with precise notations of the tribute in cash and kind that each was required to provide annually. From Persian documents we get an official listing of the chief peoples and lands over which Darius ruled, but not a satrapy list properly speaking:

> By the favour of Ahura Mazda these are the countries which I [Darius] seized outside Persia . . . Media, Elam, Parthia, Aria, Bactria, Sogdiana, Chorasmia, Drangiana, Arachosia, Sattagydia, Gandara, Sind, Amyrgian Scythians, pointed-cap Scythians, Babylonia, Assyria, Arabia, Egypt, Armenia, Cappadocia, Sardis, Ionia, Scythians from Across-the-[Black]Sea, Skudra, petasos [broad-brimmed hat]-wearing Ionians, Libyans, Ethiopians, men from Maka, Carians.[4]

One people absent from this tally is worth noting, the Jews of Judah. Three of the books of the Hebrew Bible, Ezra, Esther and Nehemiah, relate wholly and directly to the Achaemenid Persian period of Judaean history, though 'history' is not precisely what they deliver. Esther, it is thought, was written well after the Achaemenid Empire had come to an end, but it does nevertheless convey a powerful flavour of the perception the Great King's more distant subjects had of life at the top in Susa:

> The King made a feast unto all the people who were present in Shushan the Palace both unto great and small, seven days, in the court of the garden of the King's palace; where there were white, green and blue hangings fastened with cords of fine linen and purple to silver rings and pillars of marble; the beds were of gold and silver, upon a pavement of red, and blue and white, and black marble. And they gave them drink

*in vessels of gold (the vessels being diverse from one another), and
royal wine in abundance, according to the state of the King.[5]*

It is not merely an incidental detail that 'all the people' would have
included high-ranking Persian women, who would participate openly
along with the men in such royal feasting. This was one of the sharpest
signifiers of Persian 'otherness' to disapproving Greek eyes. A king
would also take the women of his closest family with him on campaign, another stigma of Persian strangeness for a Greek.

Herodotus, on what authority we cannot say, feels confident
enough to record in detail what each of his twenty satrapies was bound
to contribute annually. For instance, the Greeks united in his Satrapy
number 1 paid only in monetary form, silver or silver equivalent,
whereas the Egyptians of Satrapy 6 had included in their assessment a
sum of money raised from the sale of fish caught in Lake Moeris; and
as for the Indians of Satrapy 20, as noted above, they were 'the most
populous nation in the whole known world and [therefore] paid the
largest single sum, 360 talents' weight of gold-dust'. Moreover, he
comes up with a grand total annual assessment, in silver equivalent
reckoned on the weight standard of the island of Euboea (heavier than
the more universal Athenian standard), of over 14,500 talents.*

Herodotus, perhaps surprisingly, does not include here the prod-
ucts of what we might call the 'white slave' trade – young girls to stock
the harems of the central and regional capitals, for both sexual and
reproductive purposes, and castrated boys, including Greeks, to serve
eventually as eunuch guards of those same harems and more immediately as sex-objects.[†] Herodotus moreover was unaware of, or chose
not to record, how a province's military obligations might be met indirectly by a complicated system of 'franchising'. Rich Babylonians, for

---

* To put this in a Greek perspective, that sum would be almost thirty times the total
revenue of the Athenians' naval empire at its height in the 440s and 430s.
† Elsewhere, 8.105, he describes the Greek Panionius's trading in eunuchs as 'utterly
wicked'.

example, instead of serving in person, usually as cavalrymen, might pay a sum of money to a third party, a middleman, who would purchase the services of a substitute and pocket the difference between what the rich opt-out paid him and what the substitute cost. The records of the Murashu ('wildcat') family finance house of Nippur have survived to throw a great deal of light on this franchising system, which may also help to explain why some at least of the Persians' cavalry recruits fought with less élan, though not necessarily any less skill, than some of the Great King's wealthiest subjects.

With all the aristocratic scorn he can muster, Herodotus adds confidently[6] that 'the Persians have a saying' to the effect that, whereas Cyrus was a 'father' to them and Cambyses a 'tyrant', Darius was merely a 'tradesman' or 'retail trader' (*emporos*). Actually, that was a thoroughly Greek rather than Persian mode of classification, and it is an irony that Herodotus fails to bring out just how desperately foreign and un-Greek the whole Persian system of centralized bureaucracy was. It has been well said that everyone in the Persian empire, from highest to lowest, was on a ration scale. This emerges most strongly from two sets of texts from Persepolis, known respectively as the Fortification Tablets (a cache of more than thirty thousand, excavated in 1933/4, comprising an economic archive of Darius's reign written almost entirely in Elamite, the local language of the area of which Susa was the capital – though there was at least one ethnic Greek scribe or secretary at work there too) and the Treasury Texts (a mere 750 or so, also written in Elamite, dating between 492 and 458).

Pharnaces, for example, was specially favoured to receive as his daily – daily! – ration 90 quarts of wine, 180 quarts of flour and 2 sheep. Gobryas, Darius's helper and father of Xerxes's general Mardonius, got even more (about 11 per cent more). The scope for dispensing power and patronage that such an overblown food allowance implies need hardly be laboured. Travel rations were another kind of central dole, issued to groups and individuals journeying on official business across the Empire. Travellers thus provisioned are registered as coming from southern Elam, from Persis and even from India. Destinations mentioned include Arabia, Bactria, Babylon, Egypt, Kerman and Sardis.

The latter was the terminus of the so-called Royal Road from Susa that so impressed Herodotus. Whereas a sizeable army would typically require three months to travel that distance (almost 2,600 kilometres), a single messenger using a relay of horses along the Royal Road could cover it in little over a week. Herodotus goes into inordinate detail in his description of the Road's course and length,[7] using the technical Persian term *parasang* – though he seems to have understood this wrongly as a unit of distance when it was a unit of time. Elsewhere[8] he likens the relay of horses at the Royal Road's reportedly 111 stations, or posthouses, to the relay of torches carried by runners in races held at Greek religious festivals in honour of the Olympian craftsman-god Hephaestus. The highway started from Susa, went through one (not certain which) of the passes of the Zagros Mountains, thence to the Tigris and on to the upper Euphrates, then on through Cappadocia to Sardis – and from Sardis on to the Aegean coast at Greek Ephesus in Ionia. This was one of the reasons for the heavy Persian influence on Ephesus, extending even to its famous civic cult of Artemis, who was assimilated somewhat to Persian Anahita.

Besides the required tax and tribute contributions there were other forms of economic exploitation available – for example, the confiscation of Greek lands by the satrap or even by the Great King himself, and their redistribution to favoured Persian or even Greek grandees. But, as already noted, the imperial yoke was not apparently felt to be an especially heavy one in economic terms, and so long as the contributions came in regularly and on time, subjects were not massively oppressed.

Religion featured prominently in imperial Persian propaganda. Twice in the documents quoted above Darius refers to Ahura Mazda, 'Lord Wisdom'. He was the great god of light of the Irano-Bactrian religion founded or codified by the prophet Zoroaster (or Zarathustra), who was born in Bactra (Balkh) probably sometime between the tenth and sixth centuries BCE. An even more explicit commitment to Ahura Mazda was made by Darius in the famous trilingual rock-cut inscription at Bisitun not far from Ecbatana.* The languages were Elamite, Babylonian and Old Persian. The latter was an official, chancellery language rather than an imperial lingua franca, and all the more imposing for that, though Darius seems to have been the only Achaemenid king who had proper texts composed in it, and took pleasure in doing so.

The Bisitun texts were inscribed some 66 metres above ground level in the living rock of a mountain on the slope of which have been found the possible remains of a Median fortress. The name 'Bisitun' is derived from an Old Persian word meaning 'place of the gods', and of those gods first and indeed only place was given to Ahura Mazda, whose image – a winged symbol – accompanied and indeed dominated the inscription:

> Darius the king says: '. . . By the favour of Ahura Mazda I am king. Ahura Mazda bestowed kingship upon me . . . They [specified countries] were my subjects; they brought tribute to me . . . By the favour of Ahura Mazda these countries obeyed my law . . . Ahura Mazda bestowed this kingdom upon me. Ahura Mazda brought me aid until I had held together this kingdom. By the favour of Ahura Mazda I hold this kingship.'

The insistent repetition is very striking; it parallels the deliberate repetitiveness of the figural decoration of the royal palaces. Striking too is the fact that, unlike the Pharaohs of Egypt, the Persian Great Kings were not themselves considered divine. They were instead the vicars on earth of Ahura Mazda, of whom in another inscription Darius fulsomely says: 'Ahura Mazda is a great god, who created this earth, who created the sky, who created humankind, who created happiness for humankind' – and then segues seamlessly into 'who made Darius king, one king of many, one lord of many.' Or, to quote a slightly

---

*   This, since it made it possible for Henry Rawlinson to decipher cuneiform writing, has been called the most important text for the study of the history of the entire ancient Near East. But others would make the same claim for the Hebrew Bible.

The facade of Xerxes's tomb at Naqsh-i-Rustam displays the king in an attitude of homage to the same winged-disc symbol of Ahura Mazda as his father Darius had employed at Bisitun.

variant version from an inscription of Darius incised on the façade of his tomb at Naqsh-i-Rustam near Persepolis: 'Ahura Mazda is a great god, who created this excellent work which is seen, who created happiness for humankind, who bestowed wisdom and courage upon Darius.'

As the anointed of Ahura Mazda, Persian Great Kings were owed maximum respect, symbolized by the performance of a ritual of public greeting that the Greeks called *proskunêsis*. This consisted, depending on the status of the subject performing it, either of a full prostration or of a deep bow from the waist coupled with a blown kiss. This sort of gestural body language, *de bas en haut*, was entirely appropriate to the Persians' pyramidal sort of society and political system.

Monarchy was the apex of the Empire's governing order, without any possibility of question. The Great King, King of Kings, had his duties assigned to him from heaven above, mainly to protect land and people from natural and manmade incursions. But this monarchical political system did not – quite – reflect an imposed imperial monotheism. For there were other gods and goddesses in the Persian pantheon, Anahita and Mithras for example, and despite all Darius's and other Great Kings' efforts to make it seem otherwise, the Empire as a whole remained polytheistic in outlook and behaviour.*

The erection of the Bisitun inscription towards the beginning of Darius's reign was obviously propagandistic. It was designed to demonstrate – and illustrate – that central order and control had been reimposed following a very widespread bout of disaffection and indeed outright revolt following the death, in murky circumstances, of Cambyses son of Cyrus in 522. There is no hint that this disaffection and revolt had been caused by religious opposition. But unrest leading to open revolt at the close of Darius's reign in the provinces of Babylonia and Egypt does indeed suggest that Ahura Mazdism came at a cost in regions where the political order was shaped or dictated in accordance with the perceived wishes of other all-powerful deities. In both those key provinces the senior priesthoods (of, respectively, Bel-Marduk and Amun) were apparently the most active forces behind the rebellions, and it was they whom Xerxes chose to punish, perhaps rather heavy-handedly, as his first acts as Great King.

In the case of Persian official dealings with the Greeks, a rather telling piece of epigraphic evidence goes in precisely the opposite direction. The text in question was cut into a marble block in the second century CE in the Greek city of Magnesia (on the River Meander in Ionia), probably at the instigation of priestly authorities keen to establish publicly the sacredness of the land at issue. But there is every rea-

---

* The great exception was of course Judah, where Cyrus had earned the title 'Messiah' from Deutero-Isaiah for restoring the exiled Jews from their Babylonian captivity.

son to think that the document is an authentic copy of an imperial order of Darius originally delivered to Gadatas, satrap of Lydia and Ionia, in about 500 BCE:

> *The King of kings, Darius, son of Hystaspes, speaks to Gadatas, his slave, thus: 'I find that you are not completely obedient to my orders. Because you are cultivating my land, transplanting fruit trees from the Province Beyond-the-Euphrates [Syria-Palestine] to the western Asiatic regions, I praise your purpose . . . But because my religious dispositions are nullified by you, I shall give you proof of a wronged [King's] anger, unless you change your ways. For the gardeners sacred to Apollo have been made to pay tribute to you; and land that is not sacred they have dug up at your command. You are ignorant of my ancestors' attitude to the god, who told the Persians all of the truth and . . .*[9]**

Darius's tactful reference to his ancestors would have been music to a Greek subject's ears, since to the Greeks tradition, the honouring of their gods 'in accordance with the things of the fathers' (*kata ta patria*), was of the essence of their religious custom (*nomos*) and belief. Greeks were perhaps on the whole not quite as devoted gardeners as the Persian Great Kings; it is to the Persians that we owe the Edenic term 'paradise' (from *pari* 'around' and *dieza* 'wall'), meaning originally a cultivated hunting park. Yet they too appreciated the distinction between the sacred and the not so sacred, between precincts (*temenê*) 'cut off' as special places for their gods and land that had not been so sanctified and sacralized. And they would have found Darius's toleration of a foreign, Greek cult entirely congenial and culturally familiar too.

But Darius's use of the phrase 'all of the truth' in the truncated last sentence was peculiarly Persian. Herodotus insists that the whole of a Persian's education between the ages of five and twenty was devoted to the instilling of just three virtues or skills: riding a horse, shooting

---

*   The rest is lost.

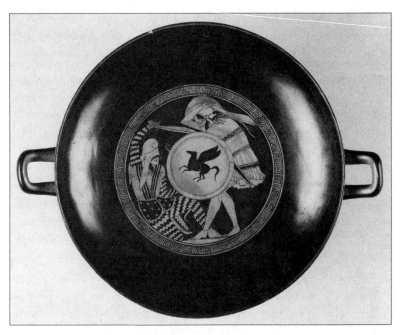

Another in the early fifth century. Athenian series of Persian vase scenes, this cup of c. 480 by the so-called Triptolemos Painter shows a defeated Persian on the (sinister) left, carrying both sword and bowcase, and a victorious Greek hoplite on the (might is) right.

the bow, and telling the truth. Telling lies was the worst possible violation of the Persians' honour code – ahead of, in second place, owing a debt. In the Bisitun trilingual inscription Darius presents himself as the very embodiment of the Truth, engaged in battling against the usurper and the rebels who incarnate the Lie. Indeed, all Persian royal inscriptions try to convey eternal verities about the Great King. Their overriding aim was not to record individual political events (though they do sometimes do that too) but to emphasize that the King's rule is divinely ordained and that the peace of the Empire is to be secured only through following the Truth, specifically by adhering to the moral precepts of Ahura Mazda.

Further confirmation of the official royal conflation of Ahura Mazda with the Truth comes from a famous document of Darius's son, Xerxes, his so-called '*Daiva*-Inscription', a *daiva* being Old Persian for a demon or devil:

> Among these countries [the thirty or so listed immediately above in the text, over whom Xerxes's data (law) was asserted to prevail] there was a place where previously demons had been worshipped. Afterwards . . . there I worshipped Ahura Mazda in accordance with Truth reverently . . .[10]

Just as specifically Persian, likewise, is Darius's use of a term that can be translated as 'slave' in Greek, even when addressing so high-ranking a Persian as a satrap, who might well have been related to him by birth or by marriage. That hateful parlance would, however, have struck a deeply false note to a Greek audience and very possibly gives a clue to what was at least part of the reason for the Ionian and other Greeks revolting against him in 499.

This revolt, like the revolts of 521–519, in which Greeks were not involved, was forcibly suppressed. But Darius did not aim merely to hang on to the empire he had inherited. He burned also, like Cambyses, to expand it. In 513, as noted, he moved his forces across the Bosporus strait from Asia into Europe and established a new satrapy in Thrace or, as it was officially known, Beyond-the-[Black]-Sea. A basis had been laid for further conquest in the southern Balkan peninsula – that is, conquest of the Greeks of Macedonia and points south. But, whether that was how it was seen by Darius at the time is another question, unanswerable on current evidence.

THREE

HELLAS: THE HELLENIC WORLD IN 485

There are many and powerful factors preventing us from doing this even if we were to wish to (which we do not) . . . For the Athenians to be traitors to all that would not be well.

Herodotus, *Histories* 8.144

IN 492, SOME twenty years after Darius's first European démarche, the Persian maw opened yet wider – wide enough to swallow up Macedonia on the fringes of mainland Greece proper. This was a direct consequence of an episode that we refer to compendiously as 'the Ionian Revolt'. This label is actually doubly misleading, because it was not only the Greeks of Ionia who revolted. They were joined by their fellow Asiatic Greeks from Aeolis to the north and from Caria and Lycia to the south, as well as by Greeks from islands lying off the Anatolian coast. Besides, it was not by any means only Greeks who revolted against their Persian masters during the first decade of the fifth century BCE. Some of the Greeks' Near Eastern neighbours joined in too, including some from as far south as the island of Cyprus, which forms a natural bridge between Anatolia and the Levant. However, the conventional terminology is at least convenient.

Herodotus is our major and only continuous narrative source for the Revolt, but his account presents difficulties. Above all, he has excessively personalized its motivations, either as a result of his (mainly oral) sources, or because of his own predispositions and predilections. He makes a very great deal hang in particular on the machinations of Histiaeus, the former sole ruler of Greek Miletus in the Persian interest, and of his supposed protégé Aristagoras. No doubt their personal contributions were significant, but by themselves they could not have brought on or sustained a revolt that quickly far overleaped the confines of Ionia and that lasted six whole summer campaigning seasons (499–494). Some objective factors had to have been operating in addition, and operating strongly.

If these were not primarily economic, they are likely to have been political or ideological. In a nutshell, the Greek rebels wanted to be free. Subjection to an alien imperial power abroad and to rule by quisling tyrants at home was no longer considered an acceptably 'modern' mode of political rule. It contradicted one of the possible definitions of freedom – freedom as political independence and self-determination – and it did so the more blatantly since the major advance in Greek freedom constituted by the Athenian Revolution of 508/7.*

It was that year, to be brief, that the Athenian Assembly endorsed the radical political reform package proposed by Cleisthenes. This was a direct form of democratic self-government, more like a dictatorship of the proletariat (that is, the poor majority of the citizens) than any version by which the electorate surrenders power on an everyday basis to a government of elected representatives.

At the root of the Athenian democratic project was a notion of citizen freedom. This was twofold: both negative freedom from external coercion (whether domestic or foreign) and positive freedom to participate in and indeed decide matters of prime importance to the community of citizens as a whole. This new-style Athenian regime at first

---

* The label 'Athenian Revolution' is not uncontroversial, since it may carry the implication that it was a consciously motivated act of political self-transformation. I would myself emphasize more the – surely revolutionary – transformation of both institutions and consciousness that flowed from the reforms.

believed it would be able to coexist with the Persian Empire, if only Persia would leave Athens alone. It therefore gave to the Persian authorities at Sardis in 507 or 506 those formal tokens of submission, earth and water, which to Darius as to any Great King signalled subordination and loss of independence. Half a dozen years later, however, in 500/499, when Ionian Greeks came to Athens to request Athenian aid for their proposed revolt, the Athenian democracy had come to think quite differently about its place in the world and specifically about its relation to Persia.

There were, in any case, strong sentimental links between Athens and the Greeks of Ionia. A century earlier the Athenian poet-statesman Solon had referred to the Athenians' home territory of Attica as 'the oldest land of Ionia', and the Athenians were keen to foster the myth that the Greeks speaking the Ionic dialect of Greek who had settled on the west coast of Anatolia had not just set sail from Athens but had done so under Athenian inspiration and leadership. Of the Ionian Greek cities the most important was Miletus, and it was Miletus that in 500 took the lead in approaching Athens. The Athenian democracy

This bronze weight in the form of an astragal (knucklebone) tips the scales at a cool 93.7kg; it was found at Susa, but the long Greek inscription indicates that it was looted by the Persians from the Greek oracular shrine at Didyma and so probably taken after their sack of nearby Miletus following the crushing of the Ionian Revolt in 494.

now believed that it could with impunity and profit lend both material and spiritual aid to its Ionian 'cousins' in their revolt against the Persian Great King.

Herodotus, who was not an Ionian (Halicarnassus spoke the Doric dialect) and possibly was guilty also of some anachronistic hindsight, took a very dim view of this Athenian decision. He contrasted it unfavourably with Sparta's sober-sided rejection of Ionian pleas for help and viewed it, Homerically, as 'the beginning of evils'[1] for all Greece. For he detected a single chain of causation running from this fatal Athenian decision through to the expeditions of reprisal and would-be conquest in mainland Greece launched first by Darius and then by Xerxes, and on into the later part of the fifth century:

> *During the three generations comprising the reigns of Darius the son of Hystaspes [521–486], and of his son Xerxes [486–465] and his grandson Artaxerxes [465–424], Greece suffered more evils than in the twenty generations before Darius was born.*[2]

This was one of only a handful of references to the period after his main subject of the Graeco-Persian Wars. Since Herodotus certainly lived to see the outbreak of the disastrous Spartan-Athenian conflict known as the Peloponnesian War, which was a sort of prolonged intra-Greek civil war, he very likely had that specifically in mind when he gave this doom-laden judgement.

It is questionable, though, whether the Revolt in general or Athens's role in it can bear the interpretative and causal weight placed upon them by Herodotus. He seems to have underplayed the rebelling parties' military and political successes, which involved unique military co-operation between Greeks and non-Greeks both on the Asiatic mainland and on Cyprus, and conversely to have exaggerated the degree of independence allowed the Greeks by the allegedly magnanimous Persians even after their final defeat. The showdown took place at sea at Lade near Miletus in the summer of 494. The result was a total victory for the mainly Phoenician Persian fleet. The rebels' disgrace was the greater because a major Greek contingent from the island of Samos had abandoned their comrades-in-arms immediately before the final battle.

Yet Herodotus believed that in 493–492 Darius's appointee as governor of the region allowed the Ionian cities to become 'democracies',[3] for all the world as if they were on a par with the – then still in fact unique – Athenian democracy.* At most, modern scholars rightly hold, some sort of local 'town council' independence might conceivably have been granted. However, by the time of Xerxes's invasion in 480 quisling tyrants had again ominously reared their less than prepossessing countenances in several of the Ionian Greek cities. Moreover, the Ionian Revolt had done nothing to deter Darius from thinking he could further expand Persian power permanently in Europe. On the contrary: the subjugation of Macedonia by Megabazus, satrap of Thrace, ensued immediately.

It was not, though, by land and through northern Greece that Darius authorized his next major military initiative, in 490. This took a sea route, through the Aegean, and was directed against first the city of Eretria on Euboea and then Athens. A more or less direct route led the mainly Phoenician fleet from its home waters off Lebanon via the largest Cycladic island of Naxos (which had caused trouble in 500) to Euboea and then on to Attica. The expedition was commanded by Artaphernes, a brother of Darius, and by a Mede called Datis (who we know from Persian records had had prior personal experience of the Empire's western sector).

The ostensible motive of the expedition was punishment. Almost a decade earlier both Eretria and Athens had dared to aid the revolting Ionians, and such defiance of the imperial power and interference in 'its' sphere, however minor in their practical long-term impact, had to be seen to be visited with severe retribution.

But it is doubtful that this was all that Darius had in mind. All

---

* The governor was Mardonius, later to be the premier general of Xerxes in Greece.

empires by a law of their nature worry about security at the fringes. For example, one of the proclaimed reasons for Julius Caesar's first invasion of Britain in 55 BCE was that the pesky Britons had been giving aid to their Celtic cousins across the Channel in Gaul. Another of Caesar's motives was to 'cross Ocean', a previously unheard-of feat. Darius in 490 surely aimed at least to deter any further mainland intervention in 'his' Asiatic sphere by turning the Aegean into a Persian lake patrolled by his Phoenician navy.

Phoenician naval superiority was not then in question. The Battle of Lade in 494 had proved it beyond a shadow of doubt. The Greeks' crippling naval defeat was due partly to inferior discipline, but no less to inferior hardware, tactics and experience. In 490 Eretria was simply rolled over. The city was taken over and torched, and many Eretrians were transported a very long way from home, deep into the heart of the Persian Empire. The Athenians, predictably, offered no naval resistance. Apart from not having much of a fleet themselves as yet, they were in no way helped by the decision of their neighbours on the island of Aegina, who did possess a significant war fleet, to give formal tokens of submission, earth and water again, to Darius's ambassadors. So the Persians landed unopposed in the broad bay of Marathon in east Attica. The issue was then whether, and how, the Athenians might put up any serious resistance on land.

Sensibly, despite the various contretemps that had afflicted relations with Sparta some years before, they sent at once for Spartan help, employing the services of the extraordinary long-distance runner Philippides (or Pheidippides). He reached Sparta from Athens, a distance of some 250 kilometres, in well under forty-eight hours.* Sparta was then by a long way the most powerful Greek military state in terms of conventional land warfare. It was under the dominant influence of King Cleomenes I, who was known to be violently hostile to

---

* The modern-day 'Spartathlon', the ultra-Marathon race inspired by him, has seen the record-winning time cut to a little over twenty hours.

Aegina. It had also, like Athens, treated Darius's ambassadors with great contempt, and indeed some irreligion, by murdering them. The Spartans now reacted positively to the Athenians' request for military aid, save only that a prior religious commitment (they claimed) prevented them from sending that aid immediately. In the event, the Spartan force arrived at Marathon on the day after the great battle, leaving Athens and its sole ally, neighbouring Plataea, to face the Persian music.

It will never be quite clear why exactly the Persian invaders lost the Battle of Marathon, and lost it so comprehensively. The role – or rather the lack of a role – played by the Persians' cavalry will probably have had a good deal to do with it. In its absence the battle was a straight fight between heavily armed Greek soldiers who, under the inspiration of the tactical genius of the aristocratic general Miltiades, were fighting over (in more than one sense) their own home soil, and the relatively lighter-armed, more heterogeneous and less motivated troops at the disposal of Artaphernes and Datis. The Greek forces came out well on top and suffered relatively few casualties: according to Herodotus, a mere 192 Athenians died, as opposed to some six and a half thousand on the Persian side. There was some concern about a possible fifth column at Athens, prepared to do a deal with the Persians, but this never in fact materialized.

Darius died in 486, presumably a less than entirely contented man as regards Greek affairs, despite all his many other staggering successes. The upshot of his failure at Marathon was that in 485 Persia's imperial writ had not yet been extended over mainland Greece proper. By then his son and successor Xerxes had established himself as Great King, had suppressed rebellions in Babylonia and Egypt, and was considering what sort of a mark he might be able to impose on his kingship and on the Empire.

Herodotus at the start of the seventh book of his *Histories* records a supposed debate between Xerxes and his closest advisers, especially an uncle called Artabanus. He also presents a good deal of supernatural apparatus that supposedly pulled Xerxes first one way, then the other. Despite Herodotus's dramatization, there was almost certainly never much doubt in Xerxes's mind that the conquest of mainland Greece was unfinished family business and a top priority for imperial action. If that motive of revenge recently weighed (as it surely did) with an elected President of the non-monarchical, democratic United States, how much more so will it have weighed with an absolute monarch motivated by personal as well as imperial considerations of revenge, security and prestige.

In 484 or so mainland Greeks south of Macedonia first got wind of Xerxes's hostile intentions and preparations. It was open to them in principle to consider true Greekness incompatible with 'slavery' – that is, subjection to the 'barbarian', non-Greek rule of Persia. And that is indeed how those mainland Greeks who decided under Spartan leadership to resist the Persian invasion in 480 did eventually decide to couch their resistance, ideologically speaking. But such loyalist Greeks were decidedly thin on the ground, and – with notable exceptions – rather thin in spirit too: they needed the beef and steel that Sparta alone was able to inject. One explanation for this lies in the very nature of Hellas – and Hellenism.

The 'colonizing' movement of the seventh and sixth centuries had left Greeks permanently settled pretty much all round the Mediterranean basin and round the Black Sea to the north-east. The resulting Greek world – or 'Hellas', to use the ancient Greeks' own term – was as much, and as little, a unity as the 'Arab world' is today or 'Christendom' was in medieval times. Politically speaking, it was not a unity or even an entity at all. Pericles of Athens with his usual gift for the memorable phrase said of his Boeotian neighbours that they were so disunited and mutually hostile that they reminded him of tall trees caught in a strong wind: their tops crashed against each other so that they acted as each other's executioners. And this, even though the Boeotians were not only fellow Greeks but members of the same Boeotian ethnolinguistic group with an actively used religious centre in common. Another illustration: Herodotus – in the context of 480, post-Thermopylae and leading up to the Battle of Salamis – reported that in his view the only reason the Phocians alone of all the Greeks north of Attica did not medize was 'simply and solely their hatred of the Thessalians. If the Thessalians had remained loyal, the Phocians would doutbless have gone over to the Persian side.'[4]

So much for panhellenic solidarity! What did unite all Hellenes were a number of other, non-political factors: myths of shared descent, ultimately from a god; other shared religious beliefs and practices, especially animal blood-sacrifice on an open-air altar; other social and societal norms and customs; and a common language (with its dialect variants). Herodotus, combining his brilliant narrative and analytical gifts, placed in the mouths of the Athenians an expression of the nature and force of this composite notion of Greekness at a deeply critical juncture of the Graeco-Persian Wars. The context is the troubled winter of 480/79. The Persians have been rocked by their defeat at Salamis, and Xerxes has returned to Asia, but he has left Mardonius with a powerful enough land army and sufficient naval support vessels to have every reasonable expectation of finally finishing off the Greek resistance the following spring and summer.

The Persians at first, though, employ a diplomatic strategy of divide and rule by bribery – a technique that would often bring them handsome dividends in dealing with the mainland Greeks over the next century and more.* To that end Mardonius dispatches his vassal King Alexander I of Macedon as an envoy to the Athenians, offering them huge amounts of money if they would desert the loyalist Greek coalition.

The choice of Alexander was in itself massively controversial. On the one hand, he claimed he was a Greek with the best interests of Greece at heart. On the other, the very Greekness of the Macedonians was fiercely contested: it was an issue then, as it has been unhappily in

---

* It was indeed the same strategy later pursued to devastating effect by Philip II of Macedon, father of Alexander the Great.

more recent times, whether and how far the ancient Macedonians were true-blue Hellenes. Mythological genealogy was on their side, since it made Macedon an early and quite central branch of the Hellenic family tree. Etymology was perhaps on their side also: philhellenic Macedonians like Alexander himself derived the name of their ruling royal house of the Argeadae (the descendants of Argeas) from unimpeachably Greek Argos in the Peloponnese. But custom and practice – what the Greeks called *nomos* – and above all language seemed to tell crucially in the other direction.

Macedonian political *nomos* did not yet extend to the construction of the characteristic Greek form of self-government, the *polis* or citizen-state. There were indeed no citizens properly so called in Macedonia, only subjects (as in Persia), and the Macedonians remained politically an *ethnos* (people) ruled by a hereditary and absolute king – or rather by a tribal warlord. Indeed, even the title of that supreme warlord to suzerainty over his fellow – or rival – warlords was questionable. For, despite the single kingship, the land of the Macedonians was not properly unified either governmentally or militarily before the Persian conquest.*

The language criterion of Greekness was vital, since the Greek verb *hellênizein*, literally 'to be Greek', basically and originally meant to *speak* Greek. And this for the Macedonians was a problem. There existed an adverb, *makedonisti*, that meant 'in Macedonian' (the language or dialect), and that betokened the fact that Macedonians could speak among themselves a language or dialect that was incomprehensible to other, more 'standard' Greek-speakers. And incomprehensible, too, in such a way as to raise the issue of whether Macedonian speech was even fundamentally Greek. There were some Greek-speakers, it is true, whose version of Greek (local idioms and/or thick accent) caused

Skip to 87

---

* After the Persians had withdrawn, an early form of political unification was first achieved by King Archelaus at the end of the fifth century, but true unification came only under Philip II (359–336).

other Greeks to sneer or laugh at them. The Spartans' spoken Greek struck the Athenians this way, for example. But there was no question of their being thought not Greek – or not wholly Greek or not Greek enough – as a result. This was, however, the case with the Macedonians' local language. It is therefore quite telling that when another standard test of Greekness was applied to the Macedonians – namely, whether or not they were eligible to compete in the all-Greek and only-Greek Olympic Games – the answer delivered by the authorities (of the city of Elis) in charge of the Games was deeply ambivalent. Only the King of the Macedonians, they decreed, should be considered eligible – meaning that the Greek status of all his subjects was left at best in limbo.

Compare – and contrast – the case of the Greeks of Sicily. This was one of the very first areas outside 'old' Greece to be 'colonized'. Syracuse, for example, was founded in the later eighth century BCE, traditionally in 733. Some Greek women were no doubt taken along on some of the many colonizing expeditions to Sicily which eventually saw Greeks settled all over the island, except in the far north-west, a Phoenician enclave. These women will have included members of priestly families, with a view to maintaining continuity of religious practice and identity with the 'old' country. Indeed, religion together with kinship constituted the closest affective ties between a metropolis (mother city) and its colonial 'daughter' foundation. And yet most of the Greek colonists will have been young, unmarried men who took for their wives and sexual partners women of the indigenous Sicel and Sican populations. Thus most Sicilian Greeks of the early fifth century will have been of mixed Greek-'barbarian' stock originally. Even so, when the tyrant of Syracuse, Gelon, claimed a share of the command of the anti-Persian resistance forces, his admittedly unacceptable and imperious demand was not rebuffed on the grounds that he was not, or not sufficiently, Greek. 'Greekness', in short, like ethnicity in probably all societies and cultures, was situationally constructed rather than naturally given. The Macedonians' problem was that typically they failed to demonstrate their claims to Greekness with sufficient

Occasionally, Greek potters and painters, such as the two men nicknamed by scholars the Sotades Potter and the Sotades Painter, ventured into elaborate vase shapes; here a rhyton, a ritual vessel for pouring libations to the gods, in the form of a ram's head with a decoration of an ivy frieze in red-figure technique, possibly imitating a Persian metal vessel captured as booty in 480 or 479.

clarity and lack of ambiguity. That Alexander was a Persian vassal-king in 480 did his cause no good whatsoever.

The Spartans somehow learned of Alexander's mission, and – revealingly – were sufficiently frightened that the Athenians might be persuaded to abandon the coalition by offers of Persian gold that they at once sent their own counter-legation to Athens. This gave the Athenians a wonderful platform – or perhaps we should say it enabled Herodotus to offer them one; and here is what the Athenians said to allay the Spartans' fears, or rather what Herodotus makes them say:

> *There are many and powerful factors preventing us from doing this [deserting the coalition] even if we were to wish to (which we do not). First and greatest of all is religion: the images of the gods*

*and their shrines that the Persians have burned and destroyed we
must of necessity avenge to the best of our capacity rather than
do a deal with the perpetrator of these outrages. Then there is the
fact of our being Hellenes: we are of one and the same blood, and
use one and the same tongue, we have in common the establish-
ments of the gods and the sacrifices we perform in their honour,
and we share the same customary ways. For the Athenians to be
traitors to all that would not be well.*[5]

The three constituent elements of the Athenians' persuasive definition of *to hellênikon*, which I have translated above as 'the fact of our
being Hellenes', are, then, common blood, common language and
common customs, especially common religious beliefs and practices.
Herodotus gave a great deal of weight to what we would call marital
and sexual attitudes and practices, and to food habits. Tell me how
and with whom you have sex, and what and how you eat, and I will
tell you who you are. But if pressed, he would probably have privileged common religious practices above all other common customs,
and not least common funerary arrangements.

So when Herodotus wanted to illustrate by means of an exemplary
parable both the differences between ethnic customs and the fact that
different ethnic groups imagine their own customs to be not just better
than those of others but absolutely the best possible, it was precisely
funerary arrangements that he chose for purposes of demonstration.[6]*
As a matter of hard historical fact, it was not the case that all Greek
societies practised identical funerary customs. Far from it. And the
Spartans' ways of death were probably the most idiosyncratic of all.

---

* See Appendix 3.

FOUR

SPARTA 485:
A UNIQUE CULTURE
AND SOCIETY

Sparta, world-famous home of a narrow military aristocracy, with its haughty pride of race, its relentless discipline and its ruthless oppression of its subjects . . .

M. N. Tod, 'Retrospect', 1944

T HE SPARTANS, notwithstanding their extraordinary patriotic pride and military prowess, were by no means entirely friends to freedom. As we saw earlier, at home in Laconia and Messenia they exercised for several centuries a ruthless domination over native Greek populations many times the size of their own, to whom they gave the derogatory collective label 'Helots', or 'captives'. Professionals in a world of amateurs, the Spartans alone of Greek cities maintained a standing army. But they were not militaristic in the sense that they enjoyed war for its own sake. That unique army was invented and maintained, first and often foremost, to dominate and suppress the Helots. In fact, their whole society was organized as a kind of standing army. It was kept ever on the alert against the enemy within, as well as against any Greek or non-Greek enemies from without. It was no accident that the Spartans' Messenian Helot problem should have figured prominently in Herodotus's account of a significant visitor to Sparta in 500.

The visitor was Aristagoras from Miletus. Not many foreigners ever set foot in Sparta, let alone foreigners from the non-Dorian Greek world of Ionia far across the Aegean Sea. But Aristagoras had a specially compelling mission: to secure Spartan military support for his proposed revolt against Persia – the Ionian Revolt, as it is known (see Chapter Three). Aristagoras was in the parlance of Herodotus's day a 'tyrant', an unelected, non-responsible sole ruler. He owed his position to the patronage of his predecessor Histiaeus and to his control of superior military force backed by the support of the Persian satrap in nearby Sardis. He was not perhaps an unmitigated despot any more than, for example, Peisistratus tyrant of Athens (died 527) had been. But his very position was enough to cause suspicion, especially as he had been ruling Miletus in effect as a pro-Persian quisling, or puppet.

As Herodotus tells the story, the Spartan citizen body as such was not consulted at all on whether they wished to support Aristagoras against Persia. This may just be an accidental omission, but it may equally well reflect the fact that Sparta's political arrangements were fundamentally oligarchic, disguised only by a veneer of popular consultation. Sparta in 500 was dominated by a powerful king, Cleomenes I, who controlled the tiny and elite Spartan *Gerousia*,* or Senate (comprising its twenty-eight elected members, together with the other king ex officio, making thirty in all). This meant he was in a position to dictate the policy of Sparta, regardless of the views of the citizenry as a whole. But Herodotus gilded the lily a little by making out that the only Spartan with any decisive influence over the King was a young girl of about eight – his only child, Gorgo (future wife of Cleomenes's half-brother Leonidas). Aristagoras was allegedly making some headway in attracting Cleomenes's support, by pandering to the known Spartan susceptibility to bribes, when Gorgo sharply reminded her father of where his moral and regal duty lay.

Herodotus in his usual way does also reveal what really told

---

* See Glossary.

against Aristagoras. In order for the Spartans to lay their hands on the wealth stored at Susa, they would have to undertake a march of some three months inland into Asia, far away from the Aegean coast. But the Spartans were essentially landlubbers. In 525, as we saw in Chapter One, they had essayed an aggressive foray as far across the Aegean as the island of Samos, in an attempt to unseat the tyrant Polycrates. But that unsuccessful attempt offered no precedent for the sort of amphibious expedition that Aristagoras was advocating. So the Milesian left Sparta empty-handed. In newly democratic Athens, however, he had far greater success, which gave Herodotus the opportunity to contrast favourably the refusal of the one Spartan, Cleomenes, with the agreement of thirty thousand gullible Athenians.*

Cleomenes's supremacy in Sparta was exercised at no small political cost. He had acquired the throne hereditarily reserved to the Agiad royal family in about 520 in controversial circumstances, since he had been born to his father Anaxandridas's second – and bigamous – wife. Dorieus was the oldest son of Anaxandridas's first, wholly legitimate wife, but he had been born after Cleomenes and his claim to the succession was rebuffed. He therefore took himself off in a giant huff and embarked upon a series of adventures in north Africa and Sicily, where he died. In about 515 the other royal house, that of the Eurypontids, experienced a much smoother succession, which brought Demaratus to the throne. But Demaratus too had a chequered past, and there was a question-mark over his legitimacy that Cleomenes was eventually to turn into a full stop. Indeed, he and Cleomenes probably never got on very well with each other; that, according to Herodotus, was a normal feature of relations between the two royal houses. In 506 they fell out spectacularly – publicly, and with fatal consequences, at first for Sparta's foreign policy and eventually for Demaratus himself.

---

* Since in general Herodotus's account of Cleomenes is hostile, and since he elsewhere says nice things about the crucial military importance of Athens being a democracy, presumably his judgement was affected here by his own conviction of the supreme folly of the Ionian Revolt.

This exceptionally handsome bronze figurine of a hoplite fighter decked out in his finest parade armour was made by a Perioecic craftsman and dedicated in a Perioecic sanctuary of Apollo in south west Messenia towards the end of the sixth century. As if to show that Perioeci could be the equals of their Spartan overlords, our hero is accompanied by his favourite hunting dog, of whom only a trace is preserved.

Sparta by the middle of the sixth century was already considered the strongest military power in mainland Greece; hence Croesus of Lydia's concluding an alliance with Sparta against the incoming tide of Persian might (though actually the alliance bore no fruit). Specifically, Sparta had the strongest land army, the core of which was its citizen hoplites. Unlike in all other Greek cities, every Spartan full adult citizen was also, by definition, a member of Sparta's hoplite phalanx. Again unusually or uniquely, hoplite arms and defensive armour were provided centrally to Spartan warriors. This was from an arsenal stocked and maintained by the labour of sub-Spartans called *Perioeci* or 'dwellers around'. Since the Spartans themselves were forbidden by law to practise any other trade or craft than warfare, their weapons and armour were manufactured for them by the free but politically unenfranchised inhabitants of some eighty small towns and villages concentrated mainly in upland and coastal Laconia but with a scattering around the coast of Messenia too. Some *Perioeci* were wealthy enough to be able to equip themselves to fight as hoplites, and Sparta came to draw ever more heavily on these support hoplites in the course of its history.*

---

* Already at the Battle of Plataea in 479 there was the same absolute number (5,000) of such hoplites in the field as of Spartans, but 5,000 was a far higher percentage of the potentially available Spartan total.

Freed by compulsory Helot labour from the necessity to earn their bread, Spartan citizen hoplites were compelled to drill, drill, drill and in other ways too to train incessantly in preparation for an immediate call to arms. The Helot underclass were always threatening to rise up in significant numbers against their masters. So, at the beginning of each new civil year Sparta's chief elected officials, the board of five ephors (overseers, supervisors), formally declared war on them. If any Helots did choose to rebel, they might then be killed with impunity, without the killer's incurring the taint of religious pollution that otherwise inevitably accompanied the shedding of human blood.

The ephors too had general oversight of the Spartans' unique educational system, the *agôgê* (upbringing). This had been devised chiefly for the boys, in order to turn them into suitable officer material as adults. Successful graduation from the *agôgê* was a requirement for a Spartan male to permit him to join the group of full citizens known as *homoioi*, or peers (literally 'similars'). But it was also applied – separately but almost equally – to the girls. From the age of seven a Spartan boy was removed from his parental home and required to live in a public dormitory-cum-barracks that served as a schoolhouse too. He was kept on very short rations, so much so that he might find himself reduced to stealing even a not very appetising wild fox. This gave rise to the iconically Spartan tale of the boy who was interrupted shortly after he had caught a fox and interrogated by one of his educators. Under the rules of the *agôgê* stealing by the boys was permitted, and even encouraged (to develop the skills of stealth, surprise and resourcefulness that might well come in handy in adulthood on campaign). But being caught redhanded in the act of stealing was absolutely forbidden and severely punishable, so the boy in the tale stuffed the fox under his tunic (the one tunic he was allowed per annum). And rather than utter a cry that would betray his theft, he stoically kept silent as the fox gnawed away at his vitals until he dropped down dead in front of his inquisitor. Exaggeration aside, the message of the necessity of stoical obedience was unambiguous – and its pedagogic effectiveness ensured that it was repeated and preserved.

Another such cautionary tale concerns a rather older, teenage Spartan youth. He made the bad mistake of crying out in pain when taking part in the vigorous physical mauling that constituted a large part of the Spartan educational cycle – or endurance test – at that stage of his life. His cries were heard by the seniors in charge, and the street cred of the teenager instantly plummeted as a result. However, unlike the boy with the fox, it was not he who was liable to be formally reprimanded and punished – but instead his lover, a young Spartan citizen. The thinking was that the older, adult mentor had failed to inculcate properly Spartan values and behaviour into his adolescent beloved.

Such literally pederastic ('boy-desiring') pairing relationships between an unmarried young adult citizen warrior (aged, say, twenty to twenty-five) and a teenaged boy (aged between fourteen and eighteen) were not abnormal or unusual; actually, they were more or less obligatory for all in Sparta, as part of the *agôgê*. The Spartans even devised a special local vocabulary for them: the older partner was called the 'inspirer' and the younger one the 'hearer'. Of course, these metaphors might well have been a cover for the relationship's carnal and earthy aspects.* Sharing in a lopsided partnership of this nature had for the junior party the force of an initiatory ritual, an essential step along the gruelling road to his achieving full manhood. It is not unlikely, either, that it could have implications for political and other sorts of relationships at later stages of a Spartan's life.†

The institutional practice of a state-run, comprehensive educational

---

* The Spartans had a reputation among other Greeks, no doubt exaggerated, for being addicted to buggery.

† The future king Agesilaus II, as a teenager going through the regular educational system (because not expected to succeed to the throne), was the 'hearer' of Lysander. Lysander later became briefly the single most powerful Spartan of his day, and so the most influential single Greek, since Sparta was then the superpower of the Greek world. Certainly, he was more powerful even than the kings, and his support and influence were by no means irrelevant or incidental to Agesilaus's attaining the Eurypontid throne in a fiercely contested succession dispute in (probably) 400.

system for all boys was unique to Sparta. Likewise unique was the parallel cycle for Spartan girls, which also placed a premium on physical fitness, though its overall aims were of course different, since in Sparta as elsewhere in Greece women were deemed the non-military half of the citizen population. Whereas the boys were being groomed for adult warriorhood, the girls could not aspire to being initiated into the mystery of martial bravery and courage encapsulated in the term 'manliness' (*andreia*) that could also mean 'courage'. Instead, the females were being officially prepared for the almost equal honour they were granted as wives and mothers, ideally the mothers of future warriors.

Sparta according to the poets was a city 'of broad dancing-floors', and this vigorous bronze figurine of a dancing (or running) Spartan female of the later sixth century was a wonderful advertisement for her city as she was exported as far afield as southern Albania (northern Epirus in antiquity).

The Spartans placed a premium on reproduction (*teknopoiia*, literally the 'making of children'), mainly, one supposes, for fear of the vastly larger subordinate population of enslaved Helots by which they were surrounded. It was, then, in the eugenic belief that physically fit women would be more successful mothers of sons that all girls were given a training in athletics, including wrestling and throwing the javelin as well as running, besides a more typically Greek schooling in singing and dancing.* Though the girls, unlike their brothers, contin-

---

* Edgar Degas, well schooled in the classics, was particularly caught by this Spartan female athleticism and reproduced it on several occasions in the 1860s in studies now in the National Gallery, London, the Fogg Art Museum of Harvard University, and the Art Institute, Chicago.

ued to live in the parental home with their mothers until marriage, what they were deliberately *not* brought up to perform were the standard domestic tasks of cooking, cleaning and clothes-making that fell to the lot of all other Greek girls and wives. Those were reserved for Helot women. Spartan mothers didn't even play the major role in child-rearing, again because of the ready availability of Helot wet-nurses and childminders. Instead, a huge amount of attention was paid to ensuring that the female half of the population internalized the state's dominantly masculine values.

Hostile non-Spartan critics took pleasure in condemning the women for failing to abide by the strict and austerely community-minded 'laws of Lycurgus'.* They were allegedly overfond of luxury and wealth. This included landed property, which, exceptionally in Greece, Spartan women could own in their own right. They were castigated too for their lack of self-discipline, and even for their cowardice in the face of the enemy. When Laconia was penetrated, for the first time ever, right up to the town of Sparta itself in 370/69, the Thebans and their allies laid the Spartans' fields waste, including those owned by women, right under their noses. Aristotle claimed that the women did even more damage to Sparta than the enemy! On the other hand, a friendly observer such as Xenophon could praise the Spartan women, rather, for their remarkably stoical reaction to the loss of their nearest and dearest menfolk at the Battle of Leuctra in 371.†

Besides developing Greece's most efficient hoplite army, the Spartans also finessed their relations with the outside Greek world

---

* Lycurgus was a legendary and at least semi-mythical lawgiver of early times to whom were ascribed pretty well all historical Sparta's laws and regulations. But despite his success with the Spartan men, he was said to have failed to win the women over to his views.

† Xenophon was a much older contemporary of Aristotle. As a guest-friend of King Agesilaus, he had lived in Sparta when in exile from his native Athens at the beginning of the fourth century, and at Agesilaus's suggestion had put his two sons through the Spartan educational system.

through carefully constructed diplomatic means. Like the educational cycle, this was prompted not least by concern about their internal security against the Helots. Within the borders of the Spartan state (known officially as Lacedaemon) there were also the eighty or so cities and towns of the free but politically subordinate *Perioeci*, who were expected to form the first line of anti-Helot defence. But it was also felt desirable to throw a further ring of confidence around Sparta's extensive home territory, which at some 8,000 square kilometres was twice the size of the next-biggest state in the Greek world, that of Syracuse in Sicily.

The Spartans' first external alliance was possibly concluded in about 550 with the nearest *polis* to the north, Tegea in Arcadia. But inside a generation their alliance system within the Peloponnese had been extended as far as the Isthmus of Corinth, and by the end of the sixth century or early in the fifth it had gone beyond the Peloponnese into central Greece, embracing Megara and the offshore island of Aegina. Allies swore one-sided oaths of subordinate loyalty to Sparta, guaranteeing to provide military support on demand in return for Sparta's preserving the allies' generally oligarchic regimes – a service that became more and more important following Athens's conversion to democracy in 508.

The one Peloponnesian state that conspicuously refused to join Sparta's alliance, as we noted earlier, was Argos, which challenged Sparta militarily in the field in about 545 but was very seriously defeated. The pattern was to be repeated quite regularly thereafter (494, 469, 418 . . .). In 525 Sparta felt confident enough even to throw its weight about in the eastern Aegean, with the crucial naval assistance of its ally Corinth. Again in 512 or so, in a bid to unseat the ruling 'tyrant' dynasty of the sons of Peisistratus, Sparta sent a naval rather than a land expedition against Athens. And this raises the general question of Sparta's attitude to foreign tyrants, or autocrats. Sparta came to acquire the reputation of opposing tyrants on principle, since it did as a matter of fact depose a good few of them. But in all cases sound pragmatic reasons for the depositions can be advanced with equal plausibility, and there were at least two occasions when Sparta so far forgot its supposed anti-tyrannical principles that it attempted actually to impose or reimpose tyrants. Both these occasions fell within an extraordinary and history-transforming period of just half a dozen years, from 510 to 504, and both in relation to Athens.

Herodotus, who placed great emphasis on the Spartans' extreme religiosity, believed that they had been persuaded to turn against the Athenians' longstanding tyrant dynasty in 510 by a constant stream of Delphic oracles. At all events, the regime of Hippias and his brother was abruptly terminated by Cleomenes's intervention, and Hippias made good his escape not merely into exile but into the arms of Persia. As a client now of Great King Darius, he nursed into extreme old age his dream of return and restoration. From a Greek perspective the nexus between Persia and mainland Greek politics had been decisively forged, confirming the link between Persia and Greek tyranny that was already institutionalized on the Asiatic side of the Aegean.

Two years later, in 508, Cleomenes was back in Athens, again with an army, and this time occupying the Acropolis for some days. But there was no chance here to claim that the intervention was in the name of securing freedom for the Athenians from oppression or tyranny, because Cleomenes was actually intervening against the clearly expressed wishes of the majority of Athenian citizens. They had declared that they favoured the imaginative and pioneering 'democratic' reforms proposed by Cleisthenes, a longstanding opponent of the old tyrant regime. Cleomenes, in the sharpest contrast, favoured a reactionary solution, the installation of Cleisthenes's opponent Isagoras as a pro-Spartan quisling tyrant. So much for Sparta's supposed opposition to tyranny on principle!

Cleomenes to his shame and embarrassment found himself blockaded on the Acropolis and forced to withdraw ignominiously to Sparta. But he retained sufficient clout to effect the temporary exile of Cleisthenes, for a second time, with a considerable number of his relations and closest supporters. That success proved to be transient. Cleisthenes soon returned, his reforms began to take root and to flourish – not least, as events were soon to prove, in the military department. So in 506 Cleomenes decided to try again to assert his will upon a recalcitrant Athens. This time he had, he thought, prepared the ground more thoroughly. The army he led was not just of Spartans, but of the Spartans and their considerable number of Peloponnesian allied states. Moreover, he had, he thought, arranged to co-ordinate his invasion from the Peloponnese via the Isthmus of Corinth with attacks on Athens from Boeotia (led by the Thebans) and Euboea (the city of Chalcis). But there were two flaws in the enterprise. The first was that, though the allies were clear at the start that the objective of the expedition was to exert Spartan power over Athens, it became clear to them only later that Cleomenes intended a repeat of his 508 ploy, the installation of Isagoras as tyrant. It seemed to some of the more important of the allies, especially Corinth, that Cleomenes was thereby overstepping his stated remit, and Corinth's memories of its own tyrant dynasty were still rather too fresh.

The second, and more damaging, flaw was that Cleomenes had failed to carry his co-king Demaratus with him, ideologically and morally; physically, Demaratus did indeed accompany the army as it headed for the Isthmus, presumably because it was then still quite normal for both kings to lead out such a major force. At a crucial moment, though, and in concert with the Corinthian allies, Demaratus simply withdrew and returned to Sparta, so that the Spartan part of the concerted pincer movement on Athens was left in complete disarray, a total shambles. The Boeotians and Chalcidians nevertheless went ahead with their attack from the north and east, only to be soundly defeated by the new-style democratic army of Athens, in high spirits as they fought not just to protect their sovereign independence but also to preserve their revolutionary new political regime. Even so, in about

504 the Spartans tried yet again. And this time, such was their desperation that the tyrant they proposed to impose on Athens was none other than the old one, old in both senses: Peisistratus's son Hippias, the 'medizing' refugee at the Persian court.

Herodotus does not actually name Cleomenes in connection with this final attempt, and it is possible that he prudently hung back, despite approving the project. What scuppered this last initiative was not Demaratus – or not Demaratus alone – but a collective decision taken by majority vote in Sparta of representatives of all Sparta's inner circle of allies. In other words, no longer could a Spartan king simply dictate to the allies, but the allies had acquired a collective voice, and a collective right to be heard. Modern scholars mark this moment as the birth of what they call the Peloponnesian League. Sparta retained the initiative vis-à-vis its allies; that is, the allies could not commit Sparta to a foreign policy of which it disapproved, and it was for Sparta to make up its own mind first in closed deliberation before summoning the allies to a public conclave to gain their approval. But the vital clause inscribed in all treaties of alliance, to the effect that an ally must 'follow the Spartans whithersoever they may lead them', had now been crucially modified to give the allies, collectively, a right of veto by majority vote.*

This was the Sparta, headed by King Cleomenes, that Aristagoras visited in the year 500, a somewhat chastened Sparta but still the pre-eminent military power on the Greek mainland. Untempted by Asiatic adventures, the Spartans were to be much preoccupied with Peloponnesian matters nearer to home in the 490s. Aristagoras had, according to Herodotus, advised the Spartans to suspend their petty local wars over pitifully poor scraps of land 'with your rivals the Messenians, the Arcadians and Argives'.[1] There is no other certain evi-

---

* The new alliance system had a rosy future: it was this that gave Sparta, and only Sparta, the claim to hegemony and supremacy in any Hellenic resistance to Persia. Most of the (few) Greek states that conducted the successful resistance in 480 and 479 were members of Sparta's Peloponnesian League alliance.

dence that Sparta was hotly engaged in dispute with any of the Arcadian cities at this time, though the issue of a coinage bearing the legend *Arkadikon* (the Arcadian federation) has sometimes been dated as early as 490 or thereabouts. This could have betokened the formation of a quasi-nationalist Arcadian federation, which would inevitably have been considered inimical to Sparta's geopolitical interests. Sparta's general policy was always to try to divide the Arcadians among themselves, the more easily to rule them, in particular keeping the *polis* of Tegea firmly separate from and opposed to Mantinea in eastern Arcadia. Nor is there other much sounder evidence that the Messenians, that is the Messenian Helots, were then posing any greater threat to Sparta than they constantly posed, though Plato does make one of the characters in his mammoth *Laws* dialogue allege that at the time of the Battle of Marathon (490) the Spartans had to face a Helot uprising.

There is very good evidence indeed, on the other hand, that in the 490s the Spartans, under Cleomenes, were clashing once again with the auld enemy Argos, and once again dishing out a slashing defeat. Indeed, it removed Argos from the board as a serious player for an entire generation. The centrepiece was a battle, probably in 494, fought at Sepeia in the Argolid region, so the Spartans were clearly the aggressors. Herodotus's interest is not in the battle's military details but in Cleomenes's actions after the battle, which he uses as yet another stick with which to beat his villain of the piece. Several thousands of Argive survivors, he reports, had taken refuge in a sacred grove as suppliants. Cleomenes unscrupulously ordered the Helots in his entourage – so that he would not himself be directly tainted with the religious pollution – to set fire to the grove, and thereby killed most of the suppliants. But so far as the Spartans themselves were concerned, this was not his only alleged offence. When he returned to Sparta, after a campaign that had after all been a huge success in pragmatic terms, he was put on trial for his life: for failing to take the city of Argos itself.

Such trials of Spartan kings were held in camera before the permanent *Gerousia* and the board of five ephors of the year; there were no popular lawcourts in Sparta ever, unlike the system that was developed most conspicuously in democratic Athens, for example. So most likely the chief accuser was none other than Cleomenes's fellow king Demaratus, his rival and enemy. The ephors, it seems, had to make a preliminary judgement – *anakrisis* – as to whether there was a charge to be met, and Demaratus perhaps had a majority of the ephors on his side. Nevertheless Cleomenes managed to get himself off, and he did so in a thoroughly cunning, because thoroughly Spartan, way. He claimed that as he had gone to offer sacrifice at the Argive Heraion, the shrine of Argos's patron goddess Hera, a portent had declared itself. A flame had shot forth from the breast of the goddess's magnificent chryselephantine cult statue. From this sign he said he knew with absolute certainty that it was not fated that he should capture the citadel of Argos, for, had that been so, the flame would have shot out of the statue's head, not from its breast. The Spartans, says Herodotus, found this 'a credible and reasonable defence'.[2]

In those few words Herodotus has contrived to say a huge amount about Sparta. Apart from its educational and military systems, Sparta's third most palpably distinctive cultural feature was its religious system. Elsewhere, and twice over, Herodotus comments on the exceptional piety, or religiosity, of the Spartans: 'they esteemed the things of the gods as more authoritative than the things of men'.[3] Well, actually all conventional Greeks did that much, so what Herodotus, himself a man of powerful religious motivation and conventionally Greek piety, surely means to imply is that the Spartans judged their duty to the gods to be much *more* absolute and binding. In a way, they applied to their attitude to the gods their outlook on life in general – one of order, hierarchy and unquestioning obedience. The gods stood, as it were, at the very apex of a tall pyramid of authoritative command. It was no coincidence that in Sparta every god and goddess was represented wearing arms and armour. The city's patron goddess was Athena, who despite her gender was regularly represented throughout Greece as wearing a helmet and breastplate and carrying a spear. But it was in Sparta, uniquely, that even the manifestly unwarlike Aphrodite (connoisseurs of Homer's *Iliad* would smile) was given an incongruously martial aspect.

This almost blind devotion to the gods explains why the Spartans went to inordinate lengths to find out in advance if they possibly could – through examining the entrails of sacrificed animals or consulting oracles, for instance – what the divine will was. We even hear of Spartan commanders, though faced with the absolute need to take an urgent decision in the heat of battle, sacrificing and sacrificing again and again until they received a divinatory answer they found acceptable and actionable. For this the Spartans were dubbed 'expert craftsmen in military matters' by Xenophon, a conscious metaphor since they were forbidden to be skilled craftsmen in the literal sense. One highly pertinent aspect of the Spartans' quite exceptional religiosity – exceptional not only in ancient Greek terms – was their attitude to death.

Plutarch in his 'biography' of Lycurgus says that the lawgiver was very concerned to rid Spartans of any unnecessary or debilitating fear of death and dying. To that end, he permitted the corpses of all Spartans, adults no less than infants, to be buried among the habitations of the living, within the regular settlement area – and not, as was the norm elsewhere in the entire Greek world from at latest about 700 BCE, carefully segregated in separately demarcated cemeteries away from the living spaces. The Spartans, in other words, did not share the normal Greek view that burial automatically brought pollution (*miasma*). They believed that the cremated or inhumed bodies of their ancestors were a source of communal solidarity and strength rather than weakness, and something to be embraced and literally lived with rather than abhorred and shunned and put out of sight as well as out of mind.

On the other hand, the Spartans did reserve two spaces for burials well outside the habitation area of the town of Sparta; though 'burials' is perhaps misleading. One was the Caeadas, a gorge that has been identified at the modern village of Trypi ('Hole') some way west of Sparta near the entrance to the Langhada pass leading through the

Taygetus mountain range into Messenia. Into this ravine were tossed the bodies of criminals condemned for capital crimes. The other space is much more interesting from the viewpoint of Spartan attitudes to life and death. The Spartans, as noted, were very preoccupied with the reproduction of their citizen population, but sheer numbers alone were not enough. Quality too mattered. Thus newborn infants (of both sexes, perhaps, but the males were at this stage much the more important) were submitted to a ritual inspection and test conducted by 'the elders of the tribesmen', as Plutarch puts it. They were dunked in a bath of presumably undiluted wine, to see how they reacted. If they failed the test, the consequences were fatal. They were taken to a place called cryptically 'the deposits' (*apothetai*) and hurled to their certain deaths into a ravine.* So too were those infants unluckily born with some serious and already obvious physical deformity or disability.

'Exposure' of newborns was by no means unique to ancient Sparta. It was positively recommended, too, in the utopian philosophical prescriptions of both Plato and Aristotle. But in other Greek cities the procedure was a good deal more gentle and differently configured. Parents – and not the state – had complete control over the process, and exposure might more often be resorted to for economic than for eugenic or state-dictated motives. Nor was there necessarily any expectation, let alone desire, that exposure would automatically mean death. At Athens, for example, there was a recognized term ((*en*)*khutrizein*) for the practice of placing exposed infants in a large earthenware pot, in the hope that some other family, childless for physiological or other reasons but materially able and psychologically willing, might pick them up and rear them.

So not only were Spartans brought up in the close company of death and burial but they were taught to be prepared for the loss of an infant deemed to be a public encumbrance, a burden on the state.

---

* Identified plausibly at the village of Parori not far from Byzantine Mistra on the flank of Mt Taygetus.

Consistently with that view, the Spartans did not feel the need to make a song and dance of the burial and mourning process; the giant exception that was the state funeral of a Spartan king proved that rule spectacularly.* So a dead Spartan man, woman or child was not buried in a lavish, let alone a visually prominent or monumental tomb, but in a simple earth-cut pit accompanied by a minimum of grave-goods; Plutarch says the regulations for an adult male burial allowed just his famous scarlet military cloak, with the corpse laid on a simple bed of olive leaves. (This, incidentally, could explain why so few Spartan graves of the historical period have ever been unearthed.)

A dead Spartan was not allowed even the relatively minor luxury of a headstone with an identifying name inscribed on it – with two exceptions. First, a soldier who had been killed in battle was allowed to have his name inscribed on a tombstone followed by just the two stark words 'in war' – a truly laconic message. Laconic (Spartan) speech was brief, curt and clipped, but proportionately every syllable was supposed to be made to tell. Such posthumous commemoration was the logical next step after the Spartans' glorification and exaltation of the warrior's 'beautiful death' in battle. This attitude goes back at least to the middle of the seventh century, as it is found already in the poetry of Tyrtaeus: 'endure while looking at bloody death / and reach out for the enemy while standing near'.[4] Tyrtaeus served as the Spartans' national war-poet, and his martial poems were preserved down the ages, being learned compulsorily by heart by boys during their education and recited by them regularly as adults when on campaign. The point about 'standing near' is that this is hoplite poetry: Tyrtaeus envisages hand-to-hand phalanx combat of the bloodiest kind.

The second exception and exemption concerned either priestesses or – but this alternative requires a serious modification of Plutarch's text as transmitted – women who had died in childbirth. Both alternatives can be given perfectly reasonable explanations within the general

---

* See Chapter Eight.

context of known Spartan communal values. The exaltation in death of priestesses would be entirely consistent with the Spartans' privileging of religion – the relationship of men to the gods – ahead of secular matters involving the relationship of men to men. The singling-out of women who died in childbed would corroborate the society's preoccupation with reproduction, as well as put the contribution of a mother (especially a mother of potential warrior sons) on a par with the social contribution of an adult male fighter: the former gave a new life for Sparta, the latter gave up his life for Sparta.

Xenophon's record of the aftermath of the Battle of Leuctra in 371 brings out just how odd were the official Spartan attitudes to the death of a relative. At Leuctra in Boeotia Sparta suffered its first major defeat in a pitched infantry battle, at the hands of the Thebans and their allies. More than half of the Spartans fighting had been killed, and their deaths had reduced the total adult male citizen population of the *polis* to under one thousand – compared to the then 25–30,000 citizens of Athens, for instance. This was a massive catastrophe, both collectively and individually, both publicly and – in so far as this distinction could usefully be drawn in Sparta – privately. (Since a lot of effort was put into the inculcation of official attitudes through education and habituation, unofficial, individual and private attitudes were probably quite similar.) Yet when the news was brought home, and individual families were told which men had died, the relatives of the slain went about with cheerful, almost delighted expressions, whereas the relatives of the survivors, so far from being thrilled or relieved, were humiliated by what they regarded as a double insult – not only had the state's army been defeated, but their relatives had lived to tell the despicable tale; so they cowered away from public view in a state of shock and self-hatred.*

In short, the Spartans – uniquely in all Greece – took the view that death in itself was nothing to be feared but rather something to be literally lived with and daily stared in the face. How you died mattered

---

* We shall return to this in Chapter Six.

no more – and no less – here than it did elsewhere in Greece; only in Sparta there was always a powerful and often an overwhelming emphasis on the public dimension of any death rather than on the private and purely familial one. The searing relevance of this attitude and behaviour to the Thermopylae campaign becomes almost painfully apparent.

With Argos out of the way and himself cleared of the capital charge, Cleomenes was free to direct Sparta's attention for the first time across the Aegean and towards the rising Persian menace. This is the sole occasion on which Herodotus bestows on him unqualified praise. In 491 the ruling aristocracy of the strategically key island of Aegina in the Saronic Gulf ('the stye in the eye of the Peiraeus', as Pericles was to call it) decided to medize: they gave earth and water to Darius's envoys as tokens of their willingness to submit to Persian imperial hegemony. Cleomenes at once marched and sailed to Aegina, where he met fierce resistance led by an aristocrat called Crius, or 'Ram'. Crius accused Cleomenes of having been bribed (yet another example of this standard accusation against Spartans) by the Aeginetans' enemies, the Athenians. For, he said, if Cleomenes's intervention in the affairs of an allied but independent state had been formally authorized by the Spartan state, both kings would have come, not just Cleomenes alone.

Crius here was certainly playing on and hoping to exploit the known enmity between Cleomenes and Demaratus, but he might also have been appealing to a possible constitutional requirement that both kings be in agreement on such matters of external intervention. However that may be, Cleomenes was not to be brooked or balked. After uttering a typically laconic remark – 'You had better get your horns sheathed in metal, Ram' – he returned to Sparta, engineered the deposition of Demaratus, and replaced him with the more amenable Leotychidas.*

---

* Leotychidas was a Eurypontid, but only a distant relative of Demaratus. He was also a deadly personal foe, since he had once literally stolen Demaratus's well connected and wealthy fiancée from him and married her himself.

As in the Argos episode of 494, Cleomenes found himself compelled to resort to religion against Demaratus, but here he overreached himself. Sparta had long had a special relationship with the uniquely authoritative oracle of Apollo at Delphi, and maintained a hotline to the priesthood there by way of four permanently appointed ambassadors to the shrine, known as Pythioi. These Pythioi were crown appointments, two of them chosen by each of the Spartan kings. In 491, however, Cleomenes's Pythioi did not merely consult the oracular priestess and priesthood of Delphi. They also brought filthy lucre to bribe them to say what he wanted Apollo to declare, namely that Demaratus was a bastard: in the legal sense – not the legitimate son of his father, the late king Ariston. And, moreover, the Delphic officials allegedly accepted the bribe and delivered the desired verdict. In the short run, the ploy worked brilliantly for Cleomenes: Demaratus was declared a bastard by divine utterance and therefore deposed and replaced, and Cleomenes was free to return to Aegina, take Crius and other leading Aeginetans hostage, and force them to renounce their pro-Persian, or at least not anti-Persian, policy. It was for this that Herodotus praised Cleomenes to the skies, as one 'acting for the common good of all Hellas'. However, the carefully woven plot then unravelled – disastrously for Cleomenes. The bribery was discovered, and the Delphians involved were dismissed from their posts. Cleomenes seems to have gone literally mad.

Herodotus says that he had always been slightly touched, not quite right in the head.* But the effect of the exposure of his extreme irreligiosity and his consequent self-exile to Arcadia was said to have been to make him behave so irrationally on his return to Sparta that the authorities felt they had to clap him in the public stocks. He was placed under the guard of Helots, but so persuasive was even a demented Cleomenes that he induced one of them to lend him his dag-

---

* He was probably faithfully retailing what he had been told by his anti-Cleomenes informants, who may well have included descendants of Demaratus still living in the region around Troy in north-west Anatolia.

This damaged marble mask was found at Marathon; it belongs stylistically to the first quarter of the fifth century, which could well tie it to the famous Battle of Marathon in 490. It probably depicts a god, rather than a hero, and possibly therefore Pan, who crucially aided the Athenians by spreading his eponymous panic fear among the Persians and was awarded an official religious cult in return.

ger. With that, he allegedly committed an appalling sort of hara-kiri, slicing himself into pieces from his feet upwards.

A huge amount was at stake in Cleomenes's death: Sparta's foreign policy and its standing with its allies abroad, and the health of the dyarchy at home. Not unnaturally, therefore, it has been suspected that Cleomenes did not actually kill himself but rather, having become an extreme embarrassment all round, was prudently done away with, possibly even by his own blood relatives. We shall never know for sure, but we do know the immediate outcome of Cleomenes's death, which was the succession of his younger half-brother Leonidas. It is intriguing to ponder that, had Cleomenes still been alive and still king ten years or so later – he was only in his fifties when he died, in the early 480s – then we might have been celebrating not Leonidas, but Cleomenes, of Thermopylae.

The 480s in Spartan history are pretty much one vast blank in terms of evidence. The consequences of the Battle of Marathon, and of Sparta's non-participation in that triumphant Athenian success, will have rumbled on. The Spartans might well have followed the internal politics of democratic Athens with great interest, and even been informed of developments as they occurred by their Athenian guest-friends. Increasingly in Athens, the various parties and factions adopted polarized positions on both domestic and overseas political issues, above all on the question of democratic institutions, and attitudes to Aegina and Persia. They resorted frequently to the new, democratic device of ostracism: this was a sort of reverse election, in which the defeated candidate among the most influential politicians was exiled by popular vote for ten years.

Soon after 485, however, the Spartans too were again being asked as a matter of urgency what attitude to Persia *they* should take.

FIVE

THERMOPYLAE I: MOBILIZATION

*My Lord, you know that among living creatures it is the mighty
ones that god strikes with his thunderbolt, in envy of their excessive
pride. It is always the large buildings and the tallest trees that
are blasted by lightning. It is god's way to bring the lofty low . . .
For god tolerates pride in none but himself.*

Artabanus to Xerxes, Herodotus, *Histories* 7.10

AT THE beginning of what we know as the seventh book of Herodotus's
Histories the historian stages a dramatic reconstruction.* He
describes how Xerxes came to the Persian throne and gives his entirely plausible opinion that it was Atossa the Queen Mother, daughter of
Cyrus the Great, who in effect fixed the succession for him. He then
takes us to the heart of the Persian Empire to the court at Susa, and
into the innermost chamber of Xerxes himself, indeed into the very
mind of the Great King. And he titillates us with the possibility that
Xerxes might have decided otherwise, might not have decided to
invade Greece in 480 after all. Indeed, he presents the invasion as not
Xerxes's own idea at all, but that of Mardonius – who, as his readers
would know, was to be Xerxes's defeated generalissimo at the decisive

---

* This is the book immediately after the description of Marathon and the first of the
three final books that deal with the battles of 480–479, the Graeco-Persian Wars proper.

Battle of Plataea in 479. He owed that appointment no doubt in good part to his own prowess, having already been entrusted with major commissions by Darius. But the facts that he was Xerxes's first cousin (son of a sister of Darius) and that his father was Gobryas, one of Darius's six co-conspirators in bringing Darius to the throne in the late 520s, will not have harmed his career prospects one bit.

To the promptings, or rather urgings, of Mardonius to invade were added the importunities of a number of medizing Greeks. Most prominent among such were the members of the ruling dynasty of Larissa in Thessaly – the region of Greece next over the border of the then Persian Empire, which ran as far as the southern frontier of Macedonia – and members of the Athenian ex-tyrant family of the Peisistratids. Such medizers had mixed motives, probably. For some, it was a fatalistic *sauve qui peut* attitude that predominated: the Persians were going to win, they calculated, so let's be on the winning side, or at least not stand out too visibly as opponents of the victors. For others, there was a positive feeling of warmth towards the idea of a future Persian imperial rule: had not the Persians not merely tolerated but actively supported 'tyrants' among the cities of their east Greek subjects? For both sorts, too, there was probably more than a dash of the (characteristically Greek, it has to be said) 'my enemy's enemy is my friend' syndrome.*

Herodotus imagines Xerxes calling a council of war, as he surely did, but the precise words spoken in conversation between Xerxes, Mardonius and Xerxes's wise old uncle, Artabanus, need bear no close relation to the actuality. In a sense Artabanus is a stock character of Herodotus's, the 'warner' figure who sees that the situation to be faced is not black and white, who foresees the possible impediments to a project and the difficulties in fulfilling it at least as clearly as its likely success. He is thus a foil both to Xerxes, the relatively young, inexpe-

---

* It is all the more noticeable therefore that Herodotus does *not* introduce the ex-Spartan king Demaratus, an obvious medizer of the first water, into his narrative here. He is saving him for greater things later.

rienced and excessively bullish figure, and to Mardonius who – at least in Herodotus's scenario – was gung-ho for the invasion.

One passage of Artabanus's set speech goes to the heart of the matter, at least as it was constructed retrospectively by Herodotus. Through 'dramatic irony' it foreshadows Xerxes's ultimate failure:

> My Lord, you know that among living creatures it is the mighty ones that god strikes with his thunderbolt, in envy of their excessive pride. It is always the large buildings and the tallest trees that are blasted by lightning. It is god's way to bring the lofty low . . . For god tolerates pride in none but himself.

This is tragic, in the precise sense in which this sort of sentiment was worked out on the Athenian tragic stage, most relevantly in Aeschylus's surviving tragedy *The Persians*, first staged in spring 472. There is good reason also to suppose that Herodotus, conventionally and deeply pious as he was, did indeed believe this was how the sublunary world worked.* But what then follows in Herodotus's teasing narrative is an episode that is almost comic. At first Xerxes is furious with Artabanus, the only one of his intimate counsellors to have advised against undertaking the Greek war. Next, on maturer reflection, he is persuaded of the wisdom of the older man's view. But then Artabanus changes his mind, whereupon Xerxes instantly reverts to his original, pro-invasion opinion. The reason given for these sudden switches by Xerxes and Artabanus? The intervention of dreams, a classic manifestation of the divine in Herodotus's book but also a thoroughly Homeric literary device: a neat way of reminding readers of the epic nature and scale of the impending conflict, and of what was at stake in it for the future of East–West relations. This sort of dramatized account has the further advantage, for a Greek historian, of revealing the weakness, irresolution and lack of understanding that fatally flawed the Persians' main man, the King of Kings.

---

* See Appendix 3.

Yet Thucydides, Herodotus's greatest successor as a historian, strikes a very different note, a chilling note of realism, in his account of the causation of the Atheno-Peloponnesian War of 431–404. He brings matters firmly down to earth. He had, it is true, a jealous professional interest in claiming that all wars previous to 'his' war were lesser affairs, and he probably had Herodotus's war specifically in mind as a target. On the other hand, Thucydides's account of the cause of all great wars, not just the Atheno-Peloponnesian War, smacks more of persuasive insight and intelligence than does Herodotus's tragicomic confection.

For, as Thucydides has his Athenian speakers tell the Spartans at the beginning of his *History*, there are three main motives that drive all interstate relations, irrespective of whether the state is an absolutist monarchy of the Persian sort or a democratic republic of the Athenian kind or a modified oligarchy like Sparta. These are, in their usual order of precedence: strategic concern for a state's collective security; ideological-psychological concern for its status, reputation and honour; and desire for economic advancement or profit. Thucydides's Athenians expressed them more starkly as fear, honour and profit. A combination of these three will also explain why Xerxes made the decision he did, namely to invade mainland Greece with a view to conquering it, and why he had to make that decision and no other.

In his concern for imperial security, and especially about what nastinesses might conceivably come from just over the furthest border, in 513 Darius had invaded Europe from Asia across the Bosporus strait. Later, he had authorized Mardonius's conquest of European Thrace. There were Thracians on either side of the two straits, the Hellespont (Dardanelles) and the Bosporus. The idea was that, by incorporating both, the Empire was made that much more secure. But was it, really?

Status operated as a causal factor both personally and collectively. Xerxes was at least as much in the shadow of a famously dynamic hyper-achieving father as Alexander of Macedon was to be, initially, in that of Philip of Macedon. Both sons staked their claim to parity, Alexander even to superiority. But of the two only Alexander succeeded

Great King Darius I (r. 521–486) was the first human in history to have his own portrait stamped on coinage of his own issue. The eponymous 'daric' was struck in both gold (as here) and silver, and performed key diplomatic as well as economic functions both outside and within the Persian empire. On the obverse (front side) a crowned Darius is represented in profile moving purposefully to the right, spear in his right hand, bow in his left – a combination that Greeks found utterly alien, as they found a great deal about the Achaemenid monarchy.

in making his claim good. Collectively, there was the pesky Athenian issue to settle. The Persians' defeat by Athens and Plataea at Marathon had still not been cancelled out, let alone erased from memory. And if Athens was to be put in its place, why not the rest of mainland Greece too while Xerxes was at it, so as to teach all the mainland Greeks not to meddle in a sphere not their own, nor even to think of inflicting a defeat on Persia ever again – a lesson they'd never forget?

It might seem extremely implausible that Xerxes could have been tempted into invading Greece by the prospect of further material gain. As Demaratus was going to observe rather poetically to Xerxes,[1] Greece and Poverty were foster-sisters.* A further hint that economics may not have been the most cogent of the arguments comes from Mardonius's wild claim to Xerxes that Greece was a veritable garden centre, just full of all sorts of trees. This was no doubt an argument designed to appeal to a garden-loving Persian monarch, but on purely empirical grounds it was not especially persuasive, one might have

---

* When Themistocles requested support in 480 from the Aegean island-state of Andros, the Andrians told him they were unable to help, constrained as they were by two implacable goddesses, Poverty and Incapacity (Herodotus 8.111).

thought. Nevertheless there were some silver and gold mines to be lusted after, and the revenues from some trading emporia to be harvested.

The news of Xerxes's preparations will have reached Sparta fairly soon after the order for mobilization had gone out from Susa in, let us say, 484. Sparta had friends in the offshore islands and coastal cities of the Persian Empire, and they in turn will have had their own contacts with the two local satrapal centres of Sardis in Lydia and Dascyleum in Hellespontine Phrygia to the north. The reaction in Sparta was one of great dismay. Being exceptionally pious, and believing fervently in divine retribution, many Spartans including members of the top political elite feared that a destructive Persian invasion might be heaven's way of punishing them for gross impiety. The gross impiety in question, they believed, was their murder of Darius's heralds, or envoys, in or about 491. For heralds of whatever nationality or ethnicity were universally considered to be sacred; that is, their persons were considered sacrosanct. To kill a herald in cold blood was to incur an unusually strong form of religious *miasma*.

How, the Spartans asked themselves, might they absolve themselves of this stain; how might they pay due retribution and restitution to Xerxes? The answer seemed straightforward in principle. They would send to Xerxes a human sacrificial victim as a return offering. Were he to accept that, then conceivably he might call the whole expedition off. But there remained the practical problem of finding a suitable and willing victim. Herodotus tells us that the Spartans (contrary to their normal practice) held many consecutive assemblies of their citizen body of warriors, each with just the one item on the agenda: which Spartan would be prepared to offer himself as this aversionary, retributive human sacrifice to Xerxes? Eventually an answer was found, and the strength of the Spartans' faith in this solution, or at any rate of their wishful thinking, is to be inferred from the fact that not one but two noble Spartans did offer themselves and were accepted by the Assembly. They were noble, too, in more senses than one, since they probably belonged to the hereditary Spartan aristocracy of self-styled 'descendants of Heracles'.

Sparta liked pairs: two kings; two divine symbols and guarantors of the twin thrones in the shape of the Dioscuri, Castor and Pollux; Zeus paired with Athena as objects of devotion in more than one Spartan cult; and so on. But beyond this cultural predilection, and beyond even the act of collective religious faith involved, what is most noticeable and noteworthy in hindsight is this willingness of the Spartans to put the good of the community, the city, and even of some notion of 'Greece' above purely personal or individual advantage: in other words, to sacrifice themselves for a larger good and a greater goal.

The two would-be victims, Sperthias son of Aneristus and Boulis son of Nicolaus, duly set off for the Persian Empire. They were received first at Sardis by the satrap Hydarnes and were told that, when they reached Susa, at the other end of the Royal Road, they would have to pay *proskunêsis*, obeisance or the kowtow, to Great King Xerxes. They recoiled in horror from the very suggestion[2] and, being bluff Spartans, spoke their mind to the satrap. Such reverence, they said, was fit only for the gods, not for a mortal man. This was not to be the last time that Greeks deliberately or unconsciously misunderstood this custom of royal etiquette.* For the Persians *proskunêsis* was not an act of religious worship, since the Great King was not considered divine. It would be interesting to know whether Herodotus himself laboured under this delusion too. At any rate, he seems to have used *proskunêsis* as part of his case against the Persian monarchy, and specifically against Xerxes, on the grounds that it transgressed the proper boundary line separating mortals (no matter how exalted) from the gods.

When the two Spartans did reach Susa, they were ushered into the royal presence. There would have been no problem in finding a trans-

---

* A notorious recurrence resulted in the execution of Alexander the Great's official historian Callisthenes in 327, when he refused to kowtow to Graeco-Macedonian Alexander as the new Great King.

lator (*hermeneus*) to convey to the Great King what – and in this case also whom – they were offering. But there was still plenty of scope for the sort of cross-cultural misunderstanding that had afflicted Spartan–Persian relations since Cyrus's gibe about never trusting men who come together to trick and cheat each other in the marketplace.[3] Xerxes, Cyrus's grandson, is said merely to have laughed at the pair, haughtily, and dismissed their doubtless sincerely meant and religiously motivated gesture as a joke. But the joke was on Xerxes, did he but know it. Precisely this sort of cultural misunderstanding was to be repeated in reverse by Xerxes in the Thermopylae campaign, when he was foxed by the Spartan warriors' custom of combing out their very long locks as they were preparing to fight and, if necessary, die.

The vehicle Herodotus used to expose this deeply damaging misunderstanding was Spartan ex-King Demaratus. This was not without its irony, since Demaratus was not the most obvious choice to represent and uphold good Spartan values in relation and opposition to barbarian Persian ones. After being deposed from the Eurypontid throne in about 490, Demaratus had for a time remained in Sparta as a de facto commoner, though still a man of high distinction. He was distinguished enough at all events to be entrusted with organizing a religious festival. But while undertaking this task, in Herodotus's account, he was mocked publicly and viciously for his fall from royal grace – by Leotychidas, the relative and personal enemy with whom the powerful Agiad king Cleomenes had seen to it that Demaratus was replaced. Demaratus's pride understandably prevented him from stomaching the insult, whereupon he took himself off from Sparta, for good.

What Herodotus's account does not satisfactorily explain is why Demaratus should have taken himself off where he did – to the court of Xerxes. Why could he not just have gone into dignified exile much nearer to home – somewhere sympathetic in Arcadia, for example, as Cleomenes had done before and as other Spartan ex-kings, or kings sent into exile, were to do after him? As it was, Demaratus not only fled to the heart of the Persian Empire at a time when its hostile intentions towards at least some Greek cities – especially Athens and Plataea – were already manifest. He even managed to worm his way into the innermost circle of Xerxes's foreign advisers. It was as a member of this privileged group that he returned from Persia to Greece in 480, in Xerxes's train; and in the pages of Herodotus – though with what degree of historical authenticity it is hard to judge – he makes a series of suggestions and recommendations to his new royal master that Xerxes would have done well to heed. As, of course, he did not, and with ultimately disastrous consequences.

When a Persian Great King undertook an expedition of this gargantuan scale, its preparation was a matter not of weeks or months, but years – about four years in this particular case. Orders would have been sent out first to the two most intimately concerned local satraps, those of Sardis in Lydia and Dascyleum, well placed up there in the north to control the Hellespont strait (Dardanelles). It would be their job and that of their satrapal counterparts in the other provinces involved to raise the troops required, ensure that provision was made for the supply of weapons and armour, see to the condition of the roads, co-ordinate the commissariat and so forth.

Xerxes's uncle Artabanus, interestingly, is said to have advised firmly against using the subject Asiatic Greeks to fight against their cousins across the water. Either, he thought, they would indeed fight them, but badly, or they would endeavour to take the mainland Greeks' side against the commands of their Persian overlord. But Artabanus was overruled, again; and in fact in 480–479 Xerxes would have many more Greeks fighting with him, on his side, including many 'volunteers' from the mainland as well as his duty-bound subjects of Asia, than against him, and not to any noticeably detrimental effect. At least, it was not mass disaffection or poor performance by his Greek troops that was to prove chiefly responsible for his eventual defeat.

Two extraordinary engineering projects also had the effect of broadcasting the intended invasion well in advance. Thousands of conscript corvée labourers were impressed and sent to carve a canal actually through Athos, the easternmost prong of the three-pronged Chalcidice peninsula jutting into the northern Aegean.* Mt Athos is today known as 'Holy Mountain' and is a key centre of Greek Orthodoxy, but Xerxes's motives were entirely secular. In 492 an earlier Persian expedition against mainland Greece, sent by Darius to take revenge on Eretria and Athens for their complicity in the Ionian Revolt, had suffered what Herodotus calls 'fearful losses'. Before they could round the promontory of Athos they were caught by a gale that blew them on to the rocks. Herodotus believed that as many as three hundred ships and some twenty thousand lives were lost, but even if these figures should probably be scaled back, the losses were still immense enough to abort the expedition, which confined itself to land operations in northern Greece. Almost as significant is that the commander of that failed expedition had been Mardonius son of Gobryas, then recently married to a daughter of Darius. One begins to understand Mardonius's extreme enthusiasm for Xerxes's new grand expedition.

The other preparatory *grand projet* of Xerxes was to build a bridge of boats across the Hellespont. This was not the first time a large Persian force had been conveyed by this route from Asia to Europe – Mardonius had done likewise. Nor was it the first bridge of pontoon boats carrying a Persian expedition from Asia to Europe – Darius had crossed the Bosporus strait from Chalcedon to Byzantium in this way in his expedition of 513. This time, however, its designers and constructors were not Greek. Xerxes was taking no chances of sabotage. So he set to the task some of his principal maritime subjects, Phoenicians and Egyptians, who wove and plaited huge, thick ropes out of papyrus (the Egyptian native speciality) and flax and strung them across ships lined up side by side so as to span the divide: from Abydus on the Asiatic side of the narrows to Sestus on the European.

As these works progressed, and as news of the great mobilization

---

* For three years in the early 1990s Dr B. J. Isserlin directed a topographical and geophysical expedition to trace the canal's basic characteristics.

going on in Asia filtered across to the Greek mainland, it ceased to be a case of individual Greek cities being required to decide whether or not to make a stand against Xerxes. Some form of concerted Greek resistance was clearly obligatory. The germ of it was indeed already apparent in the events of 490. The Athenians, when faced with the invasion led by Datis and Artaphernes that foundered so signally at Marathon, had sent to ask aid from the Spartans. For Sparta alone commanded the sort of multistate alliance that could serve as the core of a military resistance by land. The sea, however, was quite another matter. The Spartans were notoriously a land-based power, and the one truly significant naval state that probably was within their 'Peloponnesian League' alliance was Aegina. But Aegina, the island-state in the Saronic Gulf within sight of Athens's ports, had medized in the late 490s.

Athens, therefore, was already looking for ways to neutralize the threat posed from the sea by Aegina, when in 483 a fortunate strike of an unusually rich seam in the Athenians' state-owned silver mines at Laureum came to their aid. By then the threat from Xerxes was already all too apparent to at least one Athenian: Themistocles (his name means 'famed for Right'). Though well born and wealthy, Themistocles came from a relatively obscure family – as is perhaps indicated by his father's name, Neocles ('new to fame'). Themistocles would prove to be the single most influential figure on the Greek coalition side. He had first attained some political prominence when elected as chief archon (executive officer) of Athens for 493/2 and, as such, had inaugurated the turn to the sea that was to be the making of the city's fortune and fame. He had been the first to suggest that Athens's main naval as well as commercial harbour should be Peiraeus, and not Phaleron as before. Ten years later his hour had come, occasioned by the discovery in the silver mines. *

---

* Almost all the silver was extracted by slave labour under the most appalling physical conditions. The silver was contained within seams of lead and had to be separated from it by a process called cupellation. The resulting ore had to be washed and processed before it was usable for coinage. The primary extraction and ancillary industries, at their peak, may have soaked up the labour of as many as 20–30,000 slaves.

Normally, it seems, such an excess yield of silver would not have been minted into coin but distributed in exactly equal shares to every Athenian citizen in the form of bullion. It was reckoned that the strike of 483/2 would have been enough for a universal distribution of a sum equivalent to a couple of weeks' wages for a skilled artisan. But Themistocles had another, and better, idea. The whole extra sum, he argued in the Athenian Assembly, should be devoted to public purposes, specifically to the building of a fleet of the very latest model of oared warships, the trireme.* Now, Athens was an egalitarian and direct democracy. Everyone's vote by raised right hand in the Assembly counted for one, and no one's for more than one. The will of the majority would prevail. And the majority of Athenians were poor men, mostly farmers rather than skilled urban workers. To them, a couple of weeks' wages, silver cash in hand and up front, must have seemed a mighty attractive proposition. But Themistocles persuaded them otherwise, entirely bearing out Thucydides's retrospective encomium of him as the most naturally gifted politician with the greatest insight into the present, the greatest foresight for the future, and – therefore – the greatest ability to improvise appropriate solutions.

Thucydides might have added – as he did explicitly apropos of Themistocles's greatest successor, Pericles, who seems to have inherited a great deal of his outlook as well as enjoying many of the same natural endowments – that Themistocles had also to be almost superhumanly persuasive to make his arguments tell decisively. Since it was not clear to him that the majority of Athenians were yet fully apprised of the nature and imminence of the Persian threat, he claimed that the fleet whose construction he was advocating was for use against not Persia, but Aegina – a very present and indeed visible enemy. Athenians would have remembered, or been firmly told, that the Aeginetans had been no help to them whatsoever in their dire emergency of 490. They would have needed no telling or reminding that after Marathon there

---

*   See Glossary.

had been naval hostilities between them and that the Athenians had by no means come out of those the better. Themistocles's persuasive point, then, was that by replacing their relatively few and outmoded warships with a spanking new fleet of a hundred (or two hundred – the sources differ) new-style triremes, they would see off the Aeginetan threat for good and all.

The issue was in fact a much larger one. Indeed, it is hard to make sense of a series of bitterly fought personal political contests at Athens throughout the 480s, from which Themistocles uniformly emerged the winner, unless some major foreign policy factor such as Persia lay at the root of them. One by one those leading Athenians who either did not see the Persians as a threat, or imagined that they might somehow do a favourable deal with them, were eliminated from the Athenian political scene – physically, by means of the procedure of ostracism, for which Themistocles was always a serious 'candidate'. There is even archaeologically preserved evidence of cabals of his enemies ganging up against him and using foul rather than fair means of persuading the voters. All to no avail. Themistocles always 'won', and by the late 480s had emerged with renewed strength and enthusiasm as the unopposed champion of not merely the anti-Aeginetan but the anti-Persian cause.

But Athens could not do it by herself, any more than could Sparta. How, then, was a coalition of the more or less willing Greek resisters to be cobbled together? This was the question facing the delegates of a number of Greek cities at the first meeting they called in 482, or more likely the autumn of 481, to debate the issue of united resistance to Xerxes. According to Herodotus, that first meeting was held at the Isthmus of Corinth, within a shrine dedicated to Poseidon Lord of the Sea. But according to a much later source, 'Baedeker' Pausanias (the Periegete, or 'Traveller')* writing a nostalgic historicizing travelogue of Greece in the second century CE, it was at a site in Sparta called the Hellenion ('Place of the Greeks'). Whom should we believe?

---

* See Chapter Eight.

That there was a structure in Sparta called the Hellenion in the later second century CE (the date of Pausanias's visit) there is no cause for us to doubt. There is good reason, too, for supposing that it had been there since the fifth century BCE, along with the Persian Stoa, or colonnade, built to commemorate Sparta's key part in the famous victory over the Persians in 480–479. But was it already there before Xerxes's invasion in 480? I personally doubt it. It seems far more likely that it was constructed after 479, as a war memorial, like the Spartans' Persian Stoa. It would therefore have served as a very useful site for generating the myth that it was there that a united 'Greek' resistance had been first decided upon.

The Spartans, moreover, had a particularly strong reason for wanting to claim this as the site. Though there was never any real question but that they would have to be the overall leaders of any sort of unified Greek resistance to the Persians, their track record as leaders in 480 and 479 was not unimpeachable. It gave rise to the view – promoted heavily by Sparta's enemies in the generations after the Graeco-Persian Wars – that Sparta had been less than one hundred per cent eager and willing to commit to the defence of central Greece beyond the Peloponnese, 'their' sphere of influence. Such hostile rumours started to fly around as early as 480, despite the heroic defence at Thermopylae, and were especially rife during the run-up to the decisive Battle of Plataea in 479, when it was alleged that the Spartans were more interested in sealing themselves off behind a wall stretching right across the Isthmus than in sending an army into Boeotia in central Greece to face Mardonius. In short, there was all the more reason for the Spartans in the years that followed to have promoted the notion that they had been gung-ho for maximum resistance from the word go – after all, had they not taken the initiative and summoned the Greeks to Sparta, to the Hellenion, for a war conference in 481?

Actually, they probably had not. It is far more likely that the meeting would have been held at some more central geographical point, and most appropriately of all at an already existing panhellenic – all-

Modern Sparta was not to be outdone by the on-site modern memorials to Thermopylae and proudly displays its own 'Leonidas' on the exact same model, heroically posed at the end of the city's main thoroughfare with the modest Spartan Acropolis and far more imposing Taygetus for backdrops.

Greek and only-Greek – site containing a major religious sanctuary. For the only thing that then united Sparta and its allies with Athens and some other central Greek states, apart from the extreme necessity imposed by their common threat from Xerxes, was their 'Greekness'.* Though not specifically a political concept, the common qualities that 'Greekness' stated or implied might on occasion result in unified political action – and one of those, very rare, occasions was in the brief but climactic period from 482 or 481 through to 479.

The four existing panhellenic sites were Olympia, the Isthmus of Corinth, Delphi and Delos. The tiny Aegean island of Delos, birthplace of Apollo and sacred to the god, was ruled out automatically since it was in effect already within the Persian sphere. The Persian fleet controlled most of the Aegean, and Delos in the centre of the Cyclades was too near to the Persian-held Asiatic coast of the Aegean and its offshore islands to be allowed independence. Delphi, the holiest place in the whole Greek world, was the site not only of a panhellenic shrine and oracle but also of one of the meeting-places of an alliance of neighbouring states known as the Amphictyonic League, that embraced Sparta as well as Athens but more than half of whose permanent members came from Thessaly. The loyalty of Thessaly to any anti-Persian cause was doubtful in the extreme, thanks not least to the longstanding blatant medism of the Aleuads, the aristocratic ruling clan of the chief city Larissa, and in the event all Thessaly fell to Persia without a blow. Besides, the Delphic priesthood, as the events of 480 in particular were to expose, was by no means committed to advocating any resistance to Persia whatsoever. Partly for lofty religious reasons, and partly for wholly mundane and selfish ones, its line on Persia was at best quietist, at worst frankly defeatist. So Delphi was no more appropriate a venue for a crisis resistance conference than Delos. That left Olympia and the Isthmus.

Olympia, devoted to Zeus of Mt Olympus, was indeed a venerable

---

* See Chapter Three.

panhellenic shrine. It had been such since at least the eighth century BCE, when – according to learned calculations by the local polymath Hippias of Elis in the later fifth century – the first panhellenic athletic contests had been held, in 776 BCE. Moreover, there was at Olympia an oracle sacred to Zeus, father of Apollo of Delos and Delphi, which may imply that this oracular shrine was even older than that at Delphi. However, there was one major obstacle to the choice of Olympia for the resistance conference: namely, what might well have been perceived as the undue influence of Sparta over the sanctuary.

The city that managed the shrine and the Olympic Games, and had done so for centuries, was Elis, and Elis was an ally of Sparta within her Peloponnesian League. Besides, as the archaeological as well as the literary evidence shows, Sparta maintained an unusually close and continuous interest in Olympia, both officially and unofficially, and Elis reciprocated that concern. One of the more interesting objects now gracing the Olympia Museum, for example, is a handsome marble seat with an inscription carved upon it. The inscription, which dates the seat to about 525, states that it was made for the Spartans' *proxenos* at Elis; that is, the citizen of Elis who served as the Spartans' local diplomatic representative, a sort of consul. The *proxenos*'s name was an unusual one, Gorgos, recalling that of Gorgo (born about 508), the daughter of the contemporary Spartan king Cleomenes and future wife of King Leonidas. It is by no means impossible that there was a personal relationship of *xenia* between the Elean Gorgos and the family of Cleomenes.* At any rate it was presumably Sparta that paid for Gorgos's fancy seat, and Elis that permitted it to be erected prominently at Olympia. It would have enabled him to cut a proper figure at the Games as well as watch them in some style and comfort.†

With Olympia too ruled out, only the panhellenic shrine at Isthmia

---

* See Glossary.

† It was a peculiarly Spartan sort of gift, since one of the chief marks of respect that a junior could pay to a senior at Sparta was ostentatiously to yield his seat to him.

was left, dedicated to Corinth's patron god Poseidon (brother of Zeus). Initially, it might be thought that this site too would suffer from its connection with Sparta; Corinth, like Elis, was a member of Sparta's Peloponnesian League. However, against that could be set Corinth's record of proven independence from, indeed outright disloyalty to, Sparta. It was the Corinthians who, in concert with King Demaratus, had scuppered Cleomenes's expedition against newly democratic Athens in about 505. That might have made the Athenians, the next most important state after Sparta among the potential resisters to Persia, look quite favourably on the Corinthians even twenty years later, especially as we know that in the late 490s or early 480s the Corinthians had loaned the navy-poor Athenians twenty warships in their struggle with the Aeginetans. But what tipped the scales decisively in favour of Isthmia were surely several other factors in combination. Isthmia was still just within the Peloponnese, for Sparta, and within relatively easy striking distance, for Athens. Geopolitically, it was central for all southern mainland Greeks. It also had just the right religious symbolic association. Poseidon was the Greeks' universal sea god, and whatever else resistance to Persia would involve, it would undoubtedly involve a combined Greek navy, of which the Athenians would contribute the lion's share.

Now, the Isthmus is where Herodotus said the delegates of the would-be resisters first met; I think he should be believed. But that the delegates met at all is memorable enough in itself. When Herodotus at a climactic moment of his narrative (after Salamis, before Plataea, in winter 480/79) invokes a definition of Greekness, the list of unifying factors he cites signally does *not* include political co-operation, let alone union. In the event, what seems to have emerged from the meeting is some sort of loose coalition, an alliance for mutual defence based on and constituted by the oaths sworn mutually in the name of the witnessing and guaranteeing gods. This way, a breach of the pact would be sacrilege in the sight of heaven as well as a purely human, mundane and secular transgression.

The 'league' thus formed seems to have been called, simply but expressively, 'the Greeks' (*hoi Hellênes*). Its acknowledged leaders were to be the Spartans, thanks to their unique fighting prowess and because they already headed the only non-religious, non-ethnic multi-state Greek military alliance then in existence, the Peloponnesian League. Spartan precedence is made clear, not explicitly by Herodotus but by the text of a monument, once magnificent but now visible only as a poor shadow of its original self. It squats today forlornly in the hippodrome, the race-course, of ancient Constantinople. But originally it had been erected proudly at Delphi.

After the fighting was all over in 479, and Delphi had been forgiven for its medism, the Greek coalition set up in Apollo's sanctuary there as a thank-offering and war memorial a cauldron supported by three bronze coils topped by snakes' heads. On the coils was written, in truly laconic style, the following message: '[By these] the war was fought . . .' There follow the names of thirty-one Greek states/cities, identified in the usual Greek way by the collective name of the citizens. First comes 'Lacedaemonians', the Spartans. Of the other thirty, no fewer than fourteen were members of Sparta's Peloponnesian League: Corinthians, Tegeans, Sicyonians, Aeginetans, Megarians, Epidaurians, Erchomenians,* Phleiasians, Troezenians, Hermionians, Tirynthians, Mycenaeans, Halieians and Lepreans. Of the remainder, the Cycladic island of Melos, Dorian by ethnicity, claimed to be a 'colony' (*apoikia*) of Sparta. That would have given Sparta and its immediate allies and satellites an overall controlling majority – if votes were needed, and if the procedure that operated in the Peloponnesian League congresses was also adopted by 'the Greeks'.†

Such was Sparta's pre-eminence that it was agreed the city would

---

* A variant spelling of Orchomenians, referring to the men of Arcadian Orchomenus, not to be confused with its Boeotian homonym, since all Boeotians except for the Plataeans and Thespians had medized.

† Decisions at League congresses were taken by majority vote, with each city represented having one vote apiece, regardless of size.

formally exercise command of coalition forces by sea as well as by land – a travesty, in practical terms, though fortunately the fact that a Spartan was technically admiral-in-chief in both 480 and 479 had no decisively negative consequences. Athenian postwar propaganda did like to make out that Athens would have made an equally good over-all leader of the Greeks, or at least joint leader, by taking over the direction of affairs by sea. It was even claimed that the Athenians had graciously, if ostentatiously, declined to bid for such a rightful posi-tion. But that was just wishful invention. Really, in 481 there would have been no debating or questioning Sparta's title.

A third party, however, is also said to have claimed a share in the overall command. Because its claim is so intrinsically implausible, it is probably authentic. Gelon was a major Sicilian Greek tyrant ruler in the first quarter of the fifth century. He made himself tyrant first, in about 490, of Gela on the south coast,* and then in about 485 of the most important Sicilian Greek city, Syracuse (founded from Corinth in the 730s), ceding Gela to his brother Hieron.† By alliance and conquest Gelon created in Sicily what can fairly be called an empire, and, as an (admittedly relatively petty) imperial ruler and a Greek, he felt entitled to stand up to Xerxes in the name of all the Greeks. So – allegedly – he made the coalition Greeks an offer they could and did refuse: he said he would throw the weight of his mili-tary forces behind the resistance on condition that he be granted half of the overall command.

There was a further, serious dimension to this offer, though, which provides the first major linkage between eastern and central Mediterranean Greek history since the seventh century. For Gelon had his own troubles with invading 'barbarians' much closer to home, in the form of the Phoenicians of Carthage in north Africa (modern

---

* This was where Aeschylus was to die and be buried in 456.
† Their father was Deinomenes, so the tyrant dynasty is known as the Deinomenids, on the model of the Peisistratids at Athens.

Tunisia). They, like the Greeks, had planted a number of 'colonies' in Sicily, mainly in the far west of the island. And they both envied Gelon his hegemony and wished to safeguard their lucrative trade routes, which ran from north Africa westwards via Sicily to Spain (and even Britain – to the tin mines of Cornwall). So while the Greeks of 'old' Greece were threatened from the East by the Persians, the Greeks of 'new' Greece, the golden West, were threatened by barbarian invaders from the south. There was even talk of co-ordination between the two sets of barbarians, since the Phoenicians of old Phoenicia (Lebanon) formed the elite of Xerxes's navy. At any rate, Sicilian Greek tradition fervently maintained that the Battle of Himera in north-western Sicily, in which the Carthaginians were defeated and repulsed by Greek forces under Gelon and Theron, the ruler of Acragas, was fought on the very same day as the Battle of Salamis off Attica, at the end of September 480.

Practically, however, the Greek West was to play no direct part in the coalition's eventually successful resistance to Xerxes. The real issue that remained outstanding even after the formation of the coalition in 481 was strategic. What strategy was the coalition to adopt in face of Xerxes's impending invasion, and how was it to be co-ordinated – both as between the land and the sea, and as between Sparta and Athens? Given the apparent fragility of the coalition when under direct fire in 480, and the seemingly unpreprogrammed switches of strategic policy, it would probably be fair to infer that between the first meeting of the loyalists at the Isthmus and the coalition's first (not terribly) co-ordinated act of military resistance in summer 480 they had not got very far in their strategic planning.

After that first meeting the proto-coalition had sent out a reconnaissance party to spy on Xerxes's forces, but more practically it had set about resolving through diplomacy a number of longstanding intra-Greek quarrels. Thus Aegina and Athens were quick to patch up their particular feud. Yet this advance was tempered by setbacks elsewhere. For example, so great was Argos's hatred of

Sparta that it refused to serve in any force led by her. Instead, it maintained a formal neutrality that bordered uncomfortably on lending aid and comfort to the Persian enemy. Nor was Argos by any means alone in not being motivated decisively by any form of panhellenic fellow-feeling.

The more consolidated coalition met for a second time, again probably at the Isthmus, in spring of 480. But, if any credence can be placed in Herodotus's detailed account of the upheavals within Athens following on news that Xerxes was on the march in European Greece, even this meeting would not appear to have reached any very firm strategic conclusions. At any rate, whenever news of the formation of this resistance coalition reached Xerxes, he is unlikely to have quaked in his boots (or rather, his regal saffron-tinted slippers with the distinctive upturned toes). Bring 'em on! he would have said, and in early summer that year the Persian juggernaut finally began to roll. From Sardis Xerxes moved towards the Hellespont via Troy (where he offered a thousand oxen to Athena – ten times a 'standard' hecatomb sacrifice). Was that historic defeat of Asia by Europe at Marathon now finally to be avenged?

The Persians' crossing of the Hellespont from Abydus to Sestus by a double pontoon bridge of boats constructed by Phoenician and Egyptian engineers was a major logistical operation. The distance to be bridged was over two kilometres, the winds were strong, the currents – partly as a result of the winds – even stronger. The crossing, inevitably, took a long time: precisely seven days and nights, according to Herodotus. But it would have taken even longer, we are given to understand, had whips not been used *pour encourager les autres*, with Xerxes looking on from the Sestus side of the narrows.

This was not just a neutral report of a factual occurrence. For Greek readers and listeners it was another of those culturally coded pieces of information with which Herodotus studs his history. Whips, to Greek eyes, were only for slaves, not free men, who (with but very few exceptions) were by definition exempted from corporal chastisement. Indeed, in Greece whips were used by free, slave-owning men precisely to symbolize and solidify this fundamental division of status. Xerxes's later order to have his troops whipped into battle at Thermopylae will not therefore have surprised Herodotus's Greek audience.

From Sestus the army marched north-east along the Thracian Chersonesus (the Gallipoli peninsula), then turned sharply west into western, Odrysian Thrace.* That Xerxes was leading the expedition in person was a sure sign of its prime importance to him. At a place called Doriscus, close enough to the coast, and where there was a conveniently large plain, he called a halt and a forces review.

Herodotus, here at his most Homeric, seizes the opportunity to rival Homer's 'Catalogue of the Ships' in Book 2 of the *Iliad*. But whereas Homer had to catalogue only the thousand or so Greek ships launched by the face (and other bodily parts, no doubt) of Helen, Herodotus had teeming masses of land troops from a rainbow of subject nations to describe, as well as the relatively more homogeneous Persian navy. Nor would the irony have been lost on his original readers that, whereas Homer was cataloguing the forces of the eventual victors, Herodotus was cataloguing those of the losers – as if to imply that size was not everything.

Modern scholarly readers, however, are less easily satisfied. I dare venture with some confidence that there is not a single professional historian today who believes in the accuracy of Herodotus's reported figures of 1,700,000 Persian land troops and over 1,200 warships registered at the initial European muster at Doriscus in western Thrace. (Later, adding in the forces raised in Europe, Herodotus gives even higher figures, such that the total number on the march with Xerxes numbered over five million souls – 5,283,220 to be (im)precise!) Perhaps some rivers en route really were drunk dry, as he says; this was all hap-

---

* Ancient Thrace is roughly modern Bulgaria, plus the coastal strip in the south that now forms part of the modern state of Greece.

pening in early summer, not winter or spring, and large deep rivers were not all that common. But his figures have been cut down regardless, by other commentators, to as (relatively) few as 80,000 and 600 respectively. Perhaps 80,000 is rather excessively low. However, any serious reduction would have the effect of putting the Greek coalition's achievement in a somewhat different light, and that, I suspect, is one of the major reasons why Herodotus was so keen to maximize the enemy numbers.

Sceptics have also claimed that Herodotus's sources were Greek and therefore either misinformed or deliberately disinformative; for example, it has been argued that it is unlikely all the subject nations of the Persian Empire would in fact have been represented. Against that, it has been countered – plausibly, to my mind – that the presence of the Great King himself at the head of the united army and navy would have entailed a maximally representative force. It is also possible, as in the case of his accounts of Darius's accession and of the tribute of the Empire, that Herodotus somehow gained access to authentic Persian sources here too.

Here are some highlights from Herodotus's 'catalogue' (translated in full in Appendix 2) which also give some sense of the – incurably amorphous – shape and stretch of Xerxes's forces. Relatively few of them had of course ever fought together before, and even fewer on this Greek terrain. Herodotus's infantry list begins naturally with the Persians, the inhabitants of what the Greeks called Persis in southern Iran. They were commanded by Xerxes's father-in-law Otanes (whose daughter Amestris was the Great King's long-suffering principal wife).

> On their heads they wore the tiara, a soft felt cap, about their bodies an embroidered and sleeved tunic, [over which was fitted a covering] of a coat of chain mail that looked like fish-scales, and around their legs trousers (anaxurides). They bore shields of light wickerwork, below which were slung quivers; short spears, but long arrows with reed shafts; and daggers hanging down from a belt beside their right thigh.[4]

Three things would have struck a Greek reader very forcefully about this description. Unlike the typical Greek hoplite infantryman, with his large and heavy, basically wooden shield and his long, iron-spiked thrusting spear, the Persians were light-armed. Second, they were archers as well as hand-to-hand fighters, whereas the Greeks partly for social reasons kept those two kinds of soldiers radically distinct. Third, horror of horrors, they wore trousers (the wrong ones, presumably). That might seem to us eminently sane and practical, but dress codes are never wholly rational, and the Greeks chose to make of this item of apparel a marker of ineradicable cultural difference. Real men don't wear trousers! Herodotus, however, did not let that get in the way of his measured and objective view that the native Persians were Xerxes's best fighting troops, trousers or no trousers, as well as the most magnificently equipped. They included above all the elite 10,000-strong Persian infantry force known to the Greeks as the Immortals, who were a sort of glorified royal bodyguard.*

To a Greek eye, the Persians' way of war had other alien features besides. They brought along with them on campaign vast numbers of 'camp-followers', their women and servants, who were conveyed by and indeed lived in elaborately fitted-out covered carriages. They ate especially elaborate food, transported by an immense baggage train of camels and mules. But what seems to have struck Herodotus most is the sheer amount of gold that every one of the Persian soldiers carried and wore about his person, which glinted and glistered amazingly in the sunlight. Gold, to a Greek, was an ambivalent symbol – highly desirable but also potentially hazardous, if not fatal.†

After the Persians come, inevitably, the Medes of northern Iran. At

---

* See Glossary; and for their prowess at Thermopylae, see Chapter Seven.
† The Greeks borrowed from the East the notion of a Golden Age, when all was for the best in the best of all possible worlds. But gold was not native to Greece, with just a couple of minor exceptions, so the metal retained a whiff of exoticism that acquired a strongly negative connotation by its association with barbarian Persia – especially through the imperial 'daric' coinage (see Glossary).

Bisitun lies not far from Hamadan (ancient Ecbatana, capital of Media in northern Iran). Here Darius I had carved into the rock the visual equivalent of a royal chronicle, designed to demonstrate how he personally had restored order to a kingdom troubled by rebellion and had brought the ringleaders of revolt literally to heel. Above the submissive rebels hovers the winged sun-disc symbol of Ahura Mazda, great Zoroastrian god of light and emblem of the Achaemenid monarchy; behind the king are carved two key court officials. To accompany the visual images, Darius also had incised in the rock a trilingual message – in Old Persian, Elamite and Babylonian – spelling out how and why, and in whose name (Ahura Mazda's), he had saved Persia. This trilingual inscription proved crucial to the decipherment (by Henry Rawlinson) of Old Persian cuneiform (wedge-shaped) writing, which enables us to read a host of primary bureaucratic texts.

least here Herodotus was able to tell the two peoples apart, though he does add that the Persians' dress and equipment were originally borrowed from the Medes. Whether this is technically true or not, he is certainly right to remind his readers that the Medes had 'been there' before the Persians. Cyrus the Great and his Achaemenid successors had a solid base of Median empire on which to build, and the fact that the Persian Empire became a truly world empire, the first ever, was crucially due to this prolonged and mostly harmonious co-operation between the two related peoples of the Iranian heartland.

It was entirely appropriate, therefore, that the Median contingent was commanded by a member of the Achaemenid Persian royal family, one Tigranes.* Of the other nationalities and peoples who were also said to be equipped more or less in Median fashion it may be worth singling out those who lived on offshore islands in the Persian Gulf; for these islands were specially used by the Great King as penal resettlement colonies for recalcitrants and rebel subjects, Greeks among others.

After the Persians and the Medes we encounter a number of other Iranian and adjacent peoples, among them the Cissians and the Hyrcanians, the latter under the command of a Persian who survived the fiasco in Greece to achieve the plum post of satrap of Babylonia (now southern Iraq). From further north in Iraq came the Assyrians, descendants of the once formidable imperial power that had been laid low by the Medes at the end of the seventh century.

From what is today northern Afghanistan came the men of Bactria, home of the two-humped camel that under Persian aegis was exported as far west as Egypt. Another trouser-wearing people were the Sacae, a subgroup of the Scythians of the Caspian region, one of whose kings had been represented on the Bisitun relief of Darius. The

---

* This was a name destined to echo down the corridors of ancient Middle Eastern history for many centuries to come, as the Romans would become only too well aware in their attempts to control Armenia.

Bactrian contingent and the Sacae were commanded as a mark of their importance by a full, older, brother of Xerxes, Hystaspes, named after their paternal grandfather. The Parthians and Chorasmians of Iran were commanded by Artabazus, son of Darius's major administrator Pharnaces.

Moving, next, to the east of Iran and beyond the Hindu Kush mountain range of eastern Afghanistan, we meet Xerxes's Indians. By India was meant essentially the Punjab, and so a province that is mostly located in Pakistan today with only a very small portion running over the modern border into the state of India. It had been conquered by Darius but was in fact lost well before the arrival of Alexander the Great in 327. In his listing of imperial revenues, Herodotus had noted the huge amount of gold-dust the Indian satrapy was obliged to hand over by way of annual tribute; here he provides an early mention of the celebrated Indian cotton, the fabric of the Indians' clothing.

Moving back to the west of Mesopotamia, we get to Anatolia. Here one non-Greek people from south of the Black Sea stands out in Herodotus's account, the Paphlagonians:*

> *The Paphlagonians served with plaited helmets on their heads, small shields and moderately sized spears, light javelins and daggers; on their feet they wore native boots reaching to mid-calf.*

This last was a detail of some interest to sandal-wearing Greek infantrymen. Other non-Greeks mentioned include the Macrones and Mossynoeci, who were commanded by a Persian based, only just, in Europe: Artayctes son of Cherasmis, governor of Sestus.† The crucifixion of Artayctes by the victorious Greeks in 479 is the last event

---

* Paphlagonia was a major source of the slaves privately owned in, for example, Athens. Partly for this reason, Aristophanes caricatures the leading Athenian politician Cleon as a Paphlagonian house-slave in his comedy *Knights*, staged in 424.

† Both Mossynoeci and Macrones reappear in Xenophon's *Anabasis* describing exciting events of 401–400.

Blacks were always a minority subject in Greek art, but Greek painters of the early fifth century knew an Ethiopian ('burnt-face') when they saw one, and valued them for their exotic appeal on olive-oil flasks such as this alabastron, a fancy version of an everyday utility object for people who used oil for rubbing down and cleansing after exercise.

described by Herodotus in his continuous narration of the Graeco-Persian Wars and practically the climax of the entire work.

Where, though, in the infantry catalogue are the Asiatic Greek hoplites and light-armed? The short answer is – nowhere: apart from the one cryptic statement that 'The Lydians bore arms and armour [*hopla*] very like the Greeks.'[5] Earlier, however, Herodotus had cleverly made Xerxes point out to Artabanus in one of their supposed conversations that the 'Ionians' were effectively hostages: 'Why should we fear that they will cause trouble and disaffection,* when they have left behind their children, wives and property in our domain?' 'Our' here is in the fullest sense the possessive form of 'the royal "we".'

So much for the Asiatic contingents of Xerxes's taskforce. Moving south and east to Africa we find first the Arabians, then the Ethiopians both eastern and southern (that is, the Nubians), then finally the Libyans. Herodotus specially noted the (southern) Ethiopians' painting

---

* Literally, 'something too new' – a very Greek expression.

of their bodies, half with chalk, half with vermilion, their tight curly hair, and their wearing of the skins of leopards and lions, all thoroughly exotic to Greek eyes.

Last come Xerxes's European infantry contingents, both non-Greek and Greek. Spanning the Asia–Europe divide were Thracians, most of whom were Europeans.* Herodotus then lists the six Generals of the High Command, the marshals of the army.

In first place, Mardonius son of Gobryas, keenest advocate of the expedition after (if not before) Xerxes himself. Next follows Tritantaechmes, son of Artabanus (Xerxes's wise adviser) and so Xerxes's first cousin. Then Smerdomenes, a son of the great Otanes (one of the original co-conspirators with Darius in the late 520s), another nephew of Darius and so another first cousin of Xerxes. Next Masistes, another full brother of Xerxes – with whom, as Herodotus was to detail lovingly towards the very end of his work, Xerxes was later to fall out so spectacularly on account of the Great King's fatal passion for Masistes's wife. Then, fifthly, Gergis son of Ariazus, and finally Megabyzus son of the Zopyrus whom Darius is said to have rated as a benefactor to Persia second only after Cyrus (and, we presume, himself). In a separate category, between the High Command and the Great King himself, falls Hydarnes, son of Hydarnes the very high official who had received the two Spartan ambassadors at Sardis in about 484 and given them a lesson in Persian etiquette that they took very ill indeed. He was privileged to command the Immortals[†]

---

* Herodotus does not include a description, or even a mention, of the Macedonian troops under Xerxes here (he does include them later on), perhaps because the muster occurred before the army had reached Macedonia. But he does quote a Macedonian source saying that the Thracian Brygi of Asia had once lived in Macedonia. One probable member of this ethnic group has acquired a certain fame among art-historians: he was a potter, or the owner of an outstandingly successful pottery workshop, at Athens in the first quarter of the fifth century and employed an artist known to scholarship as the 'Brygos Painter', who specialized in powerfully dramatic scenes of human and divine life.
† See Appendix 2.

and was to play a key role, or even the key role, in winning the Battle of Thermopylae for Xerxes.

Xerxes's cavalry troops played no significant role at Thermopylae, although the defeat of the cavalry around Mardonius, himself on horseback, was an essential preliminary to the eventual rout of the Persians at the finally decisive battle at Plataea the following year. Only eleven non-Greek peoples provided cavalry (once again, the Greeks – of Macedonia and Thessaly – are not catalogued). Two are especially striking: first, the Sagartians, because they were cowboys – their weapon of choice was the plaited-leather lasso (though they also carried daggers); and, second, the Arabians, because they rode not horses but a type of fast camel specially bred for use in war. There were two supreme cavalry commanders, both sons of Datis the Mede. Clearly, their father's upset at Marathon, where the Persians' cavalry was conspicuous in the defeat only by its absence, was not considered a reason not to appoint them.

The third main element of Herodotus's massive catalogue was a Catalogue of the Ships, all – allegedly – 1,207 of them. Herodotus rightly begins with the Phoenicians (of modern Lebanon) and the neo-Assyrians to their north, all of whom inhabited a land known then as 'Palestine'. They together contributed 300 ships, about a quarter of the total fleet. Then came the Egyptians with 200, the Cypriots (both Phoenician and Greek) with 150, and the Cilicians (of south-west Anatolia) with 100. These figures are all probably rounded. None of the other non-Greek ship-contributors managed to reach three figures, the highest contribution being the Carians' 70.

In the case of the fleet catalogue, Herodotus does inescapably include Xerxes's Greek subjects, who furnished a combined total of 307 ships. This was divided five ways between the Hellespontine/Bosporan Greeks (100), the Ionians (100 – Herodotus at any rate could distinguish Ionians from other Asiatic Greeks), the Aeolians (60), the Asiatic Dorians (30), and the offshore islanders (a mere

17).* This total, if correctly given, was the highest of all, and, though Herodotus does not spell it out, the implication was crystal-clear. This was to be not only a war of Greeks against Persians, but also a war of Greeks against Greeks; what he called elsewhere[6] with great sadness an *emphulos stasis*, a civil war within a single people or ethnic group.[†]

All the Persians' ships, Herodotus continues, had a large complement of marines, as indeed did the ships of the loyalist coalition's fleet. This feature of sea-fighting in the period 480–479 was one that Thucydides would later sneer at by comparison with the more sophisticated fleets of his own day in the Atheno-Peloponnesian War. The naval combats of the Graeco-Persian Wars seemed to him more to resemble land battles on the sea than proper sea battles in which the ship itself was the main weapon. Herodotus, too, is exceptionally dismissive of the lower-level naval commanders, who he says were mere 'slaves' (*douloi*), meaning slaves of Xerxes ultimately. But he lists honorifically by name all the Persians of the naval High Command, and they include a number of members of the royal family and its extensions by marriage. For example, the Egyptian squadron (200 ships) was commanded by Xerxes's full brother with the dynastic name of Achaemenes; and the joint Ionian and Carian squadron (170) by a son born to Darius and a daughter of Gobryas father of Mardonius.

Herodotus also lists by name a number of individuals whom he calls 'the most nameworthy' or 'the most celebrated' (*onomastotatoi*) after the high admirals: three Phoenicians, a Cilician, a Lycian, two (Greek) Cypriots and three Carians. All, as one would expect and predict, were male. But then, quite extraordinarily, he bursts into a

---

* The islanders apart from those of Samos had suffered major losses at Lade in 494, the final battle of the Ionian Revolt, and Persian generosity in victory had clearly not extended to allowing, let alone encouraging, the rebuilding or maintenance of serious navies.

† See Appendix 3.

This calcite jar was made in the reign of Xerxes (486–65) and is inscribed 'Xerxes Great King of Persia' in trilingual script (Old Persian, Elamite, Babylonian – the same three languages as on the Bisitun rock-cut inscription of Darius). But it was found in the Mausoleum of Halicarnassus, which was not built until over a century later, so perhaps originally it had been a gift to the shrine of Artemis at Halicarnassus, preserved as a valuable heirloom, and appropriated by Mausolus's widow and successor as Persian vassal to shed dynastic lustre on her late brother-husband's memory.

paean of praise for one woman, finding it a marvel (*thôma*) in itself that a woman should have taken any part whatsoever in the campaign, let alone played such a prominent role. The woman was Greek – it would be hard to imagine a non-Greek woman being allowed any sort of role under Xerxes, perhaps – the daughter of a Halicarnassian father and a Cretan mother, and her name was Artemisia (a 'theophoric' name, based on that of the virgin huntress goddess Artemis). She commanded five Greek warships from four Greek cities or islands (Halicarnassus, Cos, Nisyra and Calynda). She did so, Herodotus reports, in virtue of being a *tyrannos*, an autocratic sole ruler, who had inherited this position from her late husband. Put differently, she was a Persian quisling. The reason for believing any or all of this is that Herodotus too was a native Halicarnassian, born too late to have known what Artemisia was like at first hand but patriotic enough to want to give her – and therefore his city – a place in the sun, even if it did happen to be shining on the Persian side.

This presumably explains why in her case uniquely Herodotus anticipates his narrative of the Wars by adding that Artemisia not only furnished the 'most reputable' (*eudoxotatai*) ships in the entire fleet – apart from those furnished by Phoenician Sidon – but also allegedly gave Xerxes the 'sagest counsels' (*gnômai aristai*),* 'man-to-man' advice, as it were, because Herodotus again uniquely applies to Artemisia, a woman, the Greek word for bravery that meant literally 'manliness', *andreia*. When he comes to depict her in action, at Salamis, he has her displaying not only a manly bravery of sorts but also a cunning worthy of an Odysseus. To make good her escape from a coalition Greek ship, she rammed and sank a Greek ship fighting on the Persian side, making it look as though it were an enemy vessel. This deceptively noble exploit reportedly provoked from Xerxes the wondrously gender-bending exclamation 'My men have become women, my women men!'

Artabanus is said by Herodotus to have commented to Xerxes on this truly awesome armada:

> No one in his right mind, my Lord, could find any fault with the size of your army or the numbers of your ships.[7]

But he sagely added that the sheer size and numbers of them would inevitably mean that Xerxes was going to have trouble finding adequate harbours to shelter the fleet and providing adequate supplies of food. He therefore counselled him to take a worst-case-scenario view with respect to planning, but to act boldly and decisively in execution of the plans once they had been prudently formulated. At which the younger, less experienced and more optimistic but also more impetuous Great King supposedly expostulated:

> It's better to run every risk and take the negative consequences in half of them than to be paralysed by fear and never have any positive consequences at all.

---

* Whether she did in fact advise Xerxes intimately in the way that, say, Artabanus certainly did, is perhaps doubtful.

The dramatic irony would not have been lost on Herodotus's audience, who knew well that the dice had not rolled favourably for their Persian adversary.

For all his eagerness for the invasion and conquest of Greece, it is nonetheless noticeable that Xerxes took his time to get from Doriscus through Macedonia to Thessaly. A number of different reasons accounted for his slow progress. First, simple logistics – Persian armies did not travel light, and baggage-trains such as his did gravely impede an army on the hoof.* Nor was movement facilitated by a specially built Royal Road. Second, notions of royal grandeur were at stake. Xerxes wished to make and to leave behind him an impression of stately magnificence. Third, and by no means least, he was keen to encourage the further spread of what had come be known to the Greeks as 'medism'. The more slowly the juggernaut advanced, and the more irresistible, inevitable and inexorable its progress appeared, the more likely were wavering Greeks to follow the example of the Aleuads of Thessalian Larissa and cross over to the Persian camp. Eventually, sometime in July, Xerxes's land forces reached the border between Macedonia and Thessaly, the vale of Tempe, which is the main route for motor traffic from Macedonia through Thessaly to central Greece.

Tempe was also the first line of defence picked by the Greek resistance coalition. Two commanders had been placed in overall charge, to reflect the dual leadership of Sparta and Athens: respectively, Euainetus and Themistocles. But it has to be said that each was a rather puzzling choice. The absence of a royal Spartan commander from this first coalition initiative is noteworthy; typically, all land expeditions involving Spartan forces were led by a Spartan king. On the other hand, it seems odd of the Athenians to select Themistocles to lead a defence that apparently was to be conducted at first solely by land; Themistocles was nothing if he was not a naval man. Indeed, it is Herodotus's treatment of this earliest phase of the resistance that has

---

* The Roman word for baggage trains, *impedimenta*, says it all.

caused some scholars to wonder whether he really understood the inevitably amphibious nature of any conceivable resistance to Xerxes's blatantly amphibious invasion force. It has even been asked whether Herodotus possessed any strategic sense at all. The puzzle is only compounded by the speedy abandonment of the Tempe 'line', when it was discovered – as it ought surely to have been much sooner – that the pass could be 'turned', that is outflanked.

The likeliest explanation is that the 'Greeks' comprising the resistance coalition had not yet really worked out a viable, co-ordinated strategy of any sort. Hence the hugely increased significance of the first seriously defensible and genuine line that was chosen next: the amphibious Thermopylae–Artemisium axis. Though, according to Herodotus, even that was selected only after some last-minute hesitation and dissension among the coalition loyalists had been knocked on the head by Leonidas. Appropriately enough, when the extraordinary threat posed by Xerxes's transit through Thessaly past Tempe had become unmissably acute, Sparta reacted in the most extraordinary and extraordinarily decisive manner imaginable.

SIX

THERMOPYLAE II:
PREPARATIONS FOR BATTLE

*[The Spartans] are the equal of any men when they fight as
individuals; fighting together as a collective, they surpass all
other men.*

'Demaratus' to Xerxes, Herodotus, *Histories* 7.104

T HE CONQUEST OF GREECE would necessarily depend on co-
operation between the Persians' land army and the naval forces
that would help, crucially, to supply it. Advance by land west and
south from Doriscus, where in June 480 Xerxes had conducted the
massive muster of his forces, was unproblematic if slow. All territory
up to the northern border of Thessaly was already under the control
of the Great King, and after the resistance coalition had abandoned its
abortive notion of defending a Tempe line with ten thousand troops in
July, Xerxes was able to make his stately way past Mt Olympus and
through Thessaly unimpeded (except by his huge baggage train). The
progress of the fleet was more chequered, but eventually it did reach
Cape Sepias opposite the northern tip of Euboea as planned.

What should the reaction of the 'Hellenes' of the coalition be? If
they were genuinely serious about putting up resistance, it was obvious where the next line should be drawn: at the axis between the pass
(more accurately passes, as there were three) of Thermopylae, by land;

and, by sea, at the point known as Artemisium (the site of a shrine of Artemis) at the north end of the island of Euboea. Some professional geologists and geomorphologists have sought to prove that Thermopylae was not the pass it was cracked up by the ancients to be; that Xerxes did not have to force this, but another, pass in order to proceed into central Greece. But if that were so, it is remarkable just how often the ancients, including many Greek natives as well as possibly benighted foreigners (such as a band of migratory and marauding Celts in 279), kept making this same stupid blunder.

However, there were other, manmade obstacles to the coalition Greeks' conducting such a serious defence at this time, or conducting one whole-heartedly and in full force. Most conspicuously, allowance must be made in the case of the non-Spartan loyalists for a considerable ingredient of sheer panic fear that the Persian host was simply too large to be resisted, either at Thermopylae or possibly anywhere else. After all, the vast majority of the several hundreds of other Greek mainland cities had already voted with their feet and decided to join or at least not actively oppose the Persians rather than try to beat them back at any cost.

Fear of that sort is unlikely to have gripped the Spartans, however. They were war-hardened, and ever war-ready. For them, as we noted earlier, the requisite sort of martial bravery was a core value inculcated by formal public education from the earliest age, not something to be summoned up uncertainly to meet an ad hoc emergency. All the same, the situation facing them in summer 480 was the greatest emergency any Spartans had ever faced or would ever be likely to have to face. It threatened not just their lives and livelihood, but their very way of life.

Yet the Spartan force sent to defend Thermopylae was only about two-thirds the size of the one Sparta had just recently dispatched to, but withdrawn from, Tempe. The reason for sending what was advertised as only an advance guard was shared by all members of the coalition, though it was applicable to the Spartans above all. For the Olympic Games were due to be celebrated; these took place every four years, probably at the second full moon after the summer solstice, so

A sombre and bearded bronze Heracles, mythical ancestor of both Spartan royal families, wears his distinguishing lionskin and cuts a vigorously masculine military dash in this sixth-century Laconian-manufactured bronze figurine.

sometime in August. This was a panhellenic religious festival, a major celebration in honour of the most powerful of all the Greeks' gods, Zeus of Mt Olympus. So every four years the 'Olympic truce' was declared to enable any Greeks who wished to participate or spectate at Olympia to make their way to the site in the north-west Peloponnese in safety, immune from the usual risks and dangers of travelling through the territory of other and all too often hostile Greek cities. It would have been hard, therefore, for pious Greeks to divert their minds from their customary Olympic Games preparations.

For the Spartans, and even more imminently, there was the further religious obligation to celebrate the annual Carneia festival in honour of Apollo, one of the main events of their religious calendar. All their principal religious festivals were dedicated to Apollo – the Hyacinthia and the Gymnopaediae as well as the Carneia; and the Spartans, as in the case of their non-appearance at the Battle of Marathon in 490, were exceptionally, indeed egregiously, scrupulous in their observance of such festivals. So they too felt they could not commit their full military strength to the defence of the pass at Thermopylae.

But 'Greece' desperately needed the Spartans, the coalition's leaders, to act somehow, and to act effectively. They had to make at least some positive gesture of resistance, and if possible more than a gesture. There were several other factors, all religious or quasi-religious, that would have tugged the Spartans in favour of a Thermopylae defence. First, it was on Mt Oeta, not far to the west of Thermopylae, that their ancestral hero Heracles was thought to have met his end on earth before being borne away to a permanent afterlife as a god on the summit of Mt Olympus.* Below Mt Oeta to the south stretched the territory known as Dôris. Mythically, Dôris was the aboriginal home of the Spartans' Dorian forefathers before they made the Great Trek south

---

* The Spartans' two kings were supposedly descended lineally from the two great-great-grandsons of Heracles who had founded the city of Sparta, making Heracles the Spartans' ultimate ancestor. Ancestral piety including ancestor worship was a Spartan speciality.

into the southern Peloponnese at least seven centuries earlier, as the fifth-century Spartans would have envisaged the timeframe.

The other quasi-religious factor favouring a firm Spartan commitment to defending Thermopylae was Delphi. On the council of the religious association known as the Amphictyonic League, the Spartans were represented only indirectly, as members of the Dorian people (*ethnos*). They took great pains to maintain a separate and direct hotline to the Delphic oracle through the Pythioi, the four permanent ambassadors appointed by the kings.* In the lead-up to Xerxes's invasion, the oracle had been issuing to the Spartans' coalition partners in Athens a stream of negative, blackly tinged forebodings about the uselessness of resistance. To put it bluntly, the Delphic priesthood was medizing. Herodotus reports a similarly pessimistic Delphic response allegedly delivered to the Spartans. Either, it said, they must sacrifice the life of a king, or the Persians would destroy them and occupy their land. Many scholars have seen this as a classic case of *vaticinatio* post eventum, a prophecy after the event: the Spartans did in fact sacrifice a king, and their land was not occupied. They suggest that Delphi put out this invented oracle retrospectively both to show how powerful its prophetic powers were, and also to try to wipe away some of the stain of medism incurred by its earlier, pessimistic outpourings.

But if opinion in Sparta, as elsewhere within the coalition, was wavering somewhat in the summer of 480 – at any rate over the tactical issue of whether to meet Xerxes north of the Isthmus of Corinth, as opposed to at the Isthmus itself – then it might well have required some external authorization as powerful as that of the voice of Delphic Apollo to win the waverers round. It is my hunch that for this reason King Leonidas would have used his official contacts to engineer this oracle; not for nothing was he the half-brother of Cleomenes. He would then – leading vigorously from the front, as strong Spartan kings could – have made sure that it was he, not his co-king Leotychidas, who was chosen

---

* See Chapter Four.

by the Assembly, on the advice of the *Gerousia* and the ephors, to perform the sacrificial regal role at the Hot Gates. It is no mere coincidence, I feel, that there is a distinct similarity between this act of self-sacrifice and that of Sperthias and Boulis in about 484, also on Leonidas's watch.

For all these reasons the Spartans decided to entrust the defence of the Thermopylae pass, not to a commoner such as Eurybiadas (the coalition navy's admiral of the fleet), but to one of their two kings. Characteristically, they gave this decision too a religious spin.

What do we know of Leonidas? The answer, sadly, is remarkably little – apart, that is, from what he actually did during those few hectic and climactic weeks of August 480. He was not destined by birth to become king at all, and did so only because his older half-brother Cleomenes I died without male issue.* The fact that he was married to Gorgo, Cleomenes's only daughter, making him Cleomenes's son-in-law and indirect heir as well as half-brother, will have eased the succession, presumably. But Leonidas is likely to have felt that he had a lot to live up to, and quite a lot to prove besides.

On the other hand, precisely because he had not been expected to become king, Leonidas would have gone through the normal educational cycle from which the crown princes in each of the royal houses were – alone – exempted.† He will therefore have had a very good idea of Sparta's 'true interests'.‡ No less important, Leonidas will have

---

* Cleomenes died a gruesome, allegedly self-inflicted death. It has been suggested that Leonidas may have had a hand in this and in the subsequent cover-up. At all events, he it was who most benefited from Cleomenes's untimely demise.

† This was true also of Eurypontid King Agesilaus II, who also succeeded an older half-brother; he reigned from *c.* 400 to 360 and was for a time the most powerful of all mainland Greeks.

‡ In his 1776 republican pamphlet *Common Sense* Thomas Paine acutely observed: 'Men who look upon themselves [as] born to reign, and others to obey, soon grow insolent; selected from the rest of mankind their minds are early poisoned by importance; and the world they act in differs so materially from the world at large, that they have but little opportunity of knowing its true interests, and when they succeed to government are frequently the most ignorant and unfit of any throughout the dominions.'

shared the common Spartan warrior temper, of which the taskforce of three hundred appointed to serve under him at Thermopylae would represent the flower and acme.

Why, precisely, were 300 chosen, some four per cent of the total Spartan army of 7,500–8,000, and why these particular 300? First, 300 was a manageable figure for an elite taskforce, one that recurred elsewhere in Greek history at different times.* Second, the figure of 300 had strong symbolic and practical overtones in Sparta, as it was the fixed number of the regular royal bodyguard. The bodyguards were known as the *hippeis* ('cavalrymen'), though in fact they served as infantrymen in the dead centre of the hoplite phalanx, where the commanding king would be stationed. They also performed a number of ceremonial or espionage functions off the battlefield. The three hundred *hippeis* were specially selected in an intense competition from among men in the ten youngest adult citizen year-classes, aged between twenty and twenty-nine.

Leonidas's Thermopylae advance guard of three hundred, however, was to be selected with one crucial additional criterion. Besides being exceptionally brave, skilful and patriotic, each of the chosen few must also have a living son. In practice, since Spartan men typically did not marry until their late twenties, this is likely to have meant that at least some and perhaps many of the Thermopylae three hundred were aged thirty or over. As for their commander Leonidas, who by my calculations was aged about fifty in 480 and had apparently married Gorgo surprisingly late in life, he met the criterion imposed on the three hundred through his young son Pleistarchus.

The condition that each of the three hundred must have a living son – which is merely reported by Herodotus without further comment

---

* Most famously in the Sacred Band of Thebes, which flourished from 378 to 338 and consisted of 150 homosexual couples. The Spartans practised official pederasty involving an adult with an adolescent, as noted in Chapter Four, but did not officially encourage, let alone institutionalize, for military purposes homosexual relationships between two adult men of fighting age.

– has been interpreted variously in modern times. For some scholars, it was a device to ensure that they fought exceptionally well and bravely; but they were conditioned to do that anyhow. The reason, rather, was social – or, more precisely, societal. It was so that the sons would be there in place to carry on their father's name, that is, to perpetuate their *soon-to-be-dead* father's name and patriline. These particular sons would thus constitute an elite within an elite, the nucleus of the next adult generation's star fighters, bursting with pride to emulate the feat of their late fathers. For the Thermopylae three hundred were to be in effect a suicide squad, of a peculiarly Spartan kind – entirely consistently with their upbringing and with the way in which Leonidas had conceived and pitched his own role. This was as peculiarly Spartan a thing to do as eating black broth in the mess.

Since 9/11 the issue of suicide/homicide in the name of a higher cause, sometimes also known as voluntary martyrdom (bearing witness, usually religious), has intensely and continuously engaged both the public media and the serious scholarship of the West. What makes the suicide/homicide assassins tick? Attention has focused naturally enough on Israel–Palestine, Lebanon, Iraq, Sri Lanka, Turkey and Chechnya, as well as those actions masterminded or inspired by Al-Qaeda (for instance, in Casablanca and Istanbul besides New York and Washington, DC). A number of possible generic motivations or explanations have been advanced – economic frustration and self-promotion to the posthumous status of hero and martyr, as well as religious devotion and political, especially nationalist ideology – together with, in individual cases, psychopathological disturbance. However, none of those suicidal/homicidal deeds was carried out officially and openly in the name of a legitimate state organization or governmental agency, no matter how much covert support they may have received from particular governments. The tactic is increasingly used for preference in civil wars. Nor are most of these actions at all discriminating in their targets, since they murder civilians and children as readily as armed combatants; and, unlike the fully adult Thermopylae three hundred, the perpetrators tend to be young men between adolescence and full manhood.

The nearest modern analogy, therefore, to the Spartans' behaviour at Thermopylae – and it is by no means an exact one – is the officially ordered suicide hits by Japanese kamikaze ('divine wind', literally 'spirit wind') aircraft pilots, human bombs and manned torpedoes in the Second World War. These share with the Thermopylae action the motivation of an overriding commitment and loyalty to the good and the absolutely overriding dictates of the state, in the Japanese case those of the God–Emperor, and the belief that the enemy in some sense represents an overwhelmingly evil force against which tactics of last resort including the supreme sacrifice of self are entirely legitimate, in fact heroic. Also common to both are the notions that the spirit of resistance they symbolize may be as literally vital as the physical damage they inflict on the enemy, and that there is intense dishonour to be incurred through failure to carry out the suicide.*

They share also, even more importantly, an underlying philosophy – which is not by any means the dominant underlying philosophy of war in the West today. For most Westerners the point of war is to win – and survive. Western philosophy teaches by and large how to live, not how to die. But a key element of the Spartans' world outlook was acculturation of the males from a very young age to the expectation of a non-natural, early death; indeed, their whole society was shaped so as to enable them to cope with this.† This is not entirely different from the Japanese *bushido* ('way of the warrior') honour code that prevailed under the ancien régime of the Samurai. It has been claimed by progressive Japanese intellectuals, such as the septuagenarian film director Yoji Yamada who has specialized in making Samurai movies, that this honour code makes no sense today, given its emphasis on death as the ultimate career move. But it would have made an awful lot of sense, I

---

* See the case of the Spartan Aristodamus, Chapter Eight.
† See Chapter Four.

think, to the Spartans, and not least to Leonidas and his three hundred. The Spartans alone out of (all) the Greeks could have both conceived the Thermopylae vision of self-sacrificial suicide and gone on to carry it off to such stunning effect.

Besides the Spartiate (full Spartan citizen) soldiers, the Spartans automatically sent to Thermopylae a non-combatant complement of Helots, perhaps as many as a thousand in all, a couple of whom are individually mentioned by Herodotus. On the other hand, Herodotus fails entirely to notice or mention the 900–1,000 *Perioeci*, or 'outdwellers', who accompanied the Spartans, even though their presence is required to make up the global figure of four thousand Peloponnesians fighting at Thermopylae that he does report. These are mentioned by later sources, and they were presumably volunteers, like those who we know volunteered a century later for another Spartan campaign in northern Greece. Leonidas vetted them carefully, no doubt, both for their proficiency and, no less important, for their morale. Nor does Herodotus report the alleged medism of Perioecic Caryae in northern Laconia on the frontier with Arcadia. If the allegation were true, it would add a spicy extra dimension to Spartan deliberations over the wisdom of committing large numbers of Spartiates outside Laconia, let alone outside the Peloponnese.*

The women of Sparta were considered exactly the non-military half of the population. But, as Herodotus was the first to emphasize in a historical work, they were nevertheless a vital ingredient in Sparta's overall military comportment and profile. They also achieved wide fame – or notoriety – elsewhere in Greece for not being properly

---

* The story of Caryan medism is told by the Roman architect and engineer Vitruvius in connection with the type of female-figure architectural member in the form of a column known as a 'caryatid', which means literally a female from the town of Caryae. But I am inclined to think it's made up retrospectively, since in 370 Caryae did defect from Sparta, and the Spartans might well have invented a tale of Caryae's medism in 480 in order to blacken the name of the men of Caryae and justify their taking harsh steps to recover and punish the town.

feminine. According to one of Plutarch's *Laconian Apophthegms*, Spartan wives and mothers were in the habit of barking the peremptory command, 'With it – or on it!' to their husbands or sons, as they were about to set off on campaign. 'It' was the warrior's hoplite shield. The men were either to come back alive, with their shield (to throw a shield away was a major hoplite crime), or to come back gloriously dead, carried upon their shield by their comrades. That phrase echoed throughout antiquity. It was seen as encapsulating the Spartan women's fighting spirit and their total internalization of Sparta's martial – and overrridingly masculine – values. It was in the same vein of anecdote that Gorgo (wife of Leonidas, daughter of Cleomenes I) was once allegedly asked by a critical – or envious – non-Spartan woman, 'Why is it that you Spartan women alone rule over your men?' Gorgo adroitly evaded the question and shot back, 'Because we Spartan women are the only women who give birth to [real] men'!*

One of the most prominent of these real men was Spartan ex-King Demaratus, between whom and Xerxes Herodotus stages two revelatory discussions on the subject of the Spartans in the run-up to Thermopylae. At the first of these, supposedly immediately after the description of the Doriscus muster, Xerxes asks Demaratus ironically, expecting the answer 'no', will the loyalist Greeks have the guts and gumption to 'raise their arms against me and resist'? Before answering his lord and master, Demaratus makes great play with the notion of truth; this was an idea that was dear to the Persians from their

---

* Evidence of this sort has led the bestselling novelist Steven Pressfield to add one further, wholly fictional factor to the Thermopylae 300 equation in his *Gates of Fire* (Pressfield 1999). As he tells the story, Leonidas personally chose the 300, but paid special attention to the likely comportment of their soon-to-be widows and the effect that their premature bereavement would have on the morale of Sparta as a whole. He has based this persuasive intuition not on any direct evidence but on the attested comportment of the female relatives of the Spartans who either died in or, worse, survived the disastrous defeat at Leuctra in 371 (see Chapter Four).

upbringing, and to none more than the Persian Great King, who was the sworn and (as noted) declared enemy of 'the Lie'. Does Xerxes want the truth, Demaratus replies, or merely to be humoured? Here Herodotus captures very well the flavour of any such encounter beween a courtier and the immense majesty of the Great King, who had the power to swat like a fly even the greatest of his subordinates – a Mardonius, say – since all alike were equally 'slaves' in his eyes. But Herodotus has a further agenda too – dramatic, indeed tragic, irony. For Demaratus will tell Xerxes the truth, the whole truth and nothing but the truth, and yet – Cassandra-like – he will not be believed.

Demaratus begins by stating his supreme respect for the Spartans, out of all the Dorian Greeks. Partly this reflects the fact that most of the Greeks who would stand up to Xerxes were Dorians. But it was also a way of diminishing the impact of Demaratus's formal treachery to his native city of Sparta. He then spells out that what he will say applies solely to them. His eulogy is bestowed on two grounds. First, 'they will never come to terms with you and so bring slavery to Greece'. Second, the Spartans will not merely resist but will fight as no others, no matter how few against however many. Xerxes has a bit of a laugh and a smirk at this, on the grounds of the immense disparity of numbers between his forces and the Spartans. He concedes that maybe, with the judicious application of the whip, 'a few might hold out against many', but even if the numbers on each side were equal, he would still back the Persians to win.

One is meant to notice the Great King's elementary, ethnocentric error. The Spartans, as Herodotus's readers would have needed no reminding, did not have to be whipped to make them fight with all their might, even against the most massive odds. Whips were only for slaves, not free men; they were appropriate for a barbarian master to use on his slave subjects, but out of the question for the citizen soldiers of a free Greek *polis*.

Demaratus counters with two knockout ideological punches. First, the Spartans 'are the equal of any men when they fight as individuals; fighting together as a collective, they surpass all other men'. Second, the reason the Spartans will resist is that they have made a conscious decision to obey not any one human, let alone an absolute dictator (such as Xerxes), but the Law (*nomos*): both the individual laws and customs that they themselves make, and the general concept of the political obligation to be law-abiding. The most relevant law in this particular case, according to Demaratus, is 'not to retreat from the battlefield even when outnumbered, to stay in formation, and either to win or to die'. Demaratus even tells the Great King, unbelievably to Xerxes's ears, that the Spartans fear Law as a *despotês* ('master') far more even than his subjects fear *him*.*

What Demaratus is therefore saying on Herodotus's behalf is that there was an unbridgeable gulf fixed between the kind of political system and authority embodied personally by Xerxes and the kind represented by Sparta. Since Sparta's system stood for freedom, it follows that the Great King's stood for slavery.† Xerxes, for once, Herodotus tells us, did not get angry with Demaratus for speaking his mind plainly, and tried to turn their dialogue of the deaf into something of a joke. But it was the Spartans who would laugh last and longest.

Their second supposed interview is related in the immediate prelude to the story of the fighting at Thermopylae itself. While Xerxes had his troops drawn up and waiting just outside the western end of

---

*   To anticipate, the reminiscence here of the language of Simonides's Thermopylae epigram is palpable and surely conscious. Simonides's Spartans lie dead in the pass, 'obeying [present tense] the *rhêmata* of the Spartans'. *Rhêmata*, literally 'sayings', is derived from the same root word as *rhêmata*, and *rhêmata* was the term the Spartans used both for their basic constitutional law (which they ascribed to the Delphic oracle via their lawgiver Lycurgus) and to a number of other lesser laws.

†   This point seems to me to be crystal-clear and unarguable, even if Herodotus was also trying to convey another point about the Spartans: namely, that their society was by Greek standards unusually authoritarian. All military discipline is indeed hierarchical, unidirectional and top–down; and Sparta was a uniquely military society.

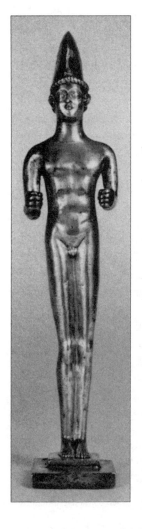
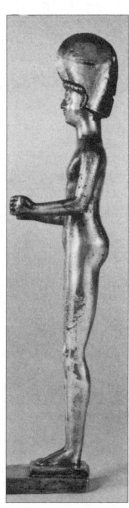

An extraordinary collection of precious objects from what had once been a major local religious shrine on the Oxus (Amu-Darya) River in Tajikistan in central Asia (part of ancient Bactria) found its way to the British Museum via Afghanistan and Pakistan in the late nineteenth century; this presumably fifth century silver statuette of a heroically nude youth wearing a tall headdress of Median type is perhaps a Greek-inspired local work.

the pass, he sent a mounted Persian scout to spy on the Greeks' behaviour. The Greeks he observed happened to be Spartans. This was the incident in which, utterly astonished and bemused, the Persian reported back to an equally bemused and astonished Xerxes that the Spartans were engaged either in gymnastic exercises or in combing out their (exceptionally) long tresses.

Ancient Greek males famously practised their physical exercises and competitive athletic sports fully nude – hence the name given to the place where they practised and worked out, the gymnasium.* Such nudity was shocking to a non-Greek oriental. It was another of those cultural markers of otherness via which the Greeks persuaded themselves of their cultural superiority to all 'barbarians'.

As for the Spartan men's long hair, that was sufficiently unusual among Greeks, let alone Persians, for it to cause comment. Most Greek males cut their hair short, or shorter, on attaining puberty or full civic manhood. The Spartans, by contrast, chose that moment of socio-sexual passage from one status to another to let the hair grow, precisely as an outward and visible sign of adult male warrior status. Various rationalizing explanations have been offered, both for the cause and for the origin of the practice's adoption, but its symbolic meaning was most likely the most significant: real men grow their hair long. The Spartans' wives, in symmetrical inversion, had their hair shorn on marriage and kept permanently short thereafter.

The Persians too, or some of them, had long hair. But on the brink of a fight to the death was no moment for Persians to be seen coiffing it in public. Xerxes allegedly could not believe that a bunch of gymmad cissies would cause him much trouble in battle. But the coiffure's symbolism and its combing out were decoded for Xerxes by Demaratus, who told him it meant that the Spartans had resolved to

---

* From the Greek word for stark-naked, *gumnos*. Gymnasia were also public parks; it was in a gymnasium in this sense that Aristotle's Lyceum (institute for advanced study) was located at Athens.

fight to the death. The Great King's total failure to grasp the Spartan mentality and the import of key Spartan social customs was Herodotus's way of foreshadowing his ultimate defeat and of throwing doubt from the start on the wisdom of such an unsoundly based enterprise.

For the other Greeks of the coalition at Thermopylae there were other locally specific factors at work besides the common excuse – the imminence of the Olympic Games – for sending only an advance guard. Out of the twenty-five thousand or so fighting men potentially available, the Peloponnesians sent only about four thousand.* No doubt this was partly due to their reluctance to commit troops beyond the Isthmus of Corinth, outside Fortress Peloponnese. But loyalist Greeks from north of the Isthmus were also present in very small numbers at Thermopylae. There were no Athenians at all on land there (though there were many thousands with the fleet at Artemisium), nor Megarians. More controversially, there were only a few Boeotians, including a mere four hundred from the Boeotians' principal city of Thebes.

Later, after Thermopylae, all the Boeotians except Thespiae (an enemy of Thebes) and Plataea (an ally of Athens) medized, so that when the Persians were eventually beaten back in 479 the Thebans' reputation was besmirched.† But was this entirely fair to the four hundred Thebans present at Thermopylae? Were they there, as Herodotus's version has it, only because Leonidas had compelled them to be, as hostages, of a kind, for the loyal behaviour of their compatriots back home? If we follow sources other than Herodotus, a quite opposite view emerges.

---

* This is the figure reported by Herodotus as having been inscribed on a commemorative postwar document.

† So black indeed were the Theban traitors painted that 150 years later Alexander the Great could still hope to disguise or at least mitigate his brutally pragmatic destruction of Thebes in 335 by referring back to the Thebans' medism in the Graeco-Persian Wars.

The Thebans of the 420s, the grandchildren of the men of 480, had a different explanation – or plea of mitigation – for their ancestors' unpatriotic behaviour, as reported by Thucydides. Thebes then, they said, had been ruled by a narrow oligarchy – somewhat akin, perhaps, to the Aleuad dynasty of Larissa in Thessaly who had been prominent and proactive medizers – whereas since the 440s Thebes, like the rest of Boeotia, had been governed by a more broad-based, and much more politically moderate, oligarchy. Other sources, including the Boeotian Plutarch (from Chaeronea), went even further in their rehabilitation. Plutarch was incensed by what he took to be Herodotus's anti-Boeotian prejudice. For him, it was these four hundred Thebans who were the true patriots. Being opponents of the ruling regime in Thebes, they had volunteered to serve under Leonidas. It is not easy to decide between these two diametrically opposed versions of the four hundred Thebans' presence. Apart from them, there were certainly present about a thousand troops each from the two local Greek peoples most directly affected, those of Phocis, and those of Opuntian Locris. The not very grand total of Greek resisters was perhaps some seven thousand in all.

No doubt the Thermopylae operation was generally seen very differently by the other Greeks present than it was by the Spartans. Herodotus actually reports that even as late as when they first clapped eyes on Xerxes's horde a panic-stricken parley was called to discuss whether it might still be prudent for them to beat a retreat. Even Leonidas is said to have had some sympathy with this view, until he was swung back to his original intention by the anger of the Phocians and Locrians. Implausible as that report is,* many of Leonidas's non-Spartan troops probably believed at the outset that a brave resistance at Thermopylae would be followed, for the survivors, by an honourable retreat in order to fight or die another day.

---

* It's a product, I think, of the mainly Athenian anti-Spartan strain within Herodotus's oral sources. This represented the Spartans and other Peloponnesians as always keener on maintaining a defensive line at the Isthmus.

Another factor caused them all legitimate alarm. The Tempe line had been abandoned when it was learned that it could be outflanked fairly easily by not just one but two other passes. It was now learned from the local Greeks of Malis that Thermopylae too could be turned, by a single path (or trail) called Anopaea. This snaked over Mt Callidromus to the south of them and emerged somewhere near the East Gate. Anopaea was, however, a path, not a pass, and wide enough, in places, only for single-file human traffic. One of Leonidas's first decisions on the spot was to attempt to seal this potential gap. He detached the local Phocian contingent of one thousand in its entirety to guard Anopaea. These were men familiar with the terrain and conditions and who had immediately the most at stake and to lose. Had Leonidas had the spare manpower, he would probably also have sent a Spartan officer to command them, according to the normal procedure of the Peloponnesian League. But at Thermopylae precious little was normal.

For all the ifs and the buts, the shilly-shallying and the recriminations, the Greek coalition did indeed mount a serious defence at Thermopylae; and thereby – after a build-up lasting at least four years – finally precipitate the first serious head-on encounter between the Persian invaders and the resisting Greeks. The season was by now high summer, and the Gates were shortly to become Hot in more senses than one.

SEVEN

THERMOPYLAE III: THE BATTLE*

*Anyone who retells the story has to come to terms with this
genius [Herodotus] and his narrative, second only to Homer in
the literary legacy of the ancient world.*

Robin Lane Fox, *The Classical World*

T HERMOPYLAE IS A tapered plain extending some five kilometres from west to east, with mountains to the south (including
Callidromus) and the sea to the north, in the shape of the Gulf of
Malis. Disregarding the area's present greatly changed topography,
we must imagine for 480 a narrow pass between mountain and very
nearby sea, scarcely wide enough for two chariots or wagons to pass
each other comfortably, and punctuated by a series of three 'gates'.
It was at the so-called Middle Gate, a stretch of the pass some 15 to
20 metres long where the cliffs rose unnegotiably sheer on the land-
ward side, that the loyalist Greek defence force took up its position.†
It was deep summer. At that time of year a haze of heat and dust
often squats uncomfortably over the plain, and temperatures rise

---

*   See Appendix 1 for a deailed discussion of the source question.
†   Greek excavations in the last century uncovered a stretch of walling over 100
metres long; originally built by the local Phocians to resist enemies coming at them
from the south, the structure was now refurbished and reoriented by the Spartans to
face north.

to the high 30s C (100°F). Water supply was not a problem, but the flies were.

After Xerxes's vast Persian forces arrived at the pass's western end, a three or four days' delay intervened before he launched his assault. This was perhaps designed to pile yet further psychological pressure pressure on the Greeks; the tension must have been well-nigh intolerable already. The delay would also have enabled Xerxes to establish the vital communications link with his storm-tossed fleet now finally safely in harbour at Cape Sepias. The Greeks' naval station was at Artemisium, opposite.* In this pre-battle pause Xerxes allegedly sent a peremptory message to Leonidas: 'Hand over your arms!' Leonidas is said to have sent back a classically laconic response (just two words in Spartan Greek – *molôn labe*): 'Come and get 'em yourself!'

Herodotus presents Xerxes as seething with rage that there were any Greeks there at all with the presumption and gall to resist him. That may explain why Xerxes did not at first simply sit back and let his skilled archers try to pick off the small Greek force. But archers by themselves could have done little damage to a wall of Greek hoplite shields or against rapid hoplite infantry charges. Anyhow, they could never have completed the job from scratch. And the rest of his troops, stretched out in a huge column to the west of Thermopylae, were champing at the bit. When the assault was at last launched, probably on 17 August by our calendar, it became Day 1 of an epic three-day encounter.

The Great King sent in first his Medes, some two thousand strong; they were not quite his very best troops, but near the top of the class. Given their inferior armour and weapons, they could make little headway in dislodging the defenders. Their javelins were no match for the

---

* Herodotus is not at his best in making clear the inextricable link between the land and naval forces of the two sides, but he does at least mention the key role played by Leonidas's liaison officer, the ship-based Abronychus of Athens, a trusted lieutenant of Themistocles. More than once he had to run the 7 or so kilometres between the Gulf of Malis and Artemisium.

Regular hoplite warriors wore a one-piece bronze helmet with an attached horsehair crest running front to back, but this determinedly brooding cloaked figure sports a transverse helmet crest, which may mark him out as a general, perhaps even a king. The strands of long hair escaping from under his helmet confirm the figurine's stylistic indications that he is a Spartan warrior – like those whose coiffing at Thermopylae so astonished and confused Persian Great King Xerxes.

longer, sturdier lances of their enemies, they wore neither metal helmet nor greaves, and their shields though broad were made of wickerwork. In the confined space available, besides, Xerxes's men were unable to make sheer superiority of numbers tell.

The Spartans were the best equipped and trained by far of the Greek defenders, all of whom were apparently heavy-armed infantry hoplites. Over their long hair the Spartans wore a bronze helmet, skilfully raised by Perioecic or Helot armourers from a single metal sheet. Atop the helmet a horsehair crest ran from front to back – though possibly Leonidas's was distinguished by having the crest run transversely across the skull from ear to ear.* A helmet like this provided good cranial protection but it severely restricted vision and hearing, so staying literally in touch with one's immediate comrades was utterly crucial.

To cover the torso a cuirass (*thôrax*) was worn. Other Greeks had by now abandoned cuirasses made of bronze for lighter and more flexible versions made of quilted linen, or for felt or leather jerkins, but it is my hunch that the traditional Spartan still preferred to wear the old bronze cuirass made in two halves, a front and a back. Underneath the breastplate from shoulders to mid-thigh ran his sleeveless wool tunic, dyed red from the milky fluid extracted from murex molluscs native to the Laconian shores off and near the island of Cythera. His trademark cloak was of the same fabric and dye, but would be discarded for the actual fighting. A Spartan hoplite covered his legs with a pair of springily protective bronze greaves, but disdained footwear of any sort. From earliest youth he had run barefoot over rocky, prickly terrain, so that his soles were battle-hardened as no other part of his body.

On his left arm, in an unalterably fixed position, the Spartan hoplite bore his large round shield (*aspis*), measuring about 1 metre in diameter. Basically made of wood, with a bronze rim, it was covered all over with a thin facing of bronze sheet. On to this sheet was affixed a letter in the shape of an inverted 'V'. This was the Greek letter *lambda*, 'L', the first letter of *Lakedaimonioi* ('Spartans').† Besides the regulation initial letter, Spartans were also permitted a choice of personal blazons. A gorgon death's-head mask, perhaps, or a lion or a fighting cock were normal choices. (But one Spartan allegedly opted for a life-sized fly. When asked why, he replied that he would be fighting close enough up to his enemies for them to see it.)

---

* A transverse crest is depicted on the little bronze figurine of a cloaked Spartan hoplite now in the Wadworth Athenaeum, Hartford, Connecticut.

† The replica Spartan hoplite statue standing proud in Sparta, Wisconsin, has an 'S' inscribed on his shield, so as not to confuse the ordinary local viewer; but in antiquity 'S' stood for Sicyon. In a battle in the 390s Spartan hoplites wickedly picked up discarded shields belonging to men of Sicyon, precisely so as to confuse their enemies.

His shield was the single most crucial element of a hoplite's armour, since it was rightly said to be worn for the good of the line as a whole as much as, or rather than, for the benefit of its individual wearer. It was this item above all that made a hoplite a hoplite, a close-order phalanx fighter. The Spartan phalangite carried a short, straight sword, more a dirk or dagger really. His weapon of choice was his spear, two to three metres long, with a shaft of cornel or ash and a heavy iron tip and butt-spike of bronze.

No doubt the Medes and the serried ranks of troops that followed them did the best they possibly could under the judgemental eye of their king. But it was not enough, and they suffered heavy losses: so much so that on three occasions, allegedly, Xerxes leapt up in horror from his specially constructed throne, appalled at the carnage and slaughter of some of his best men. The Spartans added to the Persian forces' discomfiture by deploying the sort of tactics that only the most highly trained and disciplined force would have been capable of even contemplating, let alone executing successfully.

From behind the protection of the refurbished Phocian wall Leonidas's men resisted by fighting in relays. This was a clever if obvious device given the conditions, since it maximized the efficient output and the conservation of their limited resources and energies. The Spartans also practised a far less obvious tactic, not one used in regular hoplite battle, and so yet another mark of their superb professionalism and adaptability: they managed to pull off a series of feigned retreats followed by a sudden about-wheel, then a murderous onslaught on their overconfident and disordered pursuers. Eventually, towards the end of daylight, Xerxes felt he had no option but to send in his elite royal bodyguard, the ten thousand Immortals, under the command of Hydarnes – but again to no avail and again to the detriment of serious casualties.

Sweat streamed, gore flowed, entrails spilled; piles of quickly rotting corpses mounted up, and flies swarmed: neither a pretty sight, nor a sweet smell. As Day 2 went on much as Day 1 had, the decisive breakthrough still not achieved, the frustration and irritation of Great King Xerxes became increasingly palpable. Next, in an attempt to spread the risks and the damage somewhat, and to counter the excellence of Leonidas's men with his own multinational 'picked' force, he is said to have chosen from every national group under his command the men who seemed to excel in courage and boldness.

It was sometime on Day 2 that Xerxes had his lucky break, though quite independently of the main engagement. A Greek traitor opportunely appeared, a local Judas from Malis who knew all about the outflanking Anopaea path, and was prepared to tell the Persians what he knew. His name, Ephialtes, has gone down in infamy: *ephialtis* is today the modern Greek word for 'nightmare'. In his own day too he was drowned in a cauldron of boiling condemnation. Partly this was to deflect attention from the medism of so many Greek cities and peoples. But it also reflected the fact that it was Ephialtes's betrayal that set in train the eventual undoing and decimation of Leonidas's proud and valiant resistance.

Xerxes acted at once on Ephialtes's intelligence, and took no chances. He confided the special mission to members of the royal guard of Immortals, and led by Ephialtes they set out in silence at nightfall, aided by a full moon. After a heroic climb through the Anopaea, up to 1,000 metres, they easily brushed off and bypassed the thousand Phocian guards posted by Leonidas. These troops had been ill-prepared, as unprofessional Greek hoplite troops usually would have been in the circumstances. All the forewarning they had was from the rustling of the dry leaves – left over from last winter, and recently increased by those blown down in a storm – as the Persians stepped warily through them. Having posted no pickets, the Phocians were taken completely by surprise. At first light the Persian outflankers descended to east of the Middle Gate near Alpnei. Xerxes now had Leonidas's men fatally bound in an unloosable pincer grip, caught from the rear as well as the front.

But suppose Xerxes had been assassinated in his tent that very night. The Great King was for the Persians all in all. Crushing the head of the snake might very well have caused the whole expedition to be called off. But though a later source* claims such an assassination attempt was ordered by Leonidas, as a response to news of the betrayal by Ephialtes, Herodotus makes no mention of it, and his silence should be respected.

At all events, Xerxes was not murdered in his bed, the struggle for Thermopylae and Greece did continue, and on the night of Day 2 and early morning of Day 3 the Persians did outflank the defenders of Thermopylae via the Anopaea path. Perhaps Leonidas deserves to be blamed – as he certainly has been – for not reinforcing the Anopaea path with a larger or at any rate more competent, determined and effectively led defence force. But the Phocians were probably the best of the local troops, and they were fighting for their land as well as their lives, reportedly motivated further by bitter hatred for the neighbouring Thessalians who had medized.

Perhaps, too, Leonidas could have asserted his authority more unambiguously once he appreciated the desperate situation of encirclement. But judging his responsibility is difficult because the surviving accounts differ significantly as to what exactly he did do. The standard retrospective version held that he dismissed most of his remaining troops, leaving just the Spartans (not forgetting their Helot attendants), the diehard Thespians, who were animated by hatred for the medizing Thebans back in Thebes, and the four hundred other Thebans (whether loyalist volunteers or enforced hostages). The same must surely have been true of the surviving Perioecic volunteers. But a more cynical view holds that this sanitized version was just a cover-up: most of the coalition allies simply melted away when they realized the game was up and they were about to be surrounded. A variant saves

---

* The source is Ephorus as preserved by Diodorus, supported with minor variations by Plutarch and another, inferior writer. Leonidas was allegedly warned of his impending encirclement by a Greek deserter from the Persian camp, one Tyrrhastiades from Cyme in Aeolis, and not (as in Herodotus) by the Phocian guards he had posted to guard the Anopaea. The nationality of the supposed deserter is enough to make the tale suspect as a patriotic fiction, since Cyme was Ephorus's own *polis*.

Leonidas's credit a bit by supposing that, once he had learned that his position had been turned, he deliberately divided his remaining forces, sending the larger number to head off the Immortals as they emerged out of the Anopaea. But they preferred not to wait for the barbarians.

What is not in question, to even the slightest degree, is the extraordinary resolution and courage with which Leonidas, his Spartans and the few hundred other Greeks who chose to remain with him fought to the end. Apart from any other considerations, Leonidas was bound to want to stay and fight a rearguard action as long as possible. This was both to enable the troops he had dismissed (or who had withdrawn) to get away safely, and to give a chance for the fleet at Artemisium to achieve whatever it could – which turned out, somewhat surprisingly perhaps, to be quite a lot. But for Leonidas there were other, no less major considerations to take on board.

Right at the start of Day 3 Leonidas's official diviner, Megistias, had conducted the pre-dawn animal blood-sacrifice; this was a type of ritual that the Spartans were unusually punctilious about performing in all military situations.* He detected in the victim's entrails malign signs of 'impending death'. This was hardly amazing. Megistias's reaction, however, was. He begged from Leonidas the privilege of being allowed to remain and die that day, while sending away his only son to safety, along with the other Greeks who were withdrawing or had been dismissed.† Megistias gained his wish, perished heroically and achieved the posthumous accolade of an epigram by his friend Simonides:

> *Here lies Megistias, who died*
> *When the Mede passed Spercheios's tide.*
> *A prophet; yet he scorned to save*
> *Himself, but shared the Spartans' grave.*

---

* Megistias, from Acarnania in north-west Greece, was a professional *mantis*; there were various kinds of divination, not all involving animal sacrifice.

† He was motivated along the same lines as the Spartans had been when choosing the 300 from fathers of living sons.

As Megistias was sacrificing on behalf of the Greeks, Xerxes was pouring a libation to the rising sun, a power specially revered by the Persians. Xerxes then unleashed from the Persian camp what was to be the final day's assault. This was in Greek terms at 'about the time when the marketplace is full', or between 9 and 10 a.m. To make sure of its effectiveness, Xerxes had whippers-on stationed behind the troops immediately engaged, *pour encourager les autres.*

The Greeks made their last stand mostly outside the Middle Gate wall, so as to close directly with the oncoming enemy. A truly laconic quip exemplifies the heroically grim quality of this final act of resistance. When told that there were so many archers on the Persian side that their arrows would blot out the sun, one of the three hundred is said to have promptly declared: 'So much the better – we shall fight them in the shade!' Would that we knew much more about this remarkable Dieneces.

Leonidas too showed himself a true Spartan by the words with which he allegedly ordered his men to take their early-morning meal before the final encounter: 'This evening, we shall dine in Hades.'

Readers and listeners in ancient Greece, who knew their *Odyssey* backwards, would have remembered the famous description of Odysseus's descent into Hades ('the Unseen'), the Greek underworld. There he had had to supply the ghosts flitting about with blood to give them any semblance of animation. The import of Leonidas's gallows-humour was that after breakfast there would be no more dining for his troops anywhere, either on the earth or under it. The best fate that could be hoped for was that their shades would find their way underground to a comfortable pitch in the Elysian Fields, and not be consigned to the unfathomable murk of Tartarus. And the surest way of attaining that happy afterlife was by dying a beautiful death.

The Persians' losses at the beginning of Day 3 were reportedly heavier even than those sustained on the previous two days. The Greeks fought with almost reckless abandon. Shelley in 'The Mask of Anarchy' sang of those 'Who have hugged Danger in wars . . .'; few can have hugged it closer than these heroic fighters. Not even the Arabic concept of *asabiya* – 'mutual affection and willingness to fight and die for each other'* – does sufficient justice to their spirit of comradely empathy. Perhaps the derring-do of a Welsh 'three hundred' who perished fighting an alleged hundred thousand Anglo-Saxons, as celebrated in *Y Gododdin*, comes as near as any:

> They attacked with a single purpose, short were their lives,
>   long the mourning.
> Seven times as many English they slew . . . they made women
>   widows.
> Many a mother with tears on her eyelids.

Aware as I believe he was of an oracle from Delphi to the effect that only the death of a Spartan king would ensure an eventual Greek victory against the Persians, Leonidas fought and died like a man possessed: possessed by the consciousness that he was fighting for something greater than mere maintenance of the national and international status quo. His death merely intensified the Greeks' effort, for now they were fighting, Homerically, to preserve the King's body from appropriation and likely ill-treatment by the barbarian enemy. They are said to have recovered the body, after a great deal of pushing and shoving (*ôthismos*), but in the end all their efforts were naturally in vain.

With their weapons gone or broken, the Greeks fought tooth and nail – literally, using their bare hands and their mouths. Even at the finish, the Persian weapon of choice to deliver the *coup de grâce* was the arrow, safely released at a distance. And the bestial vengeance that was wreaked upon the corpse of Leonidas, including decapitation on Xerxes's express orders, betrayed the fact that the Persians had been tested almost to the limit. The Greeks had killed some

---

* The definition offered by the great Maghrebi historian Ibn Khaldun in the fourteenth century.

This 15 cm high gold plaque from the Oxus Treasure, with chased and embossed decoration, depicts a male figure clad in trousers, sporting an akinakes (dagger) at his right hip and carrying a barsom (wand) in his right hand.

twenty thousand on the Persian side, including two of Xerxes's own half-brothers.

But the mutilation of Leonidas's corpse also symbolized a key difference of culture. After the Greeks' victory at Plataea in 479, an enthusiastic Aeginetan called Lampon is said to have rushed up to the commander-in-chief, the Spartan Regent Pausanias, and urged him as follows:

> *When Leonidas was killed at Thermopylae, Mardonius and Xerxes had him decapitated and his head stuck on a pole. If now you pay them back in kind, you will win the applause of not only all Spartans but the whole of Greece. Impale Mardonius's body, and then Leonidas, your father's brother, will be avenged.*

Pausanias would have none of it, though, and Herodotus uses him to stand and to speak not only for quintessential Spartanness but also for Greekness and Greek values:

> What you suggest would be more fitting for barbarians than for Greeks, and even in barbarians we would find it repulsive . . .
> It is enough for me to win the approval of the Spartans by acting and speaking righteously.*

Of those who fought, heroically, at Thermopylae Dieneces was adjudged to have been the bravest of the Spartan three hundred, and Dithyrambus the bravest of the Thespians.† Special mention was also made of two Spartan brothers, Maron and Alpheus (or Alpheius); and as a mark of esteem Herodotus also records the name of their father, Orsiphantus. We should remember too their mother – unfortunately anonymous but no doubt desperately proud.

The Battle of Thermopylae was fought by only a very small proportion of the potentially available coalition forces. It was the Spartans' contribution, Leonidas's above all, that was the crucial one – before, during and after. The result of the battle was, in Herodotus's apt phrase, a wound (*trôma*) for the Spartans, but it was not to prove mortal either for them or for the Greek resistance. For the vital period that Leonidas held out and held up the Persian advance the Spartans gave time for the weather and the mainly Athenian Greek fleet to wreak havoc on the supporting Persian navy at Artemisium. He and his fellow Spartan dead vitally raised Greek morale. As to whether the loyalist Greeks won or lost at Thermopylae – they did both.‡

---

* Herodotus 9.78–9. Likewise emblematic of cultural difference is the story that, when the survivors of the Theban 400 tried to surrender to Xerxes, they were branded with the royal mark, as mere slaves.

† The Thespians seem to have sacrificed every one of their available hoplites in support of 'the Greeks'; it is entirely right and proper that there should be a separate modern memorial in the pass to them too.

‡ Or, as Peter Green has nicely put it, 'The ultimate victories of Salamis and Plataea became possible, in a sense, only through that splendid and inspiring defeat.'

EIGHT

THE THERMOPYLAE LEGEND I: ANTIQUITY

Go tell the Spartans, passerby,
That here, obedient to their laws, we lie.
Simonides of Ceos

SOME OF US are very partial to the luxury chocolates made by the Belgian firm of Léonidas. They come with an embossed image of a helmeted ancient Greek warrior's head in profile – meant of course to be that of Leonidas, our Leonidas. This is presumably a distant genuflection to the fragmentary marble statue in the Sparta Museum that has been given that title (erroneously, alas) and has served as the basis for the modern statue memorials at both Sparta and Thermopylae. There's a coffee-and-pastries shop not far from Liverpool Street Station in London that offers a free bite-sized Léonidas chocolate as an inducement or bribe to buy a cup of coffee. The ancient Spartans were notoriously amenable to bribes, but they would not have been tempted or amused by such self-indulgent, non-ascetic, want-satisfying fripperies as luxury chocolates. True, they might have been initially more attracted to an English brand once made by Terry's of York that was called 'Spartan', because the chocolates were 'hard-centre'. But they'd have been dismayed to find on the box an illustration not of their own temples of Artemis Orthia or Athena Chalcioecus in Sparta but of the Archaic-period temple of Apollo at . . . Corinth. At least the columns were suitably Doric.

The serious point behind all this is that such brand-names as 'Léonidas' and 'Spartan' are a characteristic contemporary version of the Spartan myth, legend or 'mirage' (the latter being the term coined in the 1930s by the French classical scholar François Ollier). This has been and indeed still very much is a key element in the European and so Western cultural tradition. The Spartan myth was crucially forged on the anvil of Thermopylae. And, though its first *written* manifestations as they have come down to us were the work of non-Spartan Greek admirers, it was launched on its global trajectory by the Spartans themselves.

Perhaps the earliest mythicist to put stylus to papyrus was Critias, leader of the junta of the 'Thirty Tyrants' at Athens, as they came to be known to their shame. He was the mover and shaker of the fanatically oligarchical and pro-Sparta regime that took over from the defeated Athenian democracy in 404 under the aegis of the all-conquering Spartan admiral Lysander. As such, he was ultimately responsible for conducting a reign of terror that lasted for about a year. Before being assisted to power in this way, he had been an associate or pupil of Socrates and thus was clearly a man of high intelligence, like his younger relative – and fellow Socrates pupil – Plato. But he was also, again like Plato, a man of high literary ambition, and he wrote plays as well as two instructional works on the Spartan *politeia* (way of life), one each in prose and in verse.

From Critias descends 'the Spartan tradition' in its most sophisticated literary form: a form that embraces along its winding and often tortuous course such giants as Plato, Aristotle, Plutarch, Montaigne and Rousseau. In what follows we shall be staying mainly with this literary version of Spartanism, and focusing within it on Leonidas and Thermopylae. But we shall stray also into other media, visual as well as verbal, and into some of its more popular as well as elite manifestations. First, though, we must pay attention to the ultimate origins of the Spartan myth-tradition.

The Spartans themselves inaugurated and sedulously developed the

Golden model of a heavy chariot, almost 19 cm long, again from the Oxus Treasure; three pony-size horses are handled by a charioteer, who is accompanied by a seated man; on the front of the chariot is a figure looking something like Bes, the widely attested demon of Egyptian origin.

Thermopylae legend, especially after the Battle of Salamis. They invited both Eurybiadas, the Spartan notionally in overall command of the loyalist Greek coalition forces, and Themistocles, the Athenian genius behind the victory, to an awards ceremony in Sparta. Each was awarded first prize, as it were – a symbolic olive wreath crown, just like the award for victors in the Olympic Games. But Themistocles was given in addition a material gift, a chariot, perhaps a racing-style chariot like those in which Spartans were exceptionally successful at the Olympics and other major Greek games (including the Athenian Panathenaic Games, at which ex-King Demaratus had once carried off the prize in the blue-riband event, the four-horse chariot race). Moreover, after the ceremony and gift-giving were over, Themistocles was provided with an official state escort, to see him safely to the frontier – and, very likely, to see him off the premises, as it were. That escort consisted of precisely three hundred men, the same figure as a Spartan king's elite military bodyguard but also the same magic number as that of the Thermopylae taskforce of only a month or so earlier.

Those Spartans who died at Thermopylae died for Greece and for freedom as well as for Sparta. However, not all of the three hundred had perished in a blaze of glory, and the stories of the two who had not managed to die at Thermopylae were also preserved and disseminated as exemplary, or rather cautionary, tales for both external and domestic consumption. First Pantites, whose only error was to have been away in Thessaly on a diplomatic mission at the time of the final encounter at Thermopylae, was said to have hanged himself on his return to Sparta, because he was 'dishonoured'. The tense used in Herodotus's Greek is the imperfect, meaning that the dishonour he suffered was a continuous state until Pantites ended it by another kind of suicide than that to which he had been originally detailed by order of the state. Sparta was an extreme case of an 'honour and shame' culture, so I suspect that it was not only the public disgrace heaped upon him but the shame he felt inwardly that prompted him to take his own life. I would judge this, in other words, to be a case of what is now recognized widely as 'survivor-guilt'.

Even more instructive, though, was the tangled tale of Aristodamus, the subject of a brilliant chapter in W.I. Miller's comparative study *The Mystery of Courage*. Aristodamus, by then the sole survivor of the three hundred, did not commit suicide in autumn 480. He somehow endured, presumably, the same public disgrace (*oneidos*) heaped on Pantites as well as his own shame at survival. Indeed, Aristodamus's case was a tougher one, since a question-mark hung over his courage. For it so happened that another of the three hundred, Eurytus, had been suffering, as had Aristodamus, from an acute inflammation of the eyes – so acute that for all practical purposes they were both blind and hardly in a position to acquit themselves at their best as fighters. But whereas Eurytus was determined to follow the orders of the Spartans to the letter and die manfully at Thermopylae, and so ordered his Helot batman to lead him into the fray, Aristodamus had – allegedly – quarrelled with Eurytus over this and decided, one presumes, that he would serve Sparta and Greece better by living to fight, much better, and die another day. This was the more favourable of the two – hostile – accounts of Aristodamus's survival. The other version that Herodotus picked up in Sparta was that, like Pantites, Aristodamus had been sent away from the camp on some errand, with another man, and though they both could have got back to Thermopylae in time to fight and die, only the other man did, whereas Aristodamus deliberately loitered to save his skin.

This extreme hostility to Aristodamus may explain why in his case Herodotus specifies in detail what form the dishonour (*atimiê*) took: no Spartan would give him light to make a fire. One assumes that applied not just in Sparta but also – and more acutely – during training in the hills and mountains around, and we must remember that winters in Lacedaemon could be very harsh. Worse still, Aristodamus would not be able to make due sacrifice to the gods. Nor was it only fire that was withheld by his fellow Spartiates. They also, as the English expression goes, 'sent him to Coventry'. It was actually part of their upbringing that Spartan boys were taught by their seniors how to become skilled at being 'laconic'. So deprivation of that talk, however little of it there might be, was actually deprivation of a very great deal.

Perhaps worst of all, in a closed society that developed its own jargon phrases and terms for all sorts of conditions and statuses, Aristodamus was publicly labelled 'the Trembler' (*tresas*). In other words, he was adjudged officially to have acted the coward, and whatever reason or excuse he himself may have put forward for his absence and survival at the decisive moment was not believed or accepted. Since this is the first mention of this technical term in extant literature, it has been suggested that Aristodamus was the aboriginal Trembler, the Spartan who brought a new category of less than fully 'peer-group' (*homoioi*) Spartans into being. That seems to me unlikely, but not being the pioneer in the field would not have lessened Aristodamus's humiliation in any way.

Perhaps he deflected and diminished this disgrace and dishonour somewhat, or sought to, by telling anyone who would listen that he would redeem himself, if given his chance. That chance came for him at the Battle of Plataea in 479. Such was Aristodamus's – perhaps grudgingly acknowledged – military distinction that he was still stationed among the *promachoi*, the front-line fighters, those whose courage and skill in hand-to-hand combat would be the most sorely tested. Spartan hoplites were trained to advance to the fray with measured step, in unison, to the accompaniment of the reeded double pipes named *auloi* by the Greeks, what John Milton called 'flutes and soft recorders'. Shield would overlap with and lock on to adjacent shield. From its enemy's standpoint the front line would thus ideally have resembled a moving wall, a counterpart to the wooden walls of the Athenian navy. But shortly before the moment of impact, Aristodamus heretically broke ranks. He turned berserker. He did not stay in his allotted position (*taxis*) but hurled himself against the enemy in a wild frenzy, precisely because he wanted to make sure he would die. So he committed suicide in effect, the suicide that he knew he ought to have committed at Thermopylae; but he did it individually, not in accordance with the collective design, and above all he did it disobediently.

Herodotus gives the statistics of the casualties on both sides and then goes into default competitive-Greek mode. In his own judgement the men of Tegea and Athens had fought best of the infantry, but top of the league as a whole were the Spartans, since theirs had been the hardest victory to achieve. Herodotus then names his 'man of the match': Aristodamus.* The Spartans themselves, however, came to a

---

* The Greek for 'best' was *aristos*; the term for a battlefield performance of excellence, *aristeia*. Aristodamus's name meant 'best of – or for – the people'.

quite contrary post-mortem judgement. For them, the 'most name-able' (*onomastotatoi*) were Poseidonius (called after one of the Spartans' most important gods), Philocyôn ('Dog-lover' – a tribute to the famed breed of Spartan hunting hounds) and Amompharetus ('Blameless virtue'). Aristodamus came nowhere in the posthumous awards ceremony.

The Spartans conceded that Aristodamus had 'displayed great deeds' – that is, fought magnificently; presumably he had taken out several Persians before he himself succumbed. But he had done so for the wrong reason, with the wrong motivation, at the wrong time and in the wrong way. He had fought in this grandstanding manner solely to get himself killed in order to expiate his state of disgrace. Instead of displaying resolute self-discipline, Aristodamus had acted in a mindless frenzy of madness; and to cap it all, he had left his rank and broken martial discipline – his most heinous crime in Spartan eyes. Put differently, he had performed the wrong sort of suicide. Herodotus so far disagreed with this judgement of the Spartans that he was inclined to put it down to mere envy. This disagreement was a sure sign of the gulf between the Spartans' ideas on life and death and those of other Greeks.

Only Spartan men who died in battle, as we saw in Chapter Four, were entitled to a gravestone with their name inscribed upon it, followed by just the phrase 'in war'. In general, indeed, the Spartans were parsimonious with any inscribed public documentation. It was therefore a mark of the extreme honour achieved in death by the Thermopylae three hundred (well, 298) that they were granted an inscribed casualty list at Sparta that served also as an official war memorial. Herodotus saw it and was proud to say that he had memorized all their names. Pausanias the Periegete, the travel-writer, also claimed to have seen it some six centuries later. The Spartans no doubt also took the leading role in persuading the Amphictyonic League of Delphi to commission from Simonides for display at Thermopylae itself one of the most famous elegiac couplets of all time:

Go tell the Spartans, passerby,
That here, obedient to their laws, we lie.

Spartans who died abroad were normally buried on the spot.* One of the so-called *Laconian Apophthegms* preserved by Plutarch reinforces the point. A citizen of Sparta's deadliest Greek enemy, Argos, proudly says to a Spartan, 'We have lots of graves of you Spartans in our city's territory'; to which the Spartan replies, 'Yes, but we have none of yours in ours' – his point being that the Argives had never managed to penetrate Spartan territory.†

There was one exception to that rule of on-the-spot foreign burial for fallen Spartan warriors. In certain circumstances the body of a Spartan king who died abroad might be brought home and given a state funeral. This was the case, eventually, for Leonidas. Herodotus elaborately conveys the extraordinary nature and quality of the Spartan royal funeral in another context, where he is describing the exceptional prerogatives accorded to all the kings in peace and in war, in life and in death. On the death of a king there was declared a suspension of state business that would last for the eleven days of official mourning. Women (presumably free Spartan women) went round the city beating kettle-drums, at which signal two members of each citizen household (*oikos*) had to don mourning garb – under penalty of a large fine for failure to do so. News of the death and impending funeral was also conveyed by riders dispatched the length and breadth of Sparta's enormous territory, to Messenia as well as Laconia, informing the whole population that all classes and statuses – Perioecic and Helot

---

* The most famous example of a foreign grave memorial can still be viewed by the informed visitor to Athens today. Sometime in or after 403 the Athenians erected in their city's most important cemetery, the Cerameicus, an impressive tomb for those Spartans who had been killed in the fighting that saw the end of the horrendous reign of Critias's Thirty Tyrants. This was part of the deal whereby Sparta allowed Athens to revert to being a free democracy, if under stringent conditions. The names of the dead were inscribed above the graves, in a Laconian hand.

† The first successful incursion was in winter 370/69 BCE.

The modern national route from Athens to Thessaloniki scythes right through the site of the Thermopylae battlefield, which is now far further from the sea than in 480. Prominently beside the road a handsome memorial was erected to the Spartan war dead in 1955, by the Greek government with Greek–American money. The statue of Leonidas seen here in left profile was modelled on the 'Leonidas' torso combined with representations of authentic ancient Greek shields bearing the device of a gorgon found both in Sparta and elsewhere (e.g., Olympia). Later, a modern memorial was also set up for the men of Thespiae who died heroically alongside Leonidas and his three hundred.

as well as Spartan – had to be represented in person at the obsequies that would take place in the capital.*

But what if a king died abroad 'in war'? Herodotus had asked this question too, and had been given the answer that a substitute image (*eidôlon*) of him would be fashioned, then carried to burial in Sparta on a richly caparisoned catafalque. The clear implication is that the actual body of the king would not be brought back but would be buried on

---

* Herodotus says this feature was the same 'in Asia' as in Sparta, meaning presumably within the Persian Empire.

the spot, like those of all other Spartans. In Leonidas's case there was a very good reason indeed for that practice, as we saw, and probably his exceptional case was the source of the supposed rule. For, according to Greek reports, despite their heroic efforts the Spartans had not been able to prevent the Persians from decapitating his dead body on the orders of Xerxes and Mardonius. By the time the Greeks gained access to it, presumably only after the Persian horde had passed on south beyond Thermopylae, it would have decomposed further, possibly even beyond recognition, and certainly beyond the possibility of embalming it with either wax or honey (supposing those materials had been to hand in sufficient quantity).* So, although the Spartans might well have wished ideally to bring Leonidas's corpse back to Sparta in 480 to receive honours 'greater than those normally accorded to a mortal man' – this was how Xenophon described the burial honours of Agesilaus's half-brother Agis II, who died in 400 – they simply could not.

About forty years later they made amends. This was a time of formal peace between the two great powers of Greece, Sparta and Athens, though also a time of great and mounting tension between them. A reminder of Sparta's role in the Graeco-Persian Wars was in order. So a Spartan detail was pointedly sent to the pass at Thermopylae, and perhaps to the small hill marked by a stone lion monument where, or near where, Leonidas had fallen.† These men duly recovered what they were persuaded were the remains of Leonidas and brought them back to Sparta, where they were reburied with all due pomp and circumstance.

Actually, all Spartan kings were automatically heroized. They were given the honorific status of semi-divine heroes after their death and were paid thereafter in perpetuity the religious worship appropri-

---

* The embalmed corpse of Agesilaus II, who died aged eighty-four in north Africa in 360, was brought back to Sparta for burial, but he had not died 'in war'.

† The Greek for 'lion' is *leôn*, a quite common Spartan personal name, understandably enough, and the first part of Leonidas's; a later poem preserved in the collection known as the *Palatine Anthology* purports to be spoken by this famous Thermopylae stone lion.

ate to heroes. But Leonidas was something special, and it comes as no surprise to find that in later centuries a formal festival was devoted to him, called the Leonidaea. Still to be seen in Sparta, not far from the acropolis, are the quite substantial remains of the religious building known as the Leonidaion that acted as the focal point of this cult worship. Predictably, too, that worship was associated with a posthumous cult devoted to the other Spartan leader in those wars, Regent Pausanias, despite the vicissitudes of his subsequent career.*

---

* Regent Pausanias (regent for Leonidas's son Pleistarchus), however, was made of different stuff. There seems no kinder way of putting it other than to say that the victory at Plataea had gone to his head. The stunning celebratory poetry of Simonides, which mentioned him by name, will not have helped to deflate his hypertrophied ego. The Spartans had to remind him, not gently, that it was not he alone who had defeated the Persians, as an inscription added on his instructions to the base of the Greeks' victory memorial at Delphi, the 'Serpent Column' – the cauldron standing on three bronze coils topped with snakes' heads (see Chapter Five) – tried to make out. Somehow or other he had himself appointed officially in 478 to some sort of command at Byzantium, the obvious nodal point for carrying on – or rounding off – the active anti-Persian naval–military campaign. But while there, he massively alienated the largely Athenian forces, and a majority of the allies clamoured for his recall and replacement. Most likely his overbearing Spartan style of command did not mix brilliantly well with Athenian democratic notions of military service. But the formal allegation made against him was far more serious than that; indeed, it could hardly have been more serious: namely, that Pausanias had been treating with Persia, either with the local satrap or with Great King Xerxes himself, with a view to doing some sort of private deal.

My own hunch is that this was black propaganda, a sure-fire way to get Pausanias recalled by the Spartans – and it worked a treat. Pausanias, however, soon returned to Byzantium in a private capacity, and it may have been now rather than earlier that he really did start negotiations with the Persian High Command and even – with the example of Demaratus before him – conceive the notion of becoming a pliant Persian instrument, possibly even satrap of 'Greece' (south of Macedonia). This, however, is all speculation. The most important consequence of Pausanias's career was the shift of the leadership of the anti-Persian campaign in 478/7 from Sparta to Athens, and the formation of the Athenian alliance that soon became an Athenian empire.

Later, on his eventual return to Sparta, Pausanias was very harshly treated by the ephors of the day, not so much for his behaviour towards Athens and Persia but

The same message of panhellenist commemoration was intended by the construction in the centre of Sparta town of two permanent monuments that served also as memorials of the Graeco-Persian Wars: the Hellenion ('place of the Greeks') religious sanctuary and the colonnade known as the Persian Stoa, the latter with remarkable architectural depictions of Persian captives.

Herodotus, however, begged to disagree with the Spartans' propaganda and sided, controversially, with the Athenians. Here is his intervention on the contested issue of which of the two Greek states, Sparta or Athens, had done most to defeat the Persian invasion:

> At this point I feel myself constrained to express an opinion that most will find objectionable, but which, since I believe it to be true, I must not withhold. If the Athenians, through fear of the imminent danger, had abandoned their country, or if they had remained but submitted to Xerxes, then there would certainly have been no attempt to resist Xerxes by sea and . . . I cannot myself see what possible use it would have been [for the Spartans] to fortify the Isthmus as long as the Persian navy had mastery of the sea. So if anyone were to say that it was the Athenians who were the saviours of Greece, that would not be very wide of the mark. It was the Athenians who held the balance of the scales: whichever side they joined would be bound to prevail. It was they who, choosing freedom, roused the Greek states that had not yet prevailed. And it was they who – after the gods – repulsed the Great King.[1]

---

because, allegedly, he had been intriguing with Helots to grant them freedom and even citizenship of some sort. He was shut up in a sacred space on the Spartan acropolis and starved to within an inch of his life, being released only so that he could die outside consecrated ground to avoid pollution. In an act of posthumous recompense and restitution the Spartans erected bronze statues of him, and at some point a religious cult to him was established, jointly with that of the other Spartan Graeco-Persian war hero, Leonidas.

This was written with all due attention to the ticklish sensitivities that surrounded the issue at the time he was composing (in the 440s and 430s) no less than in the early 470s. Hence his defensive phrase 'an opinion that most will find objectionable': this was a coded reference to the fact that in the 440s and 430s the Athenians were using their supposedly decisive liberationist role in the Graeco-Persian Wars as an argument in favour of maintaining the anti-Persian maritime empire that 'most' Greeks affected by it considered to be a form of tyranny.*

---

*   I myself, on the other hand, feel constrained to differ, strongly, from Herodotus's judgement. True, the Battle of Salamis was a stunning naval victory, one of the greatest of all time. Scholars will forever debate why Xerxes felt he could afford to negate his numerical and tactical advantage by going in to fight in the narrows around the islet of Salamis, thereby experiencing a sort of maritime Thermopylae, but a self-inflicted one rather than a natural obstacle that was unavoidable. There is no debate at all, however, about the strategic genius and other leadership qualities of Themistocles, nor about the courage and faith of the Athenians in temporarily abandoning their *polis* in the hope of returning to it again another, much better day.

Culturally and politically, too, Salamis was of the utmost significance. Aeschylus's tragedy *The Persians*, produced under eight years later in spring 472, focuses on Salamis and (the unnamed) Themistocles. Salamis confirmed the status of the Athenians' democracy as the most effective fighting constitution for them, and confirmed too the hugely enhanced position within it of the mass of the poorest Athenians who had rowed the victorious trireme warships. Victory at Salamis also led more or less directly to the Athenians' creation of an initially anti-Persian maritime empire that later turned into a major cause of the fatal bust-up between Athens and Sparta and their respective allies in the great Atheno-Peloponnesian War of 431–404. One of those Spartan allies, and not the least important in sealing the Spartans' eventual victory, was Persia, an ironic twist of fate.

And yet: in immediate military terms, the value of Salamis was ambiguous. Had Xerxes won, then the Persians would have had the Peloponnese at the mercy of a naval assault; and, if it is still not quite a foregone conclusion that they would then inevitably have won overall, by land as well as sea, their task would have been eased immensely. Victory at Salamis did not, on the other hand, inevitably mean victory for the resistant coalition Greeks in the Graeco-Persian Wars overall. From that perspective, it was not Salamis but Plataea that was the decisive battle. 'It was at Plataea, not at Salamis, that the new satrapy was lost', as George Cawkwell has crisply put it. Xerxes may have retired to Asia after Salamis, but Great Kings did not necessarily lead all major

The Athenians themselves – official spokesmen of the Athenian democracy, not isolated untypical pro-Spartan Athenians like Critias – not unnaturally agreed wholeheartedly with Herodotus, and they expressed this view openly whenever they could. First, there is the evidence of the annual Athenian public Funeral Speech (in honour of all that year's war dead). The tradition of choosing a distinguished citizen to deliver such a speech seems to have originated in the 460s. We have only a handful surviving in any form, and not all of these record real speeches as opposed to imaginary confections or reconstructions. But two of the authentic ones, those composed by the speechwriter Lysias and by the politician Hyperides, both mention Thermopylae, and in interestingly different ways, reflecting the time and circumstances of their composition and delivery.

Lysias's was composed around 400 BCE, only a few years after the Athenians' defeat in the Atheno-Peloponnesian War, the imposition of a tyranny (the Thirty) and the restoration of democracy at Athens, all at the hands or behest of Sparta:

> *While this invasion [by Xerxes] was preoccupying Greece, the Athenians went on board their ships and came to the rescue at Artemisium. The Spartans and some of the allies [of the coalition] met the Persians at Thermopylae. They thought they would be able to prevent the Persians' entry there thanks to the region's narrowness. The battles occurred simultaneously. But whereas the Athenians were victorious at sea, the Spartans were destroyed. They were not lacking in bravery, but they miscalculated the number of guards needed and*

---

campaigns in person, and he left behind, under the command of the more than competent Mardonius, sufficient forces to complete the job by land as well as by sea. But Mardonius was decisively defeated on land in the summer of 479 at Plataea in southern Boeotia in central Greece, by the largest land army ever mustered by Greeks to that date (some forty thousand in all). Herodotus – even Herodotus, whose views on the critical importance of Salamis we have just rehearsed – was forced to concede that Plataea was essentially a Spartan victory.

*the number of attackers. They were not [however] defeated by the
enemy, because they died where they were stationed to fight.*

The respect Lysias shows for the Spartans is palpable, though he
probably enjoyed writing 'the Spartans were destroyed'.*

Hyperides, on the other hand, was writing in the middle of a war
of rebellion and resistance against not a barbarian Persian overlord,
but the Greek Macedonians, whose hegemony of Greece had been
established by Philip II in 338 and confirmed by his son Alexander the
Great (reigned 336–323). Sparta, though an enemy of Macedon, was
not part of this Greece-wide resistance led by Athens in the late 320s
– partly because Athens had earlier decided not to support the
Spartans when their King Agis III raised a disastrously unsuccessful
revolt against Alexander's regent Antipater in 331. Hyperides therefore wastes no breath on praising the Spartans, but rather criticizes
them by implication: whereas 'the barbarians' (Persians) had marched
through the pass of Thermopylae when the Spartans had occupied it,
the Athenian general Leosthenes (the real hero of the piece), when he
occupied Thermopylae, 'denied Antipater entry into Greece' and
indeed shut him up in Lamia in Thessaly not far to the north of
Thermopylae.†

Alexander the Great himself is also a major contributor to
the Thermopylae legend – though his contribution has rarely been
recognized for what it is. After the first of his three major set-piece
victories over the imperial forces of Persian Great King Darius III,
the Battle of the Granicus River in 334, he ordered precisely three
hundred panoplies (suits of armour and weapons) to be sent back to

---

* Lysias was not an Athenian citizen, but a permanent resident alien of Syracusan
origin, so his speech if delivered would have been delivered by another. His family had
personal connections with Pericles, and he was immensely wealthy thanks to the prof-
its from a slave-staffed shield manufactory.
† The war takes its name from Lamia, but Hyperides has to skate over the awkward
fact that Antipater broke out from there and in 321 heavily defeated the rebels.

Athens as trophies. Punctilious as always in matters of religion, he intended these to be dedicated to Athena on the Athenian Acropolis, accompanied by the following diplomatic dedication: 'Alexander, son of Philip, and the Greeks – except the Lacedaemonians – [set up these spoils taken] from the barbarians dwelling in Asia.' Alexander does not call himself 'King' Alexander, since the Athenians were by no means enthusiastic subjects of his, and he emphasizes that this is to be an almost but not quite panhellenic offering. The panhellenism was *de rigueur*, because his whole expedition was supposedly motivated by the need and desire to avenge the sacrilege inflicted on the Greeks and especially the Athenians by Great King Xerxes 150 years before.*
So why does Alexander choose to spell out 'except the Spartans'?

Because in 334 the Spartans were conspicuous only by their absence from this new, ostensibly panhellenic campaign. In fact, to them it was Alexander, not Darius, who was the main enemy at the time, and they even collaborated (in both senses) with the Persian resistance against Alexander behind his back. How different it had all been in 480 and 479, when the Spartans were the acknowledged champions of 'the Greeks' in resistance against Persian invasion. And how, by now, were the mighty fallen. Hence Alexander's choice to dedicate specifically on the Acropolis of Athens precisely three hundred suits of armour and weapons. So much for the great Thermopylae three hundred of yore – *sic transit gloria laconica*. From those three hundred panoplies, fourteen shields were actually displayed as trophies across the eastern (front) façade of the mightiest structure on the Acropolis, the Parthenon. The surviving nail-holes bear telling witness to that lofty demonstration of Sparta's faded glory.

The Spartans fought back in these culture wars. Within the post-Alexander 'Hellenistic' period (323–30 BCE) the Leonidaion was built and the Leonidaea festival inaugurated, yet another addition to their

---

* Xerxes and the Persians had sacked the sacred Acropolis of Athens twice, in 480 and again in 479.

already crowded religious calendar. In 146 BCE Greece south of Macedon was subjugated by the new kid on the Mediterranean imperial block, the mighty power of Rome. Again, as the Roman poet Horace put it, the Greeks fought back culturally:

> *Graecia capta ferum victorem cepit, et artes*
> *intulit agresti Latio . . .*
> Captive Greece took her fierce conqueror captive, and introduced the
> arts to rustic Latium . . .

In a major philosophical disquisition, the *Tusculan Disputations*, Cicero actually translated the Simonides elegy into a more than passable Latin elegiac couplet:

> *Dic, hospes, Spartae nos te hic vidisse iacentes,*
> *dum sanctis patriae legibus obsequimur.*[2]

> Go tell the Spartans, passerby,
> That here, obedient to their laws, we lie.

'*Patriae*' – 'fatherland' – is placed centrally by Cicero in the pentameter line, and cannot fail to recall Horace's equally famous '*dulce et decorum est pro patria mori*' ('sweet and fitting it is to die for the fatherland'),[3] which has served to inspire poets and other creative artists, including now film-makers, in many succeeding generations. Within the German tradition, for example, Cicero inspired Friedrich Schiller in his 'Der Spaziergang' ('The Walk');[4] and that in its turn was the inspiration for Heinrich Böll's Second World War story 'Wanderer, kommst du nach Spa . . .?' ('Traveller, are you coming to Spa . . . ?' (1950), set in the type of elite classicizing German secondary school called a *Gymnasium*, in which Classical languages and ancient Spartan history would have been routinely taught.

Ancient Greeks for their part tended fondly to imagine that Rome had originally been a Greek foundation, since the word *rhômê* in Greek meant 'strength'. There was even talk of a biological kinship between the Romans and the Spartans, though actually this was an example of the sort of cunning deployment of kinship diplomacy that both eased the Romans' path to imperial power and sugared the pill of domination for its proud Greek subjects. At any rate, it was late in the reign of the Roman emperor Trajan (CE 98–117) that the Leonidaea festival was refounded at Sparta, probably as a response to the campaign that Trajan was then waging against the Parthians, an Iranian people related (more genuinely) to the ancient Persians against whom Leonidas had fought.

The refoundation was financed by a local benefactor called C. Iulius Agesilaus. The last of his three names is pure Spartan Greek, indeed regal. But the first two, 'Caius Iulius', bespeak the fact that a direct male ancestor of his had been granted Roman citizenship by one C. Julius Octavianus Caesar, better known as Octavian or Caesar Augustus, the founder of the Roman Empire. The Spartans had chosen to side with Octavian (as he then still was), the eventual victor in the huge civil war that pitted him, the grand-nephew and appointed heir of Julius Caesar, against Caesar's former lieutenant Marcus Antonius (Mark Antony). One key reason for their choice, unusual in the Greek world, was that the neighbouring Messenians – the descendants of the Helots eventually liberated by Thebes in 370/69 BCE – took Antony's side; and 'my enemy's enemy is my friend'. Sparta benefited enormously from this lucky decision, collectively in the form of public benefactions of various material kinds as well as individually in the shape of Roman citizenship grants to prominent Spartans.

In its Roman-period manifestation the Leonidaea festival was accompanied by a trade fair. The Spartans deliberately sought to attract travelling merchants from abroad by exempting them from the usual local sales and import–export taxes. There is even mention of a publicly regulated bank of commercial exchange operating, something the Spartans of Leonidas's own day could not have begun to contemplate, let alone tolerate or encourage. This openness towards foreigners was in flagrant contradiction of their Classical ancestors' xenophobia. As Herodotus tells us, the Spartans of his day did not distinguish in their vocabulary between non-Spartans who were Greek and non-Spartans who were non-Greek: they called them all alike *xenoi*, whereas other Greeks normally distinguished between *xenoi*, foreigners who might be either Greek or non-Greek, and *barbaroi*, foreigners who were by definition non-Greek and indeed 'inferior' barbarians. There was even a widespread view outside Sparta in the fifth century that the Spartans practised regular expulsions of *xenoi*, for both cultural and political reasons.

That, however, is less probable. While some *xenoi* might on specific occasions have been expelled (Aristagoras of Miletus in the year 500, for instance), other Greek *xenoi* were actually welcomed, especially to the annual Gymnopaediae festival. These favoured *xenoi* were the ones who had hereditary personal friendships with individual Spartans and (or) who sympathized strongly with the distinctive Spartan way of life and political outlook. If you did not happen to like them, then you might object that Spartan ways did not mix well or at all with those of other Greeks. But if on the contrary you liked both very much indeed, then, like Xenophon of Athens, you might actually send your sons to Sparta to be educated under the watchful eye of your Spartan *xenoi* – in Xenophon's case King Agesilaus II, who was very likely an ancestor of our second-century CE C. Iulius Agesilaus.

In the middle of the second century CE Pausanias the Periegete passed through Sparta, collecting material for his religiously inflected historical travelogue of central and southern mainland Greece. He was a Greek from Asia Minor, but inevitably a Roman subject too, and he suffered from chronic nostalgia, specifically for the era of the Graeco-Persian Wars. He was happy, consequently, to find that the Spartans of his day were actively cultivating and manipulating their city's architecture as a shrine to the memory of the great deeds performed by their countrymen all of six hundred years earlier. The memorial for Leonidas found a privileged place on his itinerary. So too did the tomb said to be that of Eurybiadas, the Spartan admiral of 480, and – even more to our point – the memorials for the Thermopylae dead and for Regent Pausanias, and the so-called Persian Stoa in what passed at Sparta for an *agora*, or meeting-place.

Pausanias belongs within the general Greek movement of cultural recuperation and reinvention known for short as the Second Sophistic.* For such intellectuals, the attraction of Leonidas was that he was such a glaringly obvious hero of the great Greek past (alas, long past) for contemporary rhetoricians and sophists to shower with nostalgic praise. Indeed, so regular and intense was their often fulsome eulogy of him that the practice earned a satirical put-down from the brilliantly witty Lucian.†

Plutarch (*c.* 46–120), on the other hand, would not have dreamt of satirizing Leonidas. Apart from the purely rhetorical productions of his youth (including encomia of Alexander the Great), and the host of philosophical essays of his maturity, Plutarch's major contribution to Greek literature and culture was his series of parallel biographies of the great Greeks and Romans of the more or less distant past. Among these was a *Life of Leonidas*, but it is unfortunately one of the very few of his *Lives* that did not survive from antiquity to our day. What we have are the apophthegms attributed to Leonidas in the collection *Sayings of Kings and Commanders*, or deployed by Plutarch in the extant *Lives*.

In his *Life* of the reforming, if not revolutionary, Spartan King Cleomenes III (reigned 235–222 BCE), for instance, Plutarch writes:

> It is said that, when the Leonidas of olden times was asked to give his view of the quality of Tyrtaeus as a poet, he replied:

---

* Second after the Athens-centred phenomenon of the later fifth and the fourth centuries BCE, which had made of Athens, in the phrase of Plato, 'the city hall of wisdom'.
† Another glittering ornament of the Second Sophistic, but by origin a non-Greek Syrian from Samosata (modern Samsat in Turkey) and so more easily able to maintain a slightly ironic distance.

'A fine one for firing the spirits of the young.' This was on the grounds that the poems filled the young with such enthusiasm that they stopped worrying about their own lives in battle.

This is a classic demonstration of the invention of tradition in action. Through this quotation, from a work of the early second century CE, by way of a saying attributed to a celebrated Spartan king of the early fifth century BCE, the reader is taken back imaginatively – as Plutarch intended – to the life, work and times of the Spartans' 'national' poet in the seventh century.* Plutarch contrives to suggest an immensely high level of cultural continuity over some eight hundred years, when in fact – as he and Pausanias the Periegete must surely have confessed to themselves in quieter moments of sober reflection – the world had changed, irreparably, and by no means entirely for the better, as they saw it.

In the following, third century CE the Christian apologist Origen (*c.* 185–253) had no qualms about appealing to pagan precedent in his war of words with the pagan Celsus. Origen was even prepared to suggest that the central Christian mystery of Christ's passion and death might be suitably illuminated by a comparison with the self-chosen and avoidable death of Leonidas. A century later, the struggle between pagan and Christian – not to mention between one kind of Christian and another – had intensified, to the point of not just verbal recrimination but mutual slaughter. Amidst the fray, but hoping to stand above it, Synesius of Cyrene was proud to proclaim his supposed Spartan lineage. (Cyrene had been founded in north Africa, in modern Libya, in the later seventh century BCE; its founders had come from Thera, the modern Cycladic island of Santorini (its Venetian name), and by some accounts the original founders of the city of Thera were refugees from Sparta, of which Cyrene was hence a granddaughter city.)

---

* Tyrtaeus's poetry was officially memorized in Sparta and had been sung on campaign at least until the earlier Hellenistic age in the third century BCE.

Specifically, Synesius advertised his descent from Eurysthenes, one of the twin founders of the two Spartan royal houses of the Agiads and Eurypontids (Leonidas was an Agiad). Synesius left behind his pagan roots and became a Christian bishop, and his bookishness was hardly an ancestral Spartan trait. On the other hand, his passionate devotion to hunting in his pre-Christian days would not have struck his supposed Spartan forebears as at all odd. Being away hunting was one of the very few legitimate excuses that a Spartan of Leonidas's time could offer for being absent from the compulsory evening mess meal.

Such kinship claims, made by whole communities as well as individuals, were a common phenomenon in Roman times. But they are attested as early as the fifth century BCE, within a purely Greek context, and they became such common currency in the Hellenistic era that they could be made by people or peoples without a drop of Greek blood in their veins – and made plausibly, too, in the hope of achieving recognition and acceptance. So it was that in the early third century BCE the then High Priest of Jerusalem made bold to claim the shared descent of the Jews and the Spartans from Abraham and Moses. And the Spartan King Areus responded in positive vein – or so the Jewish text of Maccabees would have it. This was the Jews' way both of finding a place symbolically in the Hellenistic world order and, more practically, of obtaining a feasible foreign ally against the encroachments of the aggressive local monarchs of the post-Alexander Seleucid house.

As for Synesius, he was immediately concerned to draw strength from an over-optimistic and self-serving comparison of his struggle against nomads ravaging Cyrenaica to Leonidas's rather more universally significant defence of Greece against the Persian invaders.

NINE

THE THERMOPYLAE LEGEND II: FROM ANTIQUITY TO MODERNITY

> Of the three hundred grant but three
> To make a new Thermopylae!
>
> Lord Byron, *Don Juan*

> Older than we are by however many ages,
> it doesn't need defending against anything.
> No more do air or fire, earth or water.
> Not even in our empty times. Neglected, it will
> go underground, or into interstellar space.

> Until out of the blue someone calls it up,
> like the Greek who cut my hair last week.
> Where was he from? 'Spar-ta', he said.
> 'You are a Spartan!' I exclaimed. 'Oh no',
> he said, 'there are no Spartans any more.'
>
> Andrew McNeillie, 'In Defence of Poetry',
>
> *Times Literary Supplement*, 16 August 2001

THE MAINLY Italian Renaissance, as it has come to be known, of the fourteenth to sixteenth centuries was explicitly a 'back to the future' movement of cultural perception and political action. Rediscovery of the wisdom, truth and beauty of the best ancient

Greeks and Romans would instigate advance and progress away from what later came to be derogated as the (benighted) Middle Ages. This Renaissance was more of a Western than an Eastern movement, more Roman than Hellenic in inspiration and reference. But there was one notable exception to that rule, Ciriaco dei Pizzicolli, a merchant more familiarly known from his town of origin as Cyriac of Ancona. Cyriac did more than anyone else, probably, to bridge East and West by bringing the East to the West. To him we owe a travelogue of 1447 that outdoes even the second-century Pausanias the Periegete's jeremiad over the lamentable present and his *recherche* of a much better *temps* that had been *perdu*. Cyriac, unlike Pausanias, approached Sparta via Mistra (a short distance to the west). Founded in the mid-thirteeenth century by the Franks, Mistra was still, just, the capital of the despotate of the Morea (Peloponnese), a junior outpost of the Byzantine world that was very soon to fall to the Ottoman Turks under Sultan Mehmet II the Conqueror. As he approached, Cyriac lamented the absence of a very long list of Spartan warriors of olden, golden times, among them – of course – Leonidas.

About the time of Cyriac's Spartan visit one of the greatest painters of the Italian Renaissance was born, Pietro Vannucci known as Perugino (*c.* 1450–1523), most celebrated now as the teacher of Raphael. His *Fortezza e Temperanza* ('Strength and Temperance') composition, in Perugia's Nobile Collegio del Cambio, includes a selection of *'uomini forti'* ('brave men', but it goes better in Latin – *viri fortes*). At the side of Horatius Cocles, great defender of ancient Rome, stands another great defender, labelled 'Leonida Lacedemonio', 'Leonidas of Sparta'. Horatius (even better known to generations of English schoolboys reared on Macaulay's *Lays of Ancient Rome*) looks up and to his left, as do the figures on either side of these two. But Leonidas, strikingly, breaks the pattern and looks down; more precisely, he looks down perhaps a trifle ruefully at the extraordinarily long sword he grips at the hilt and which he tilts at an angle with his right hand and holds two-thirds of the way down with his left. Apart from its inauthentically un-Spartan length, what catches the eye is that the sword is seriously bent out of true. The viewer is presumably intended to interpret this proleptically, as a fore-shadowing of Leonidas's heroic end.

The 'early modern' period in Europe is conventionally taken to run from about 1500 to 1800. In the second half of the sixteenth century, an interesting debate involving Spartan antiquity can be observed taking place right at the other end of Europe, in Scotland. In 1579 the humanist and historian George Buchanan praised Leonidas, along with Agesilaus II and some others, for being a true king, whereas the monarchs of his day were, he thought, too much sunk in luxury. Adam Blackwood, however, in 1581 took an opposite, constitutionalist as opposed to moralistic view. In Sparta, he believed, the kings enjoyed merely the name and empty title of 'king', rather than the substance of kingly power. In a way he was right – and certainly power divided is unlikely to have carried the same clout or implications as undivided monarchy. But careful investigation shows that those Spartans who wielded the greatest power and authority in their day – and abroad, too, not just at home – were kings: Cleomenes I, Leonidas, Agesilaus II, Cleomenes III. The one obvious exception is Lysander, but after a brief paroxysm of excessively personal power he too was cut down to a more Spartan size – by first King Pausanias and then King Agesilaus II.

At almost exactly the same time as this Scottish debate was being conducted, across the water in France the prodigious and prolific Montaigne (Michel Eyquem de Montaigne) was compiling his *Essais*. One of the best known has the arresting title 'On the Cannibals' (1580), but its contents went well beyond its ostensible subject-matter. One might not expect to find here, for example, this remarkably astute and acute observation:

> *There are triumphant defeats that rival victories. Salamis, Plataea, Mycale and Sicily* are the fairest sister-victories under the sun.*

---

* A reference to the Battle of Himera, a victory of Sicilian Greeks over invading Carthaginians, legendarily fought on the very same day as Salamis.

> *Yet they would never dare compare their combined glory with
> the glorious defeat of King Leonidas and his men in the pass of
> Thermopylae.*[1]

Fénelon, a fellow countryman and fellow *littérateur* of Montaigne,
used Leonidas almost a century later as a character in one of his
Dialogues des Morts ('Dialogues of the Dead'); he was the only
Spartan to be employed in this way. The idea and title for the work
were borrowed from Lucian, who had staged imaginary dialogues of a
historically possible and intrinsically plausible character – as well as
dialogues that were neither of these. But the notion of a dialogue
between a Spartan king and Great King Xerxes goes back ultimately
to Herodotus (though, strictly, Demaratus was by then an *ex*-king).
Like Buchanan, Fénelon depicted Leonidas as a true king, in contrast
to the merely despotic Xerxes, and painted him in thoroughly local
Spartan colours:

> *I exercised my kingship on condition that I led a hard, sober and
> industrious life, just like that of my people. I was king solely to
> defend my fatherland and to ensure the rule of law. My kingship
> gave me the power to do good without permitting me the licence
> to do evil.*[2]

Xerxes was in Fénelon's eyes simply 'too powerful and too fortunate';
had he not been so, he 'would have been a quite honourable man'.
Handel, composing his comic opera *Xerxes* in the following century,
was far less generously inclined; he shared the general anti-despotic
tendency of the eighteenth-century Enlightenment.

That Enlightenment assumed different shapes and shades in different European countries and in America, and was divided against itself
on major moral and intellectual issues. There was a broad division, for
example, in attitudes to the ancients between the modernizers and the
traditionalists. This entailed choosing, not between Athens and
Jerusalem, but between Athens and Sparta. In the Sparta corner were
the Swiss and French Rousseau, Charles Rollin, Helvétius and the abbé

de Mably, the Scottish social theorist Adam Ferguson and, in his very long 1737 epic poem *Leonidas*, the Englishman Richard Glover. Expressly going against the ancient myth of Gorgo encouraging Leonidas to his patriotically inspired rendezvous with destiny, Glover has her criticizing him for placing death for his country above life with her! Glover's Leonidas attempts to turn that criticism on its head by claiming that to die for country *is* to die for family – that is, to keep one's family free. Sparta was presented by these eulogists as both a political and especially a moral exemplar, a state whose power rested on her virtue – disciplined, harmonious, obedient. Nor was such pro-Spartanism the preserve only of elite intellectuals. In 1793 the apostate *citoyens* of the French town of Saint-Marcellin, having abandoned their Christian faith, renamed their community 'Thermopyles'.

The other side of Leonidas's exemplary public virtue is represented in Handel's *Xerxes* of 1738. This selected for its *mise-en-scène* a variant version of the unpleasant domestic plot hatched by Xerxes as recounted towards the end of the very last book of Herodotus. To cut a long story short, Xerxes will stop at nothing to get his hands on his brother's beloved. A strange subplot portrays Xerxes as hopelessly enamoured of a plane tree – perhaps a distant reminiscence of the ancient Greeks' jibe at the Great King's artificial golden plane tree that symbolized for them the utterly debauched luxury of the Persian monarchy.*

Not all the illuminati of the eighteenth century by any means agreed on eulogy of Sparta. The Frenchman Voltaire and the Scotsmen David Hume and Adam Smith, for example, were conspicuously hostile critics, Voltaire not surprisingly having no time for a city that had openly affected to despise both book-learning and luxury. But perhaps

---

* This plane tree of Xerxes is not to be confused with the oriental plane tree grown in Cambridge, at Jesus College, from a seed brought back by Edward Daniel Clarke from Thermopylae. That tree reached its bicentenary in 2002 and was duly celebrated in both Greek and Latin verse composed by a Fellow of the college, Anthony Bowen (also the Cambridge University Orator).

It is hard to beat Jacques-Louis David's own description (see pp. 184–6) of his magnificent history painting, completed in 1814 only after many years of work and without the approval of his master-patron, Emperor Napoleon Bonaparte. Heroic self-sacrifice does indeed shine out, but so too does Leonidas's sexual allure and David's predilection for naked male beauty.

the most notably hostile of all was the proto-democrat Cornelius de Pauw, in his *Recherches philosophiques sur les grecs* published the year before the French Revolution broke out. Even Leonidas does not escape de Pauw's barbed strictures – he hid behind a wall, the coward . . .

The American Revolution, like the French, was inspired in part by the founders' notions of Classical antiquity, though – like the Renaissance – this was far more a Roman than a Hellenic thing (hence there is a 'Capitol' in Washington, DC, not an 'Acropolis', and a

'Senate', not an 'Areopagus' or 'Gerousia'). But there are literally hundreds of Athenses and Spartas in North America.*

So far as the mass dissemination of ideas was concerned, the eighteenth century was still a world of the spoken word and of visual images rather than the written word: hence the importance of Louis-Jean-François Lagrenée the Elder's famous *A Spartan Mother and Son* of 1771, now at Stourhead in Wiltshire. This was painted to illustrate the devotion of the ideal Spartan mother to the state and the privileging of community above family. More famous still by far is a history painting in the strict sense (begun in 1800, completed in 1814), which takes Thermopylae, and not least the prowess of Leonidas himself, for its subject. Here is Jacques-Louis David's own view and vision of his masterwork (as conveyed in a printed note accompanying the exhibition of the painting in his studio):

> *Leonidas, king of Sparta, seated on a rock in the midst of his three hundred heroes, reflects, rather moved, on the near and inevitable death of his friends. At Leonidas's feet, in the shade, there is his wife's brother, Agis, who, after putting down the crown of flowers he had worn during the sacrifice, is about to place his helmet on his head; with his eyes on the general, he awaits his orders. Next to him, at the sound of the trumpet two young men run to take their weapons that are hanging from the branches of trees. Further away, one of his officers, a devotee of the cult of Hercules, whose arms and outfit he wears, rallies his troops into battle formation. He is followed by the high priest, who calls on Hercules to grant them victory. He points his finger at the sky. Further back the army parades.*

---

* Besides the Sparta in Wisconsin already noted, we could mention the Sparta in Tennessee that featured in *In the Heat of the Night*, the memorable movie of Southern racial hatred starring Sidney Poitier. However, the name Thermopolis in Wyoming should probably not be given any other interpretation than the purely topographical – like Greek Thermopylae, it is blessed with mineral hot springs (the world's largest), and its founding inhabitants probably did not see themselves as making a last stand like General Custer (at Little Bighorn in Montana, on 25 June 1876).

What David does not mention here is the warrior on the left who appears to be carving an inscription in the rock with the hilt of his sword.* On the other hand, he did reportedly tell E. Delécluze, a former pupil of his and the compiler of *David, son école et son temps*, that in the painting he had wanted 'to characterize that profound, great and religious sentiment that is inspired by the love of one's country'. To that uncontroversial motive, we must surely add, if not as a conscious motive at least as an effect, the strong homoerotic (not just homosocial) charge that the painting conveys. David himself had strong homoerotic proclivities, and he will surely not have been unaware of this key dimension of ancient Spartan social life nor blind to the legitimacy that appeal to the authorizing Spartan archetype might confer.

However, David's principal patron, the by now Emperor Napoleon Bonaparte, was frankly puzzled at first as to why his official court painter should have wasted so much time and effort on depicting a bunch of ancient losers. Later, however, he happily changed his mind and tune, and would presumably have responded with an emphatic *oui* to the proud painter's rhetorical question, 'I suppose you know that no one but David could have painted Leonidas?'

For the philhellenes of the early nineteenth century it was love of another country than their own, namely Greece, by which they were motivated, and for them the legends of Thermopylae and Leonidas were a gift not to be overlooked. Among the new plays on Greek or Roman themes staged at Covent Garden in the 1820s was a *Leonidas, King of Sparta*, the stage set of which boasted an extraordinary (and quite unhistorical) temple of Heracles. This was probably an Englished version of Michel Pichat's tragedy *Léonidas* that had been performed originally at the Théâtre Français in Paris in 1825, while Greek independence still hung in the balance.

---

* This is a slightly foxed French translation of part of Simonides's epigram 'Go, tell the Spartans . . .'.

Second to no other philhellene, whether English or French, and whether on paper or in the field of combat, was George Gordon, Lord Byron. He was and is the principal avatar of what may fairly be called the 'Age of Leonidas' in the early nineteenth century. Edmund Keeley, widely known for his distinguished translations of the poets George Seferis and Constantine Cavafy among others, has written sensitively of Byron's 'well-traveled path in bringing Greece to the page decade after decade'. He then cites the famous stanza from the canto of *Don Juan* – the one that is sometimes called 'The Isles of Greece' – in which Byron's noble lord, having dreamed 'that Greece might still be free', calls the valour of his enslaved contemporary Greek audience into question 'through allusions to their nobler ancient history':

> *Must we but weep o'er days more blest?*
> *Must we but blush? – Our fathers bled.*
> *Earth! Render back from out thy breast*
> *A remnant of our Spartan dead!*
> *Of the three hundred grant but three*
> *To make a new Thermopylae!*

Earlier still, in *Childe Harold's Pilgrimage* (1812), Byron had echoed and sought to encourage the early native Greek strain of liberationist patriotism displayed in Constantinos Rhigas's *Patriotic Hymn of 1798*, itself clearly inspired by the 'Marseillaise'. Rhigas had made a stirring address to the spirit of Leonidas; so here, likewise, Byron invokes Leonidas's shade:

> *Sons of the Greeks, arise!*
> . . .
> *Brave shades of chiefs and sages,*
> *Behold the coming strife!*
> *Hellenes of past ages,*
> *Oh, start again to life!*
> . . .

Sparta, Sparta, why in slumbers
Lethargic doest thou lie?
Awake, and join in numbers
With Athens, old ally!
Leonidas recalling,
That chief of ancient song,
Who saved ye once from falling,
The terrible! the strong!

But it was not only abroad, in Greece, that the Thermopylae experience could be used as an inspiration to fight for freedom. Much closer to home, and uncomfortably so – for 'freeborn Englishmen', that is, who 'never never would be slaves' – were the stirring words of the poem 'A Nation Once Again' penned by the Irishman Thomas Davis (1814–45). This was to remain one of the unofficial anthems of Irish nationalist liberation propaganda well into the twentieth century, and I quote just a snatch:

When boyhood's fire was in my blood,
I read of ancient freemen
For Greece and Rome who bravely stood,
Three hundred men and three men.
I prayed that I would live to see
Our fetters rent in twain,
And Ireland, long a province, be
A nation once again.

The Victorian British fought back. Glover's Leonidas of 1737 had been a patriot to the core, a public-spirited lover of freedom and observer of austere self-denial, opposed on principle to the luxurious Persians who languished under the 'absolute controulment of their king', the abominable and abominated Xerxes. That voluminous work can be seen as having kick-started the construction of a modern myth: one that evolved from Glover's literary paradigm into a rallying cry of moral rearmament. In the shape of the Victorian public school tradition inaugurated by Thomas Arnold of Rugby and continued well into the twentieth century by Kurt Hahn's Gordonstoun in Scotland – alma mater, if that is the phrase, of both the Duke of Edinburgh and the Prince of Wales – it has centrally informed one of the most powerful vectors of British or English political and cultural identity.

The legendary Classical exemplar of the eighteenth century thus became of central importance to the Classical tradition as a whole. This surely is what explains the nomenclature of one particular Victorian British Leonidas, whose name – or rather whose slew of culturally resplendent and resonant names: Benjamin Leonidas Arthur Lumley Griffiths – I found written out in a copy of *Hymns Ancient and Modern* donated to the church of St John the Baptist, Finchingfield, Essex, to commemorate his baptism. 'Benjamin', I would guess, is Old Testament, 'Arthur' traditional British, and 'Lumley' a family name used as a forename. 'Leonidas', last but not least, nestles among them as a modest classicizing tribute to our hero. Here is a perfect local illustration of the continually changing reception of Classical antiquity that since the Renaissance has often dominated so many aspects of European and American culture.

The Sparta of the Graeco-Persian Wars has also made many appearances in, or been the main subject of, novels and short stories, romantic and otherwise, from the Victorian period on. To name but a few of the most prominent, there have been Edward Bulwer Lytton's *Pausanias, the Spartan* (1873), Caroline Dale Snedeker's *The Spartan* (1911), John Buchan's 'The Lemnian' (1912), Jill Paton Walsh's *Farewell, Great King* (1972), Valerio Massimo Manfredi's *Il Scudo di Talos* (1988), translated on the back of the success of his Alexander the Great trilogy as *Spartan* (2002), and Steven Pressfield's epic novel *Gates of Fire* (1998). There are incidental mentions of Thermopylae, too, in such conspicuously successful Greek-related modern novels as Olivia Manning's *Friends and Heroes*, the final volume of her *Balkan Trilogy*, and the Greek-American Jeffrey Eugenides's *Middlesex*.

Perhaps the most revealing, because of the knowledge it assumes of its readers, is the following passage from chapter XIII of Charles Dickens's *The Mystery of Edwin Drood*. Miss Twinkleton, who runs an academy for young ladies, is addressing them as they leave for their Christmas holidays:

> *'And when the time should come for our resumption of those pursuits which (here a general depression set in all round), pursuits which, pursuits which; – then let us ever remember what was said by the Spartan General, in words too trite for repetition, at the battle it were superfluous to specify.'*

Scholars are agreed that 'the battle' in question is Thermopylae, but they are divided on what are the words referred to as 'too trite' to bear repetition. I myself am pretty sure that Dickens's more or less well educated Victorian readers would have had no hesitation in supplying the following apophthegm preserved by Plutarch (supposed to have been delivered by Leonidas to his wife Gorgo on the point of his departure for the battle): 'Marry good men and give birth to good children.'

In the disabused twentieth century that followed, however, one of its most potent voices, the Alexandrian Greek poet Constantine Cavafy, struck a cautionary note early on. For no matter how noble a life is lived, he argued, no one can prevent an Ephialtes, the Greek traitor at Thermopylae, enabling 'the Medes' to 'break through after all'. Hardly offering greater comfort is the final stanza of the Classical scholar-poet A.E. Housman's 'The Oracles', published in his *Last Poems* (1922):

> *The King with half the East at heel is marched from lands of morning*
> *Their fighters drink the rivers up, their shafts benight the air,*
> *And he that stands will die for naught, and home there's no returning.*
> *The Spartans on the sea-wet rock sat down and combed their hair.*

It was a local Spartan workman who dubbed this remarkable Parian marble torso 'Leonidas' when it was excavated in a British School dig below the Spartan Acropolis (where it had originally stood) in 1925; but actually the complete statue had been part of a heroic or divine group from a pedimental building and could not have been set up as a memorial to Leonidas, since it was fashioned in the 480s, while he was still alive.

Those who do not relish the thought of the Medes figuratively breaking through – as they did, for instance, via the perverted uses to which images of Sparta were put in Nazi Germany before and during the Second World War – or of dying for naught (as many perhaps felt was the case in the world war that had recently ended) will turn their minds perhaps, with relief, to the excavations conducted at Sparta by the British School at Athens betwen 1924 and 1928. In 1926 in the theatre area underneath the acropolis the excavators unearthed the head and torso of a naked male warrior executed in fine-quality white marble from the island of Paros in the Cyclades. He was instantly, and understandably, nicknamed 'Leonidas' by a Greek workman, and the name has stuck. Yet that name, for all its charm, is a factoid, not a fact.

The original complete statue was part of a group, not a stand-alone piece, and the statue group was probably affixed to the pediment of a temple, where it would have represented a hero or a god of myth, not a mortal man. Not even a dead Spartan king – 'seed of the demigod son of Zeus' (that is, Heracles), as a Delphic oracle later referred to a descendant and successor of Leonidas – would have qualified for such a representation. Besides, the date of the sculpture is, to go by the latest expert opinion (admittedly somewhat subjective and imprecise), before rather than after 480. This means that in order really to be Leonidas the statue would have had to be a portrait of a living king – and yet this was far too early for anything like a portrait statue properly so called to have been created anywhere in Greece, let alone in community-minded, anti-individualistic Sparta.

The year after the discovery of 'Leonidas' at Sparta, the Scottish poet (J.) Norman Cameron (1905–53) published a fascinating riposte to any simplistic eulogy of Spartan heroics at Thermopylae, entitled 'The Thespians at Thermopylae':

> *The honours that people give always*
> *Pass to those use-besotted gentlemen*
> *Whose numskull courage is a kind of fear,*
> *A fear of thought and of the oafish mothers*
> *('Or with your shield or on it') in their rear.*
> *Spartans cannot retreat. Why, then, their praise*
> *For going forward should be less than others'.*
> *But we, actors and critics of one play,*
> *Of sober-witted judgment, who could see*
> *So many roads, and chose the Spartan way,*
> *What has the popular report to say*
> *Of us, the Thespians at Thermopylae?*

Cameron couldn't resist a pun on 'thespians', since actors are sometimes known as such in tribute to the supposed founder of Athenian tragic drama in the later sixth century BCE, one Thespis. But his point about the nature of the self-sacrifice of the Thespians was deadly serious and has almost as long a history. It goes back all the way to Thucydides's immortal version of the Funeral Speech that Pericles delivered over the Athenian war dead in the first year (431/30) of the Atheno-Peloponnesian War. There Pericles is reported to have contrasted the Athenian and the Spartan ways of courage. Basically, his claim was that, whereas the Athenians decided consciously and voluntarily to be patriotically brave, the Spartans were merely coerced or brainwashed into being so.

This is a point that has been echoed many times in recent years, especially within the rhetoric of the ideological wars, cold and hot, waged between the 'free world' and various kinds of 'totalitarian' or authoritarian regime from the 1930s onwards. It is not without all substance, but as I have tried to show, it overstates the difference between Athens and Sparta and underplays the extent to which in Sparta too there were choices to be made and debates to be had over first principles as well as merely over operational decisions.

Cameron's poem ends with the rhetorical question:

What has the popular report to say
Of us, the Thespians at Thermopylae?

Well, actually, it now has quite a lot: there is today, for conspicuous example, an official memorial to the seven hundred Thespians alongside that erected to the Spartans at Thermopylae itself. But we should in all fairness add, as Cameron's Thespians do not, that in sacrificing their seven hundred men the Thespians seem to have sacrificed absolutely every Thespian who could afford to equip himself as a hoplite – one hundred per cent of their hoplite body, that is, as opposed to the Spartans' only 4 per cent. A sobering, but also an ennobling, thought.

Come the Second World War, and even the disenchanted W.H. Auden could seek some inspiration from Thermopylae in his post-Brechtian poem 'Grub First then Ethics'. 'All we ask for', he writes:

is a good dinner, that we
may march in high fettle, left foot first,
to hold her [our city's] Thermopylae.

For real life-and-death behaviour in the first uncertain years of that ghastly war, this summary evocation pales beside the implications of the Leonidas legend. Leonidas and his three hundred proved as important a 'Few' in ancient Greek and Spartan history as the Battle of Britain pilots hailed by Prime Minister Winston Churchill in 1940 did in British history, and the comparison between the two groups has been explicitly drawn. Contrary to a widespread misperception, England was not the only European country that in 1940 was still actively resisting Nazi Germany and the Fascist Axis powers. Greece was too, as the British ancient historian Robin Burn, parachuted into Greece like several other ancient historians to work behind the lines as a liaison officer, knew at first hand. Poignantly, he later dedicated his excellent 1962 monograph *Persia and the Greeks* 'To the Greeks of 1940', reminding his readers implicitly that the British Empire had then had just one ally in Europe who was neither yet under the Nazi–Fascist yoke, nor a subject of the Soviet empire (then still in a non-aggression pact with Germany). Burn's subtext was that the Greeks of 1940, by declaring a firm 'No' to the attempted occupation of their country by Hitler's Italian Fascist allies, had behaved in a manner entirely worthy of their forebears at Thermopylae in 480 BCE. The shade of Lord Byron would surely have nodded its agreement and approval.

Not all professional ancient historians were quite so starry-eyed, though. By June 1941 the Greeks had failed to prevent the occupation of Greece by Nazi Germany, whose land forces had entered almost inevitably through Thermopylae. Three years later, a remarkable collective tribute to the modern Greeks, *The Glory That Is Greece*, was published, in the critical year of 1944 when Greece was still occupied. In his contribution Marcus Niebuhr Tod of Oxford University, despite the temptation to extreme eulogy of the ancient Spartans' key role in ridding Greece of a foreign would-be occupier, delivered a properly balanced scholarly judgement that would not have disgraced Herodotus.*

Likewise deflationary was Constantine Trypanis's elegiac poem 'Thermopylae 1941', which ends:

> *The Stranger will still go to Sparta, but he will*
> *Announce also the death of the Australian farmer.*
> *Leonidas is only a matter of precedence.*

That jarring cultural intrusion from the New World and misleadingly flip backward reference to 480 BCE are literary tropes entirely worthy of a distinguished university professor, a Culture Minister in a Greek government, and the editor and translator of the utterly wonderful *Penguin Book of Greek Verse* (1971).

And perhaps it was no bad thing not to go overboard in praising the ancient Spartans at that particular juncture of world history. For it was not only the supposed good guys who celebrated the memory of Thermopylae during the Second World War. The Nazi Third Reich did so too. Indeed, it spawned its fair share of 'Sparta-maniacs', as the German ancient historian Stefan Rebenich has feelingly called them, people who were 'fascinated by the idea that the people on the Rhine and on the Eurotas were racially connected and had a common Nordic background'. This sort of race mysticism had prompted a frenzy of excitement in 1936, the year of the 'Hitler Games', the propaganda-ridden Berlin Olympics. The German Archaeological Institute's excavations at the Athenian cemetery in the Cerameicus yielded identifiable skeletons of Spartans, some of whom were even named in the accompanying honorific inscription.

These Spartans were among those who, as we learn from

---

* I have quoted it as the epigraph to Chapter Four.

Xenophon's Greek history, had been killed in 403 in the process of putting an end to the bloodstained reign of the originally Sparta-backed junta of the Thirty Tyrants led by the fanatical Athenian laconizer Critias.* Germany's leading physical anthropologist was at once dispatched to Athens to verify and confirm that the Spartan skeletons conformed to the classic 'Nordic' type. In the event, his results proved insufficiently clearcut, and his findings were never properly published. But it was exactly the same spirit of racialist identification that animated Reichsmarschall Hermann Göring when he addressed his failing troops during the last days of the siege of Stalingrad in 1942. He reminded them of Leonidas and the three hundred, and predicted a new reading of the famous Simonides epitaph: 'If you come to Germany, tell them you have seen us fighting in Stalingrad, obedient to the law of honour and warfare'.[3] Indeed, according to Martin Bormann, Hitler himself on his fiftieth birthday on 20 April 1945 enjoined the fellow members of his last-ditch bunker to 'Just think of Leonidas and his 300 Spartans'.[4]

The other side of that Nazi racialist coin is the desperately unhappy experience of the excellent German-Jewish ancient historian Victor Ehrenberg, who found himself condemned in the late 1930s to abandon his university post in Prague for one in London. Ehrenberg happened to be an expert on ancient Sparta and, while he was full of praise for the Spartans' defence of a concept of freedom at Thermopylae, he also soberly observed that there can be no true freedom in an 'authoritarian' state such as he believed Sparta itself to have been. In using that term, he was thinking mainly of the limits on free expression imposed by the authoritarian (others would have said 'totalitarian') regimes of his own day. These did not necessarily enslave all their subjects in the literal or legal sense. But we should not forget the Spartans' Messenian and Laconian Helots, who were indeed formally and legally unfree (and as such could be subject to instant

---

* See Chapter Eight, and the epigraph to Chapter One.

execution as enemies of the state), even though they were no less Greek than their Spartan masters and indeed on numerous occasions, Thermopylae not the least of them, played indispensable roles in their – and Greece's – support.

This debate about the character of the Spartan polity is a reminder that after 1945 the hot war of the previous six years turned into the Cold War of the next forty-five: a nerve-jangling contest of ceaseless propaganda and intermittent sabre-rattling, popularly construed as (yet again) a struggle of East versus West, a clash of civilizations. Popular culture too had its part to play in this contest, on both sides, and the massiest of mass media available for the purpose was the full-length feature film. A classic example of the genre of (not very) covert anti-Soviet propaganda movies that poured out of Hollywood and other Western studios was *The 300 Spartans* of 1962, also known as *Lion of Sparta*. This simply dripped with Cold War imagery, even to the extent of splashing across the screen uplifting slogans about the defence of freedom against slavery. It boasted a fine cast including Anna Synodinou, a great Greek stage tragedienne, playing Gorgo, and the no less great English actor Ralph Richardson as Themistocles. Leonidas, it is almost needless to add, was played – very well – by an American of Irish descent (Richard Egan).*

Strong traces of this frankly martial and celebratory outlook still persist. Arguably, it lies significantly behind the recent and current Western intervention in Iraq. Take a look, for example, at the pages of the suitably named Amazon website that are devoted to readers' reactions to Steven Pressfield's novel *Gates of Fire*. These offer an illuminating snapshot of the vitality and vibrancy of the Thermopylae myth in its latest, Western incarnations. Several of the contributions here come from (male) US veterans, some going back as far as the Korean

---

* On the historical downside, the film accepts and enacts Diodorus/Ephorus's massively implausible tale of a night commando raid designed by Leonidas to assassinate Xerxes in his bed.

War, who as well as endorsing a fairly simplistic 'us against them', 'West v. East', 'goodies against baddies' mentality praise Pressfield for having captured in a positive way what they take to be universal constants in the experience of warfare.

Likewise frankly celebratory is Frank Miller's brilliantly drawn 'comic strip' or 'graphic novel' version of Thermopylae, entitled simply *300*. Originally issued in five parts in 1998–9 as a comic book series, *300* makes an even more major impact in single book form. Miller is probably most widely known up until now for his bestselling *Sin City* series, made into a 'noir' movie in 2005. But this perception may be about to change. With its verbal echoes of Tennyson's 'Charge of the Light Brigade' (the Spartans advance fearlessly 'into hell's mouth') and visual allusions to Japanese Samurai warriors (as often, Japan is co-opted for 'the West'), this is a fairly sophisticated production, formally speaking. Its content, however, is much cruder. Leonidas and his three hundred 'boys' stand for reason, justice and law in opposition to the 'whim' and whips of the autocratic Persian monarch Xerxes, who also commits the cardinal error of believing he is a god. It is perhaps not surprising, therefore, on both artistic and ideological grounds, that it has been taken as the basis for a Warner Brothers feature film entitled *The 300* that is in production as I write and scheduled for release in 2007.*

However, such relatively gung-ho commentators and celebrators are no longer the norm. The more sombre mood regarding war that now prevails in American public discourse and elsewhere in the Western world can be traced as far back as 1978, to another movie with a Simonidean flavour and echo in its very title: the Vietnam War

---

* One small but telling visual mistake merits comment. Miller shows the Spartans with moustaches as well as beards. Yet the historical Spartans of Leonidas's day in fact shaved their upper lip in subservience to the annual injunction by each incoming board of ephors to 'shave their moustaches and obey the laws'. The famous marble statue wrongly named 'Leonidas' faithfully shows precisely this distinctively Spartan treatment of facial hair: full beard but no moustache.

movie, *Go Tell the Spartans*. Its unrelievedly bleak, flat visual style was designed, in the words of expert film-historiographer Martin Winkler, to support its 'dark view of the war'. Even President George W. Bush was said to have understood at last in 2005 that the support of the American public for war, and especially the war in Iraq, was conditional on his demanding only little of that great public. The contrast with Sparta in 480 BCE could not be starker. There and then, absolutely everything was demanded by the state not only of the adult males of fighting age, but also – and, in their different ways, no less – of their wives and other female relatives, and in general of the Spartan *demos* (people) as a whole.

Such a holistic attitude, which in Greece was not unique to ancient Sparta but was given there its fullest and most extreme expression, paid exceptional military and cultural dividends. The Battle of Marathon in 490, won by Athens with the help of little Plataea, had been essential to the development of Greece and of Athens as a cradle of democracy and high culture. Ten years later, the Battle of Thermopylae, spearheaded by Sparta, gave the tottering Greek coalition the will and the breathing-space to continue the struggle of resistance to a successful finish, and to make possible thereby the subsequent flowering of Greek culture and civilization. This florescence was eventually crucial, by extension, to ancient Greece's and ancient Sparta's continuing impact on the modern Western world, an impact that is betrayed – not least – in our English words 'spartan' and 'laconic'.

EPILOGUE

THERMOPYLAE: TURNING-POINT IN WORLD HISTORY*

If I hate the manners of the Spartans, I am not blind to the greatness of a free people . . .

Chateaubriand, *Travels in Greece, Palestine, Egypt and Barbary*, 1806

It is an ill wind, proverbially, that blows nobody any good. Terrible and ghastly as were the tragic events of 9/11, they have also, I believe, provoked a salutary spate of Western reflection on just what it is to be 'Western', on what 'Western civilization' is or might be. The process of re-examining and rethinking what is distinctive and admirable – or at any rate defensible – about Western civilization, values and culture seems to me both to have been in itself a wholly good thing, and to have had some notably positive outcomes. One ancient Greek exemplar of that civilization, Socrates of Athens, is famously reported by Plato to have said that 'the unexamined life is not worth living for a human being'. Rarely has the need for such cultural self-examination been more compelling.

---

*   A slightly different and fully annotated version of this Epilogue appeared as 'What have the Spartans done for us? Sparta's contribution to Western civilization' in the Classics journal *Greece & Rome* 2nd ser., 52.2 (2004) 164–79. I am most grateful to the journal's editor, Katherine Clarke, for permission to reproduce this reworded and mostly annotation-free version here.

This moulded head-vase, dated to the last quarter of the fifth century, depicts a bearded Persian, and on its red-figure rim-frieze shows a Persian servant with a Greek mistress; a good example of the continuing cultural interconnections between Greeks, especially Athenians, and Persia throughout the fifth century and beyond.

For instance, it makes us realize that we in the West do not necessarily have all the best tunes. Concepts and practices often imagined to be uniquely 'Western', such as reason, freedom and democracy, have had, and still do have, their active counterparts within Eastern cultures as well. Indeed, the tradition of Western civilization has been decisively shaped or enriched by Eastern – including, not least, Islamic – contributions. Had it not been for Arabic scholars, in both East (especially Baghdad) and West (Moorish Spain), in what we conventionally call the Middle Ages, a number of key works of Aristotle would have been lost to us, and Aristotle is about as central to any construction of the Western cultural tradition as it is possible to get.

Some of us Westerners, post 9/11, were provoked specifically into wondering aloud whether any definition of our civilization and its cultural values would justify our dying for them, or even maybe killing for them – as the suicide hijackers of September 11th, or the suicide bombers of the West Bank and Gaza, clearly were and are prepared to die for their brands of Islam and freedom. Those of us who are historians of ancient Greece pondered that question with especial intensity. For the world of ancient – or Classical – Greece is one of the principal taproots of our Western civilization, as I have already implied in quoting Socrates's famous aphorism, and the Spartans' behaviour at Thermopylae in 480 raises sharply the contested issue of ideologically motivated suicide.

The connection between the ancient Greeks and Us was forcefully expressed by John Stuart Mill, in a review of the first volumes of George Grote's pioneering, liberal-democratic history of ancient Greece (originally published in twelve volumes, 1846–56). As Mill put it, with conscious paradox, the Battle of Marathon – which was fought in 490 BCE by the Athenians, with support only from the neighbouring small city of Plataea, against the invading Persians – was more important than the Battle of Hastings, *even as an event in English history*. So too, arguably, or so at least I should want to argue, was the Battle of Thermopylae. Unlike Marathon, of course, Thermopylae was formally a defeat for the Greeks, a 'wound' (*trôma*), as Herodotus called it.[1] Yet it was none the less glorious or culturally significant for that, since it was soon converted into a moral, that is a morale, victory. And as Napoleon once colourfully put it, in war the morale factor is three times as important as all the other factors put together.

Indeed, some would even say – and I am tempted to include myself in their number – that Thermopylae was Sparta's finest hour. In any case, it's Sparta's Thermopylae experience that provides me with my starting-point and constant point of reference in trying to answer the question posed in this epilogue: what have the Spartans done for us? Perhaps we might begin by asking – as Great King Cyrus II, founder of the Achaemenid Persian Empire, was supposed once to have asked, in about 550 BCE – who are these Spartans?

One answer is that they were the Dorian (Doric-speaking) inhabitants of a Greek citizen-state in the Peloponnese that for many centuries was one of the greatest of ancient Greek powers. Another answer, as one of Cyrus's successors, Xerxes, found out all too painfully, is that they were a fighting machine strong enough, skilful enough and sufficiently iron-willed to play the key role in resisting and eventually repelling even his vast hordes – and so frustrating his attempt to incorporate the mainland Greeks in an oriental empire that already stretched from the Aegean in the west to beyond the Hindu Kush. Xerxes discovered these facts about Sparta in person, at Thermopylae, and his appointed commander-in-chief Mardonius discovered them again, fatally, at Plataea the following year, when it was the Spartans under Regent Pausanias who played the lead role in that famous and decisive Greek victory.

That in turn is one, not insignificant, answer to the question why today we should care who the ancient Spartans were. For they enabled the development of the civilization that we have chosen in crucial ways to inherit and learn from. What if the Persians had won in 480–479? Either that Greek civilization would have been significantly different thereafter, or/and we should not have been its legatees in the same ways or to the same degree. Another answer to the question why the ancient Spartans matter to us today concerns the impact of what has been variously labelled the Spartan myth, mirage or tradition. To put this differently: the variety of ways in which Sparta and the Spartans have been represented in mainly non-Spartan discourses, both written and visual, since the late fifth century BCE has left a deep mark on the Western tradition, on the understanding of what it is to belong to a Western culture.

To begin with, Sparta, like some other ancient Greek places, impinges upon our everyday consciousness through enriching our English vocabulary. The island of Lesbos, for conspicuous example, has given us 'lesbian', the city of Corinth 'corinthian', the city of Athens . . . 'attic'. But ancient Sparta, prodigally, has given us 'spartan', of course, and 'laconic'.

Official Persian documents were sealed by incised seal-stones like this example made of chalcedony; here the Great King himself is depicted demonstrating his manly martial prowess by spearing singlehanded a fearsome wild boar. Above them floats the familiar religious symbol of royalty.

To choose an illustration almost at random, a newspaper profile of Iain Duncan Smith, former leader of the Opposition, referred casually to his naval public school as being 'spartan' – and aptly so, in this sense: the British public school system, as invented virtually by Thomas Arnold of Rugby in the nineteenth century, was consciously modelled on an idea, or even a utopian vision, of ancient Sparta's military-style communal education.

The Spartan etymology of 'laconic' is not so immediately transparent. It comes from one of the ancient adjectival forms derived from the name by which the Spartans more often referred to themselves: Lacedaemonians, or Lakones. As noted earlier, the Spartans were the past masters of the curt, clipped, military mode of utterance, which they used alike in sending written or oral dispatches from the front line or at home in snappy repartee to an insistent teacher, for instance – so much so that the ancients preserved collections of what they believed to be genuine Spartan 'apophthegms' (I have quoted a famous one of Leonidas's), while we still call that manner of utterance 'laconic' in their honour.

Even less obviously, and much less happily, the Spartans have bequeathed us also a third English word: the noun 'helot'. This is used today to refer to a member of an especially deprived or exploited ethnic or economic underclass. It thus reflects, accurately, the dark underside of the Spartans' more positive achievements. The Greek word *heilôtês* probably originally meant 'captive', and certainly it was as captives and enemies that the Spartans treated the unfree subordinate population of Helots: more exactly, as if they were prisoners of war whose death sentence the Spartans had merely suspended so as to force them to labour under constant threat of extinction, in order to provide the economic basis of the Spartan way of life. Other Greek cities, not least Athens, were also of course crucially dependent on unfree labour for creating and maintaining a distinctively politicized and cultured style of communal life. But the slaves held by the Athenians collectively and individually were typical of the Greek world as a whole in that they were mainly 'barbarians', or non-Greek foreigners, a polyglot, hetero-geneous bunch – in fact, they were mostly owned on an individual, not a collective, basis. The Helots of Sparta, by contrast, were an entire Greek people, or perhaps (if we distinguish the Laconian Helots from the Messenian) two separate peoples united by a common yoke of servitude.

These three little words – spartan, laconic, helot – are just a small linguistic token of the fact that English or British culture, indeed Western culture as a whole, has been deeply marked by what the French scholar François Ollier neatly dubbed 'le mirage spartiate'. When he coined that phrase in the 1930s, Sparta – or rather ideas of how Sparta had supposedly worked as a society – exercised a particu-lar fascination, as noted earlier, for totalitarian or authoritarian rulers, most notoriously for Adolf Hitler and pseudo-scholarly members of his Nazi entourage such as Alfred Rosenberg. Discipline, orderliness, soldierly hierarchy and subordination of individual endeavour to the overriding good of the state were among the Spartan virtues that the Nazis and other Fascists were most attracted by – only to put them to the most perverted uses. There are still neo-Fascist organizations (one, disturbingly, in France) that are proud to follow along this same shining path.

It is this modern totalitarian or authoritarian reception of ancient Sparta that has tarnished, probably irreparably, Sparta's reputation as a political ideal or model in modern Western liberal-democratic soci-eties. Yet Sparta's idealized image had not always served such sinister or heinous purposes. In the eighteenth century, for instance, Jean-Jacques Rousseau was a huge fan of 'the wisdom of Sparta's laws', and if anything an even greater fan of its legendary lawgiver Lycurgus. In Lycurgus's ideal Sparta, Rousseau saw a society that was devoted to implementing the general will in a collective, self-effacing, law-abiding and above all thoroughly virtuous way. Rousseau helped to ensure a key role for ancient Greece (as well as ancient Rome) in the making of the modern world, and for Sparta no less than for Athens.

Rousseau was by no means the first intellectual to deploy an image or vision of Sparta as an integral component and driving force of an entire programme of social and political reforms. Among the very first on record was Plato, and it is through Plato that Sparta can claim to be the fount and origin of the entire tradition of utopian thinking and writing (utopiography). Utopia, too, acquired a bad name in the twentieth century; but in principle – the principle of hope that things can be and will be made better – it is not as bad a place as all that. In any case, it is not only for what intellectuals and others have made of Sparta, from the Classical period of ancient Greece down to our own century, that Sparta remains a choice subject of study. It is also for what the Spartans really did achieve, most conspicuously and effectively on the battlefield during the Graeco-Persian Wars of 480–479 BCE.

The Battle of Thermopylae, though a defeat, quickly became a morale victory. As such, it formed a vital and integral part of the eventual total Greek victory over the Persians. That victory, moreover, would not have been attained had it not been for the indispensable contribution made by the Spartans. The remarkably successful organization of their society into a well oiled military machine, and their development of a rudimentary multistate Greek alliance well before the Persians invaded mainland Greece, provided the indispensable core of military leadership around which a Greek resistance could coalesce. The Spartans' heroically suicidal stand at Thermopylae showed that the Persians both should and could usefully be resisted, and gave the small, wavering and uncohesive force of patriotic Greeks the nerve to imagine that they might one day defeat the invaders. The charismatic leadership of Spartan commanders of the character and calibre of King Leonidas and Regent Pausanias crucially unified and inspired the Greeks' land forces.

But what, if anything, did the Spartans bring to the feast of ancient Greek culture, the source of the Western legacy, beyond making the feast possible at all? Different modern interpreters emphasize different aspects of the classical Greek cultural achievement. I myself would privilege three distinguishing qualities or characteristics, above all: first, a devotion to competition in all its forms, almost for its own sake; second, a devotion to a concept and ideal of freedom; and, third, a capacity for almost limitless self-criticism as well as unstinting criticism of others (not least other Greeks).

The first two of these might be identified equally strongly in either of the two main exemplars of ancient Greek civilization, Sparta and Athens. The third, however, specifically self-criticism, was a distinctively Athenian cultural trait and apparently not a Spartan trait at all – or so contemporary Athenians liked to claim, and many have subsequently agreed. Pericles, for example, in Thucydides's version of his Funeral Speech of 431/30, sneered at Sparta's merely state-imposed courage; and Demosthenes a century later asserted falsely that it was forbidden to Spartans even to criticize (let alone alter) their laws.

Undoubtedly there were no Spartan equivalents of the Athenians' democratic Assembly and popular lawcourts, nor did the Spartans enjoy the Athenians' annual tragic and comic drama festivals, which provided state-sponsored opportunities for self-examination and self-criticism. Yet the Spartans were not quite the unhesitatingly obedient automatons that ancient Athenian and modern liberal propaganda have made them out to be. On occasion, grumbling at authority might turn into open defiance, both individually and collectively. Even Spartan kings, who were perched at the very pinnacle of the hierarchy of birth, wealth and prestige, might be brought low by being tried and fined – or, worse, exiled like Demaratus under sentence of death. It would be fairer and more accurate, then, to say that the Spartans' culture was not one that favoured intellectual argument or even open dissent either in the *agora* or in any other place of public assembly.

All Greeks, probably, were passionately keen on a good contest. Their word for the spirit of competitiveness, *agônia*, is the root of our word 'agony', and that etymological connection well suggests the intense, driven quality of ancient Greek competition. A war was for the Greeks an *agôn* (contest), obviously enough, as was a public debate, whether real or fictional. So too was a lawsuit, but so also was any religious festival that involved, centrally or otherwise, athletic or other kinds of competition – a festival such as the Olympic Games, for example. It was in fact the Greeks ultimately who invented our idea of athletic sports, just as they invented the prototype of our idea of the theatre, and both of them within a context of religiously inspired competition and competitiveness.

The Spartans yielded to no other Greeks in their passionate, almost fanatical attachment to competition. They even made the very act of survival at birth a matter of public competition, by entrusting elders with the task of supervising the wine-bath tests for neonates. The practice of consigning infants showing any obvious signs of physical deformity or debility to an early death at the foot of a nearby mountain ravine was not as callous or odd as it perhaps seems to us: both Plato and Aristotle advocated such 'exposure' of defective newborns in their respective Ideal States. Likewise, adult status for Spartan males could be achieved only by successfully passing the series of largely physical competitive tests that constituted the unique education or group socialization known as the *agôgê* or 'upbringing'. Even then, becoming a full adult Spartan citizen in terms of political standing and participation was made to depend on passing a further and final acceptance test – admission by competitive election to a communal dining group, or mess, at the age of twenty.

Those unfortunates who failed any of these educational or citizenship tests were relegated to a limbo of exclusion, of non-belonging, to permanent outsider status. Nor did internal competition for status end at the age of twenty for those who did achieve full citizenship status: far from it. Not for one moment did they cease to compete amongst themselves and against others, both abroad, in war, of course, and no less famously and successfully at the Olympic Games, but also at home – in local equestrian and athletic contests, for instance, or election to high office, or for membership of the elite royal bodyguard. One disappointed Spartan who had failed to be elected to the bodyguard in his twenties was said to have claimed he was delighted to know there were three hundred Spartans better than he; and even so, he went on to achieve high public distinction in later life.

As for the general Greek passion for freedom, it was said by the right-wing Athenian political writer and activist Critias, who wrote about the Spartan way of life in both prose and verse and thereby founded the literary tradition of the Spartan 'mirage', that 'In Lakedaimon are to be found those who are the most enslaved and those who are the most free'. By 'the most free' he meant the Spartans themselves, or more precisely the Spartan master class, who were freed by the compulsory labour of their enslaved workforce from the necessity of doing any productive work whatsoever, apart from warfare. By 'the most enslaved' he meant of course the Helots. These people, as noted above, were Greeks who, despite their birthright of freedom, were collectively enslaved and treated with unusual severity by the Spartans, as a conquered but permanently threatening and subversive population.

This harsh treatment at first puzzled and later deeply disturbed the more sensitive Greek observers of the Spartan scene. Plato, for example, by no means unfriendly to Sparta in general, remarked: 'The Helot-system of Sparta is practically the most discussed and controversial subject in Greece.' This controversy reached a peak in Plato's adult lifetime. For, in the aftermath of the decisive defeat of Sparta at Leuctra in 371 by the Boeotians led by Thebes, the larger portion of the Helots, the Messenians, finally achieved their longed-for collective freedom and established themselves as free Greek citizens of the restored (as they saw it) free city of Messene. I must add that the Spartans were by no means untypical, let alone unique, among the ancient Greeks in seeing no incompatibility between their own freedom and the unfreedom of a servile class, and indeed in basing the former on the latter.

These two aspects of Spartan culture and society – competitiveness and contested notions of freedom – almost by themselves make our

Spartan ancestors worthy of our continued cultural interest and historical study. But they very far from exhaust Sparta's extreme fascination.
Let's take a look at those more or less well attested Spartan social customs or practices that we have focused on in Chapter Four: institutionalized pederasty between a young adult citizen warrior and a teenage
youth within the compulsory framework of the state-managed educational system; athletic sports including wrestling practised officially –
and allegedly in the nude – by teenage girls; the public insulting and
humiliation of bachelors by married women at an annual religious festival; polyandry (wives having more than one husband each); and wife-
sharing without either party's incurring the social opprobrium or legal
guilt of adultery.

One common factor runs through much of this: the unusual
(indeed, by Greek and even most pre-modern standards, unique) functions, status and behaviour of one half of the Spartan citizen population, the women. The extant evidence is sufficiently plentiful to have
prompted a recent book on them. This is also one of several modern
studies prepared to speak of the existence of a certain 'feminism'
in Sparta. I think, however, that we should take at least some of this
highly controversial evidence with a pinch of (presumably Attic?) salt,
especially where the ideological or propagandistic intention is blatant.
Our written sources are exclusively male, almost entirely non-Spartan
and often heavily Athenocentric. But there is enough that is reliable to
enable us safely to infer that Sparta really was, in such vital areas as
marriage and procreation, seriously different, even alien, from the traditional Greek norms of political and social intercourse.

And this surely does make Sparta perpetually worth studying, not
only by historians, but also by comparative cultural anthropologists
and sociologists, among others. Herodotus, the father of (comparative
cultural) anthropology as well as of history, declared famously that he
agreed with the Theban lyric poet Pindar that 'custom was king'.
He meant that in his view every human group believes that its own
customs are not only relatively better than those of others, but the best

possible. Not surprisingly, he took a special interest in Spartan customs, practices and beliefs. Here are just a few related illustrations. All are taken from the seventh book of his *Histories*, the Thermopylae book, and all of them go to establish the point that the Spartans were not just willing, but culturally predisposed and educated, to die for their ideals: that is, to sacrifice their individual lives for the sake of some greater collective goal, whether local or national.

Shortly before the epic conflict at Thermopylae, as we saw, it was reported to Great King Xerxes by a mounted spy that the Spartans in the pass were combing and styling their very long hair. He simply refused to believe that men who coiffed like women before fighting would make serious opponents in the field. Or rather, in the case of Thermopylae, not just serious opponents but men who would of set purpose put their lives on the line in the certain knowledge that they were going to be killed. That this was indeed what lay behind the Spartans' decision to send a specially selected taskforce of three hundred under King Leonidas to Thermopylae in 480 is proven not only by the way they fought and died, but also by the fact that the men chosen all had to have a living son, so as to prevent their family lines from dying out – in other words, after their own assured deaths.

That their mission was suicidal self-sacrifice is supported further by another story in Herodotus Book 7, recounted, significantly, not long before he tells the story of Thermopylae. In the run-up to the Persian invasion of 480 the Spartans considered how they might try to persuade Xerxes to abandon it. Being a very pious people, they thought that the invasion was at least in part heaven's way of punishing them for the sacrilege of having killed, some years earlier, the heralds sent to them by Xerxes's father Darius – persons whose office invested them with sacrosanctity. So they conceived the idea of making atonement to Xerxes, and of sending two Spartans to be killed by him as restitution and compensation. Call the Spartans naive – certainly, that was how their gesture was reportedly regarded by Xerxes (who simply dismissed the would-be patriotic suicides from his presence with haughty contempt). But the spirit of self-sacrifice for a larger cause, in this case the good of all Greece, not just of Sparta, shines out.

In the event Xerxes did invade Greece and, after stiff Greek resistance, forced the pass of Thermopylae. 'Go tell the Spartans', the beginning of Simonides's famous epigram hymning the heroic Spartan dead in this encounter, has resonated in recent popular culture. As the epigram's next words, '. . . passerby, / That here, obedient to their laws, we lie', suggest, the laws of Sparta were unusually rigorous, and rigid. But another emblematic passage of Herodotus Book 7 – a supposed interview between Xerxes and the deposed Spartan ex-King Demaratus – makes clear how this last clause of the epigram was supposed to be read: as illustrating the characteristically Greek civic quality of obedience to the laws, a quality that the Spartans embodied and acted upon to the full.

Demaratus assures Xerxes that the Spartans will stand up to him, because they fear the Law more even than Xerxes's subjects fear him. More importantly still, the Spartans, unlike them, were able to make a free choice. They established their own laws for themselves by collective agreement, and they chose to obey them. They were not compelled by sheer terror or force to obey the arbitrary and lawless whim of a despot or autocrat. That, certainly, was a biased, ethnocentric judgement by Herodotus. But it also contains an essential truth, both about the ancient Greeks as a whole and not least about the leading Greeks of the Persian War period: the Spartans.

THE SPARTANS and their unique society occupy a central place in the utopian tradition. But Utopia, as the Greek-derived word's inventor, Thomas More, was well aware, is formally ambiguous. Depending on how the prefix 'U' is taken, it can mean either 'No-place' (*outopia*) or 'Well-place' (*eutopia*). The news from the Spartan Nowhere is admittedly not always good. An article in the *Times Higher Education Supplement*, featuring my earlier *Spartans* book and TV series, was introduced editorially as follows: 'They hurled babies into ravines and culled their workforce yearly. Historian Paul Cartledge thinks we could learn a thing or two from those Spartans.' Nevertheless, I should still like to think, and like my readers to think too, that a Thermopylae-inspired *eutopia* might not be the worst place on earth to find ourselves – minus, of course, the exposure of infants and the exploitation of Helots.

At any rate, the ancient ideal encapsulated in the myth of Thermopylae still resonates today: it is the concept that there are some values that are worth dying for, as well as living for. That notion, however, can be a two-edged sword. As applied by certain suicide bombers, for example, it seems to me to be wholly repellent, however justified their cause. Yet when developed in the direction taken by the Spartans and their founder-lawgiver Lycurgus, it can generate ideals of communal co-operation and self-sacrifice that qualify for the honorific label of (e)utopia.

Traditionally, and rightly, Sparta is not commemorated as a hothouse of high culture. But there was, I think, no paradox or irony when William Golding, a future Nobel Laureate for literature, wrote in 1965 after a visit to the Hot Gates:

> *A little of Leonidas lies in the fact that I can go where I like and write what I like. He contributed to set us free.*

It is worth bearing this judgement in mind as one contemplates the Thermopylae memorials on offer in Greece and elsewhere today, both in Sparta and, more poignantly if also more noisily, at Thermopylae itself.

Appendix 1
The Invention of History:
Herodotus and Other Ancient Sources

There was no Herodotus before Herodotus.
A.D. Momigliano, *Studies in Historiography*, 1966

Herodotus was dubbed by Cicero in the first century BCE 'the Father of History'. Less flatteringly, he was known also as 'the Father of Lies'. He wrote, as Edward Gibbon charmingly put it, sometimes for school-children, and sometimes for philosophers. He spun ripping boys' own yarns, in other words, and told the tallest of tall tales, but he also pen-etrated in a most grown-up way deep beneath the surface froth of events, raising the biggest of historical issues and touching upon human philosophical universals. Not the least of his major themes was the relationship between the mundane world of mere mortals and the inscrutably chancy sphere of the immortal and the divine. 'Everything is random', he makes one of his favoured characters, the Athenian Solon, claim (Herodotus 1.30). Another such, ex-King Croesus of Lydia, likens the course of human history to the turning of a giant wheel (1.207). On either view, the best policy for humans is to adopt a studied prudence. Statesmen and politicians must remember above all else that great cities and states and empires were once small – and must act on the settled assumption that ones now great will one day inevitably be small again (1.5).

One preoccupation Herodotus fully shared with our other princi-pal contemporaneous Greek written source for Thermopylae, the poet

Simonides. It was their common concern to preserve the fame of great deeds for the benefit of posterity. In this respect, as in others, both were indebted ultimately to the path-breaking example of Homer. Aptly, an ancient literary critic labelled Herodotus 'most Homeric'. He inherited, for instance, Homer's concern to project an aura of authenticity and devotion to truth-telling, even – or especially – when the subject-matter was as blatantly fictitious as the story in *Odyssey* Book 9 of the uncivilized brutes called Cyclopes ('Circle-Eyes', because they had just one large round eye in the middle of their foreheads).

Herodotus opens his exposition of the results of his enquiry (standardly *historia*, or in Ionic dialect *historiê*) with a Homeric claim: that he will aim to preserve from being lost to fame the great deeds of both Greeks and non-Greeks (meaning above all Persians). Some later Greeks, however, such as the moralizing biographer and essayist Plutarch, considered that he had succeeded all too well in preserving the fame of their ancestors' barbarian adversaries, and objected that he had been less than even-handedly generous in his treatment of some of his fellow Greeks. Plutarch, as a Boeotian from Chaeronea, was particularly incensed by what he saw as Herodotus's malignant presentation of his fellow Boeotians of Thebes as out-and-out 'medizers'. But methinks Plutarch protested too much. That he could stoop to label Herodotus quite mistakenly a *philobarbaros* (roughly, 'wog-lover') demonstrates how far Herodotus was above writing mere official, pro-Greek history.

It is sometimes said that he should yield up his title of 'Father of History' to the anonymous authors of the biblical books of Kings and Chronicles. But this is to confuse a simple recounting of possibly accurate historical facts with history proper. For besides the due preservation of fame, Herodotus announces also in his *prooimion*, or preface, an overall goal that is much more original and 'scientific': *aitiê*, which could mean either cause/explanation or assignation of responsibility. Herodotus said that he was concerned especially to discover, through *historiê*, the *aitiê* whereby and wherefor the Greeks and the non-

Greeks had come to fight the Graeco-Persian Wars. Since he does not in fact concern himself particularly with the assignation of moral praise or blame to whole communities, it is probably better to allow him to mean 'cause' and 'responsibility' in his programmatic preface. But his original readership or audience, schooled in tragic drama, would have understood there to be an inescapable nexus between cause, responsibility, guilt and blame.

Originally, *historia* meant 'research', or 'enquiry' – a meaning it still has in English in the phrase 'natural history' (the enquiry into nature). But for Herodotus it was a term of art; and by using the word prominently in his preface he was showing off a new way of looking, feeling, and above all thinking. It is very noticeable, on the other hand, that Thucydides, Herodotus's greatest successor, does not use the word *historia* at all. Why? Because according to a characteristically Greek mode of interpersonal behaviour Thucydides saw himself as a rival of Herodotus and did not want to betray even the merest hint that they might both of them be engaged in doing the same sort of thing. He was engaged in an *agôn* (contest) for priority; at stake was the cherished title of *prôtos heuretês*, 'first discoverer'.

Once upon a time – not all that long ago, actually – historians who like me were interested in the origins of their craft would have unhesitatingly ranked Thucydides above Herodotus. Thucydides was, so to say, the historian's historian, according to a view that had held sway from at least the Italian Renaissance.* More recently, beginning in the later nineteenth century, the comparison between Herodotus and Thucydides was made in terms of 'science', that being the dominant intellectual paradigm of our own modern times. Thus Thucydides's historiography was considered 'scientific', whereas Herodotus's quite simply was not. Herodotus was, admittedly, a brilliant teller of tales,

---

* Indeed, from the time of an ancient Greek 'renaissance', the Second Sophistic of the second century CE, when the hellenized Syrian writer Lucian awarded Thucydides the palm in his tract on *How to Write History*.

but that was all: too often his tales were merely tall ones. Moreover, he was in general far too credulous, even gullible, so far as his sources of information were concerned, and also (and not least) far too theological in explaining what he was told, and what he believed, had happened in the past.

One of the more positive effects of the so-called postmodern turn in historical studies is that the semi-automatic judgement in favour of Thucydides and against Herodotus has been severely questioned, even turned on its head. From the more recent scholarship on Herodotus – of which there has been an enormous amount – has emerged a very different historian from the one that was current even in the 1970s. Now, Herodotus's methods of enquiry and his reporting of the results of those enquiries are regularly seen as being entirely appropriate for negotiating the kind of contexts in which information about the past was handed on to him, and for handling the type of subject-matter he chose to research. Moreover, what Herodotus does, and Thucydides famously (or notoriously) does not do, is enable the reader to see that the past is a complex, indeterminate and messy affair, that people's perceptions of it differ greatly, being often hazy and always interested, and that history is therefore always more or less invented – by the historian – and is more or less a contemporary construction. There are no 'laws' of history to be discovered, tested or assumed.

It is important not to misunderstand the nature of Herodotus's 'research'. This was not, chiefly, a matter of delving in dusty archives or even of reading published official documents. The Greek world of his day and the relevant generations before then were not particularly document-minded, let alone archivally sophisticated. The oriental world, by comparison, was so – but Herodotus apparently could neither read nor speak any other language than his own Greek. He was dependent for gathering his oriental information either on Greek-speaking oriental informants or on Greeks who knew one or more of the key oriental languages – Persian, Aramaic or Babylonian, for instance. That he did somehow gain access to genuine oriental documents is unquestionable, but how, precisely, we cannot say. One very sceptical school of modern scholarly thought, known by its opponents as the 'Liar School of Herodotus', even questions whether he really did go to the places in the orient that he said he went to – Egypt, for example, or Babylon. (The same sort of scepticism has been applied to Marco Polo, with equally small justification.) But the majority of scholars more coolly believe that, though he did indeed go to, say, Memphis in Egypt or Babylon, his reporting of what he saw and the nature of what he was told were far from entirely accurate and realistic.

So far as his Greek informants were concerned, we have no good reason to doubt that he travelled far and wide to seek them out: as far west as to southern Italy, on the other side of the Greek world from his own native Halicarnassus in Caria in south-west Asia Minor (modern Bodrum in Turkey). Nor should we doubt that he questioned them long and hard. He practised a combination of what he called *theoriê* (critically informed travel) and *historiê*, and he exercised his *gnômê* (judgement) in evaluating the oral testimony he garnered. But his informants were sometimes no better than they ought to be, and Herodotus as a socially elite Greek would have mixed chiefly with his peers in other cities, not all of whom had an unswerving commitment to telling him the truth, the whole truth and nothing but the truth. So the outcome of his research could vary in its historicity quite considerably.

Moreover, Herodotus, like any creative artist, had an agenda of his own, and viewpoints that he wished to make his chosen sources serve. He claimed with apparent transparency that he 'related the things that were told to him, though he had no obligation to believe everything he was told' (7.152). But in hard fact the *logoi* (both narratives and speeches) that he wrote up were his own compositions. It was Herodotus who decided how, and when, to make, for example, his Spartans or his Persians speak, and how they should speak to each other. Throughout his work he shaped his narrative according to a highly sophisticated form of moral patterning.

In Book 7, in the preamble to the narrative description of the Battle of Thermopylae, Herodotus behaves very much as a dramatist might. He takes his readers – originally, of course, his hearers – backstage, and into the inner sanctum of the council chamber of Great King Xerxes himself. One of Xerxes's most favoured Greek advisers on the campaign, according to Herodotus, was a Spartan. Not just any old Spartan, but the Spartan ex-king Demaratus, who had gone over to the Persian side after being deposed from his hereditary kingship and virtually forced into exile in about 490. So at one level Demaratus was straightforwardly a traitor – a traitor to the cause of the freedom of Greece which Herodotus himself pretty clearly espouses. Yet Herodotus does not choose to represent and castigate Demaratus as such. His discourse is much richer and more subtle.

Herodotus uses Demaratus as a 'warner' figure, a sort of male Cassandra who knows the future but is not believed when he foretells it to Xerxes. He therefore has to present a Demaratus who is not wholly bad, and not wholly unsympathetic to Sparta and its ideals. This is a positive view of him that Herodotus may well have received in interviews with descendants of Demaratus still living two generations later in the Troad (the area of north-west Anatolia around Troy). The important point is that, for whatever reason, Herodotus chose to believe it and to represent it, and so his most important Demaratus narrative, or *logos* (7.101–4), is in part a version of a favourable tradition extolling the virtues of the Spartan military ethic.

Yet at the same time it is much more than that. For though Herodotus was not a fervent or uncritical admirer of Athenian democracy, he did enrich his *Histories* generally, and his Demaratus narratives specifically, with a peculiarly Athenian democratic tradition of political discourse. This rabidly anti-tyrannical tradition had originated at the foundation of the democracy in 508/7, and it found the Persian monarchy particularly congenial as grist to its mill: Xerxes, for example, was stereotyped (or caricatured) as the typical oriental absolutist tyrant. Herodotus reflects some of the colour and flavour as well as the basic ingredients of that rich concoction.

On top of the Spartan and Athenian elements in his Demaratus narratives he has added a third dimension to the mix, one that was peculiarly his own: panhellenism. This ideology was rooted in common Greek religious practices and other shared cultural customs, not least a common language, and went back many years, even centuries. Thanks largely to the Graeco-Persian Wars, it acquired an ethnocentric, almost 'racist' edge. Greek values were now contrasted, entirely favourably, to non-Greek and especially Persian values. Herodotus was by no means a simple, let alone simplistic, 'panhellenist': he could exhibit and indeed advocate quite exceptional tolerance for deeply alien non-Greek habits, practices and beliefs (see Appendix 3). But he did believe it to be a wholly good thing that the Greeks (only some Greeks, actually) had won the Graeco-Persian Wars. He went out of his way, in fact, to emphasize that this was a combined Greek, above all Spartan and Athenian, victory. Hence his use of a Spartan, even a questionably patriotic one, to express some of Herodotus's own most cherished panhellenist sentiments and tenets. This extreme subtlety and richness of discourse make Herodotus a particularly rewarding literary artist, but not an easy or straightforward historian to interpret.

He was also exceptionally adept at handling time and – for the most part – causation.* He starts his main narrative in what we call the 540s BCE. This was partly because the conquest of Lydian King Croesus by Cyrus of Persia entailed the first subjection of Greek cities to Persia, and so was the first instance of his overall theme of Greek–Persian relations. But it was also the furthest point in time at which Herodotus, using his oral method of enquiry, could hope to get back to reliable eyewitness

---

* I shall use Herodotus's treatment of Polycrates, the colourful tyrant of Samos in the 530s and 520s, in order to illustrate both. Herodotus knew Samos personally very well indeed, and he picked up unusually rich and detailed traditions both on and about the island.

testimony to events. The year 545 is roughly two generations before Herodotus's birth, or three before his maturity. Three generations, so the anthropologists tell us, is pretty much the maximum span of time over which a living oral tradition is likely to survive in anything like its original form so far as its basic factual content is concerned.

Herodotus puts the same point in another way, which would have made particular sense to his Greek hearers and listeners. Polycrates of Samos, he says (3.122), was 'the first of the so-called generation of men' to be a ruler of the sea. Herodotus has heard of the sea empire allegedly controlled long long ago by the fabled Cretan King Minos (builder of the labyrinth at Cnossos). But, for him, Minos belongs to the time of myth, to prehistorical time, well outside the limits of the 'three-generation' rule. *

Herodotus's handling of causation was not always impeccable. For example, his explanation of the breach between Polycrates and the Egyptian Pharaoh Amasis (Ahmose) in 525 seems to put the cart before the horse. It was not, as Herodotus has it, Amasis who broke off his alliance with Polycrates on the suspiciously Greek moral-theological grounds that Polycrates seemed to him to be too prosperous, but rather Polycrates who renounced his engagements to Amasis when he saw that Egypt was to be the next target of Persian imperial expansion, under the generalship of Cyrus's son Cambyses.† But overall his explanations of Greek–Persian relations from 545 to 479 tend to command respect, and the linkage between the various key stages or moments (545, 525, 499, 490, 484) is made acceptably and plausibly clear.

From the largely or wholly secular perspective that dominates mod-

---

* It is rather surprising to note that the supposedly 'scientific' Thucydides takes Minos's real historical existence as read.

† According to Herodotus's account, Polycrates had struck up a useful personal–political friendship with Amasis, but Amasis broke it off when he heard the story of Polycrates's ring. In brief, Polycrates fears that an excess of prosperity may well cause his downfall, so he hurls into the sea a specially favoured ring. But the ring is swallowed by a large fish, which is caught and presented to Polycrates by the proud and loyal fisherman – and found to contain the ring. Polycrates and Amasis infer that his downfall is inescapable. Actually this is just a Greek variant of a widely dispersed international folktale.

ern historiography Herodotus can nevertheless be dismissed as too theological. He believed, self-confessedly, in the 'hand of god' (or 'the gods', or 'the divine') as a sufficient explanation of the phenomena of human history. The utterances of oracles, if straightforwardly authentic and not 'bought' or otherwise manipulated by crooked human forces, were, he maintained, to be believed on principle as truthful. When there was a choice between different types of explanation of exceptional human happenings – such as the extraordinary suicide of Spartan king Cleomenes I – Herodotus would always automatically plump for the theological rather than the humanistic or secular explanation.

This aspect of his personal psychology was crucial to his quite extraordinary toleration of the deeply alien religious beliefs and practices of various non-Greek peoples (see Appendix 3). It has an obvious bearing too on the general presentation and colouring of his narrative. For example, he regularly pictures the Spartans as a supremely religious people, who were prepared both collectively and individually to act in ways that seemingly ran counter to rational good sense. But was it really (for instance) their sense of religious duty that prevented them setting out from Sparta in 490 in time to fight shoulder to shoulder with the Athenians and Plataeans at the Battle of Marathon? Or was Herodotus too easily persuaded by the Spartans' own religious rhetoric? If he was in fact right about Spartan religiosity – and right in part because he was a man of strong religious motivation himself – then this may be an important clue to explaining a series of what were by normal Greek standards unusually pious interpretations of civic obligation and duty.

That Herodotus was generally reliable and indeed a brilliant historian of Graeco-Persian affairs overall does not, unfortunately, rule out the possibility that he may be guilty of serious defects in his narration of events in detail.* This was partly due to the inherently defective nature of the sources available to him, but partly also to the use he

---

* This, at any rate, is the view regularly taken by George Cawkwell in the most recent scholarly account of Greek–Persian relations available to me as I wrote this book: Cawkwell 2004.

made of them. Nevertheless, Herodotus in my view remains as good as it gets: we either write a history of Thermopylae with him, or we do not write one at all.

Simonides of Ceos the praise-singer,* the other main contemporary source for the events and processes centring on Thermopylae, had a phenomenal photographic memory. He is said to have been the first to codify the art of memory by formulating rules for getting it into shape in advance and applying it to perfection in practice. At one of his praise-singing performances in Thessaly, in honour of a leading baronial family of Crannon, an earthquake wiped out all his feasting audience. He himself was said to have been saved by divine intervention – an opportune summons from the banqueting hall by the Spartan Dioscuri, Castor and Pollux, Helen's twin half-brothers.†‡ Afterwards he was able to help bereaved relatives identify the crushed corpses of their loved ones by remembering where each had been sitting.

Working for hire as Simonides did attracted a certain opprobrium, not least from his rivals, for being allegedly the first praise-poet to compose for a strict fee. Yet Simonides's younger rival Pindar surely 'earned' no less than he did in his very long career (from the 490s to the 440s).‡ And Simonides's nephew Bacchylides probably didn't care whether what he received for his encomia was called 'pay' or 'gifts',

---

* As Mary Renault entitled the historical novel she devoted to him in 1976.

† Helen (of Troy) was worshipped in Sparta, alongside her brothers: see Hughes 2005.

‡ Pindar seems never to have been commissioned by the Spartan state or by an individual Spartan, though he did manage to sneak in flattering references to the unique excellence of Laconian hunting hounds (Fragments 106, 107ab) and to Apollo Carneios, patron of the single most important festival of the Spartan annual religious calendar, the Carneia: 'Mine to sing the lovely / Glory that came from Sparta'; and to Cyrene in north Africa, that is, home of Arcesilas, the victor at the Pythian Games of 462/1 who had commissioned this victory ode. Indeed, Pindar seems to have claimed descent for himself from a Spartan who achieved the feat of conquering nearby Amyclae and bringing it into political union with Sparta.

just so long as he was remunerated and recompensed handsomely enough. (Herodotus too was allegedly rewarded handsomely, by the Athenians, for praising their decisive role in winning the Graeco-Persian Wars. But this would have been an ex gratia payment, and not cash that he had sought as a fee.)

In this as in other respects Simonides stood on the cusp between the traditional and the more modern ways of doing things. His memory rules, for example, suggest that he lived at a transitional moment in Greek culture between a predominantly oral era, when memory was the first and usually the sole resource for remembering salient facts of the past, and an era when written documents were more and more called into play to supplement or substitute for it. Yet from our standpoint Simonides looked back far more to Homer, who sang the 'famous deeds of men' (*klea andrôn*), than forward to the historiography of Herodotus and Thucydides, who sought to explain them as well as – or rather than – praise them.

Simonides wrote poems in a number of genres besides that of the encomiastic ode. He is said to have composed no fewer than fifty-six winning dithyrambs (a type of hymn in honour of Dionysus) for various Greek festivals, for instance, though not a single certain example survives. Simonides may well also be the author of an extant address to the goaty mountain god Pan (though the authorship of these lines is disputed as between him and Pindar):

> *Pan, lord of Arcadia*
> *guardian of holy shrines . . .*
> *Blessed one, whom the Olympians*
> *call the ubiquitous hound*
> *of the Great Goddess . . .*
> (trans. Richard Stoneman, slightly modified)

Pan played a particularly prominent role in Graeco-Persian affairs in 490. This concerned the remarkable long-distance runner Philippides, who brought a vital message to the Spartans, covering the 250 kilometres from Athens in under forty-eight hours. On his way either to or (more likely, I think) back from Sparta Philippides believed he was accosted by Pan himself in his native Arcadian uplands. Pan assured him that he would fight on the Athenians' side against the Persians, and so he did, at Marathon, inspiring his eponymous panic among the oriental foe.*

Praise-poets were expected to be didactic. (Simonides gets a mention on this account in Aristophanes's comedy *Frogs* of 405.) One of the choicest of Simonides's maxims was just three words long in its original Greek, but it spoke worlds about Greek political culture and gender stereotyping. *Polis andra didaskei* means literally 'a [or the] *polis* teaches a man [an adult male]'. Its rich significance may be unpacked as follows: the uniquely Greek invention of the *polis*, or citizen-state, teaches an adult male how to be in the fullest sense a man – that is, a citizen of his *polis*. Simonides elsewhere qualified Sparta as *damasimbrotos*, 'mortal-taming' or 'breaker-in of mortals'. The phrase was quoted by Plutarch in the very first chapter of his *Life* of the Spartan king Agesilaus II, who reigned from about 400 to 360 (*Ages.* 1). This was both a quintessentially apt, laconic epithet and wholly fitting for the only Greek city with a public programme of state-organized compulsory education for both boys and girls from the age of seven.

To tame is to civilize, to make the rough smooth (as in our 'polished' and 'polite'). But it was also a word that in Greek carried powerful gendered implications: one Greek word for a wife was *damar*, 'she who is tamed'. The taming in question, by the husband,

---

* The Spartans had given Philippides an assurance that they too would be present at the battle, just as soon as the phase of the moon had altered so as to free them from an overriding religious commitment. After a remarkable series of forced marches, the Spartans arrived at Marathon, but on the day after the battle had been fought, as we saw. This was a poignant moment, not without its embarrassment, and one that I am sure contributed to Leonidas's resolve to make amends at Thermopylae exactly a decade later.

was understood in exactly the same sense as the 'breaking in' of a wild animal, especially a horse. This was a particularly appropriate image for horse-loving Sparta. The whole psychology and ideology that goes with the breeding, selection and training of horses was dynamically fitted to Spartan eugenicist ideas. And many Spartans won races at both national (Olympic) and local athletic festivals with teams of horses that they had bred in their own stables. Euagoras, for example, won the victor's crown at three Olympic Games running with the same team of mares, an extraordinary – and almost unique – feat (Herodotus 6.103). It was a Spartan woman too, Princess Cynisca, sister of Agesilaus II, who became the first woman ever to win an Olympic crown: not as a competitor, of course, since women were forbidden to compete against men (or even, with the exception of a single priestess, to watch them compete), but as the owner of the winning four-horse chariot team, first in 396 – and then again in 392.

Most famous and relevant of all Simonides's many poems of praise are the three he wrote for or about Sparta in 480 and 479. The first was for all the Greeks who fell at Thermopylae, and was commissioned by the delegates to the council of the Amphictyonic League that managed the affairs of Delphi, the second most important site of panhellenic games after Olympia and even more important than Olympia as the spiritual home of religious hellenism. The Spartans were members of the League, but as representatives of the 'Dorian' branch of the Greek people, not in their own right as citizens of Sparta. Presumably, therefore, the eulogy was composed to be sung at Delphi, perhaps at the time when the famous Serpent Column victory monument was erected there in 479 after the Battle of Plataea. Here it is in full, in an elegant if free translation:

> Great are the fallen of Thermopylae,
> Nobly they ended, high their destination –
> Beneath an altar laid, no more a tomb,

Where none with pity comes or lamentation,
> But praise and memory –
> A splendour of oblation
No rust shall blot nor wreckful Time consume.

The ground is holy: here the brave are resting,
And here Greek Honour keeps her chosen shrine.
Here too is one the worth of all attesting –
Leonidas, of Sparta's royal line,
Who left behind a gem-like heritage
> Of courage and renown,
> A name that shall go down
> > From age to age.

(trans. T. F. Higham)

The special mention of Leonidas and the imperishable 'gem-like heritage of courage and renown' left by him are suggestive of a peculiarly Spartan affinity.* But the floridity and length of the eulogy for all the Greek fallen at Thermopylae are emphatically not Spartan. Contrast the elegiac couplet (a hexameter line followed by a pentameter), also commissioned by the Amphictyonic League of Delphi. This, as quoted by Herodotus and others with slight verbal variation, was for the Spartans alone:

> *Go tell the Spartans, passerby,*
> *That here, obedient to their laws, we lie.*

The elegiac couplet (to quote Anna Davies's brilliant commentary) 'derives its amplitude from a fusion of straightforward syntax with

---

* This recalls a remarkable epigram, possibly also to be attributed to Simonides, that found its way into the later collection, the *Palatine Anthology* (7.344). Herodotus had recorded (7.225.2) that the Greeks erected a stone monument at Thermopylae in the form of a lion to commemorate the deed of Leonidas and his men; there was a sort of pun involved here, since the Greek for lion is *leòn*. This poem, collected in the *Anthology*, is as if spoken by a stone lion.

poetic diction and metrical virtuosity. Music has become language carved on stone. The pressure of feeling has been controlled and transformed into two lines that contain an order to report what is neither a boast nor a fancy because it is a fact' (Davies 1981). In detail, 'their words' translates the Greek *rhêmasi*, the dative plural of *rhêma*. The root of *rhêma* is the same as the root of *rhêtra*, a word with a peculiarly Spartan resonance. It means anything uttered, so has a range of applied meanings, from law to oracle. Simonides's listeners would have picked up the echo of Sparta's own great elegist Tyrtaeus (who had used the phrase *eutheiais rhêtrais*, 'with straight rhetras') and the allusion to the so-called 'Great' Rhetra (there were other, lesser ones) attributed to the famed – or more probably fabulous – Spartan lawgiver of yore, Lycurgus. The last word of the couplet is *peithomenoi*, a participle meaning 'obeying'. Spartan obedience was in a sense the whole point of the 'man-taming' education system, the *agôgê*.

Scarcely less exciting than these two is a very recent find of another of Simonides's poems, preserved incomplete on papyrus. This shows just how well his two Thermopylae poems had gone down in Sparta. For he was then commissioned, presumably by the Spartans or at any rate by *a* Spartan, to write a great epic about the Battle of Plataea in 479, the battle that finally decided the Persian Wars on land in the Greeks' favour. The leitmotif of this poem was to depict the victorious Greeks as though they were Homeric heroes come back to life and, through the medium of the praise-poem, to confer upon them the sort of undying fame that Homer had conferred on Achilles and the other Greek heroes at Troy (see, for example, fragment 11.20–5). The unexpected recovery of this poem helps us to understand better the precise force of Thucydides's reaction against the 'mythical' in history, even if it may have unduly prejudiced him against Herodotus's unique discursive combination of the mythical and the historical.

No individual Spartan was more interested in having himself thus praised and immortalized than the overall Greek commander at Plataea, Spartan Regent Pausanias, and we learn from a later work attributed to Plato (*Letter* 2.311a) that the association of Pausanias with Simonides was much talked of. This gives especial pungency to the advice that Simonides was already known to have given to Pausanias before this new poem was rediscovered – 'remember that you are mortal'. This, however, was advice that Pausanias seems not, in the event, to have heeded.*

To sum up, Simonides was hired to give the best possible spin in memorable verse to the famous deeds of his employers and paymasters. The more they paid, presumably the more lavish – if not necessarily the more poetic – was his praise. But he was not bound by the historian's requirements of objectivity and balance.

Two other ancient sources offer something substantial on the Thermopylae campaign.† One of these passes muster as a historian: Diodorus, a Greek from Sicily who wrote a huge, compendious and

---

* Not content with setting up a boastful epigram at the entrance to the Black Sea (Herodotus 4.81.3; compare Nymphis of Heraclea, *FGrHist*. 432F9), Pausanias also had an inscription added to the base of the Serpent Column set up in 479 at Delphi, the 'navel' of the earth. Whereas the inscription on the Serpent's bronze coils merely stated that 'These fought the war' and then gave a list of the names of thirty-one Greek states, headed of course by the Lacedaemonians, Pausanias's personally commissioned epigram (quoted at Thucydides 1.132.2) virtually ascribed the combined Greeks' victory to him alone. Any even minimally alert reader of Herodotus would have predicted from this hubris that Pausanias was destined to pay the penalty of *nemesis* and come to a bad end. He did indeed come to a spectacularly bad end, being starved out – as we learn from Thucydides – in the holy shrine of the Spartans' patron goddess Athena on the acropolis of Sparta. This end by itself, in the eyes of Herodotus and many other conventional Greeks, would have wiped out the previous *kleos* (fame) that had accrued to him as conqueror of the Persians – though there were other reasons besides for thinking less than entirely well of Pausanias. Yet the exceptionally pious Spartans were anxious in case they might collectively acquire some divinely sent stain of pollution as a result of the manner of Pausanias's death in, or very near, hallowed ground. So as an act of divine atonement or restitution the authorities commissioned two bronze effigies of him to be erected on the Spartan acropolis.

† Thucydides, Herodotus's major successor as historian, offers interesting material and judgement on the Persian Wars as a whole but not on Thermopylae specifically. See Rood 1999.

oddly titled *Library of History* in the second half of the first century
BCE. The other does not: Ctesias, a doctor by profession, who hailed
from Cnidos in south-west Asia Minor (one of the two major Greek
medical centres, the other being Hippocrates's island of Cos not far
away off the same coast).

Ctesias served as court physician to Great King Artaxerxes II
(405/4–359/8 BCE) and travelled with him on campaign and other
missions. His memoirs of life at the Persian court were racy and
scurrilous enough to attract both attention and preservation. His
general account of Graeco-Persian history was still found amusing or
instructive enough to be excerpted in the eighth century by the
learned Byzantine patriarch Photius. It is his epitome that offers us
a skeletal version of Ctesias's clearly overweight and overblown
original. But it was presumably an original error of Ctesias's, and
not just his abridger's economy, that caused the complete omission of
the traitor Ephialtes from the account of Thermopylae. Gaffes like
that render his account almost worse than useless, because there are
other details in the epitome, not found in Herodotus, that may, just
possibly, be accurate.

Diodorus, however, is a different matter. He was never better than
the sources he chose to follow, excerpt and – rhetorically – adapt, and
for his account of the fifth century he by and large followed Ephorus.
The latter ambitiously composed a universal history of Greece in
thirty books. This began with the return of the descendants of Heracles
to the Peloponnese (a mythical event to be dated to the early twelfth
century on our system of chronography) and continued down to his
own day, the mid-fourth century BCE. Ephorus was a native of Cyme
in Ionia, which for part of his lifetime was incorporated within the
Persian Empire, and he may have been a pupil at the rhetoric school of
the leading speechwriter and pamphleteer Isocrates (436–338) at
Athens. The question of Diodorus's authenticity and validity boils
down, therefore, to this: what sources did Ephorus follow, if not
Herodotus? And the major interpretative issue is how seriously we

ought to take any significant detail recorded by Diodorus that is not in Herodotus.

Now, there is indeed one such detail of potentially enormous significance that Diodorus/Ephorus does include in his account of Thermopylae and that is not in Herodotus. It concerns a supposed night attack by loyalist Greeks on Xerxes's camp in the very middle of the Thermopylae campaign, with the aim of assassinating the Great King and so removing at least a major part of the *raison d'être* of the Persian campaign. What are we to make of this report? For my own – thoroughly sceptical – view, see Chapter Seven.

Appendix 2
Herodotus's Persian
Muster-Lists: A Translation

The exact authenticity and validity of both these lists are controversial. But besides serving the specific function assigned them by Herodotus within his narrative, they also afford us a colourful description of the rainbow coalition formed by the peoples of the Achaemenid Persian Empire under Great King Xerxes in 480 BCE. For that reason the lists are reproduced here in full, in my own translations (which aim to reproduce accurately the technical content and flavour of the original rather than to offer elegantly polished English).

THE ARMY (7.61–88)

(61) Those serving in the army were as follows. First, the Persians – arrayed in this manner: on their heads they wore the tiara, a soft felt cap, and about their bodies an embroidered and sleeved tunic, [over which was fitted a covering] of a coat of chain mail that looked like fish-scales, and around their legs trousers [*anaxurides*]. They bore shields of light wickerwork, below which were slung quivers; their spears were short, but their arrows long, with reed shafts; and they had daggers hanging down from a belt beside their right thigh. As commander they acknowledged Otanes, father of Xerxes's wife

Amestris. In olden times the Persians were called 'Cephenes' by the Greeks, though they called themselves 'Artaei', as they were known also to their neighbours. But when Perseus son of Danae and of Zeus visited Cepheus son of Belus and took to wife Belus's daughter Andromeda, he had a son whom he named Perses. And he left him behind there since Cepheus happened to have no male child of his own. It was because of Perses that the Persians acquired their name. (62) The Medes serving were equipped in the very same way. This mode of equipment was in fact originally Median and not Persian. Commanding them the Medes had Tigranes of the Achaemenid house. Of old the Medes were universally called 'Arians', but after Medea of Colchis arrived among the Arians from Athens, these too changed their name. This is the story the Medes tell about themselves. The Cissians who served were in all other respects equipped like the Persians but instead of felt caps they wore wound turbans. They were commanded by Anaphes son of Otanes. The Hyrcanians were armed like the Persians, and were under the command of Megapanus who later became governor of Babylon. (63) The Assyrians who served wore helmets either made of bronze or woven in a foreign style that is hard to describe, carried shields, spears and daggers (like the Egyptians), and wooden clubs studded with iron besides, and wore linen corslets. The Greeks called these 'Syrians', but non-Greeks knew them as 'Assyrians'. Their commander was Otaspes son of Artachaees. (64) The Bactrians in the army wore helmets pretty much identical to those of the Medes and carried native reed bows and short spears. The Sacan Scythians wore caps [*kurbasiai*] that rose to a point and were set upright and stiff, and trousers, and carried locally made bows and daggers, and besides these wielded the battle-axe called *sagaris*. These were called 'Amyrgian Sacae', though they are in fact Scythians, for the Persians call all Scythians 'Sacae'. Hystaspes son of Darius and of Atossa daughter of Cyrus commanded the Bactrians and Sacae. (65) The Indians wore clothes made of wood ['tree-wool', i.e. cotton] and carried reed bows and arrows of reed with iron heads. Equipped in this way, the Indians were assigned to the command of Pharnazathres son of Artabates. (66) The Arians were equipped with Median bows but in all other respects were like the Bactrians. Sisamnes son of Hydarnes commanded the Arians. The Parthians, Chorasmians, Sogdians, Gandarans and Dadicans who served had the same equipment as the Bactrians. Artabazus son of Pharnaces commanded the Parthians and Chorasmians, Azanes son of Artaeus the Sogdians, and Artyphius son of Artabanus the Gandarans and Dadicans. (67) The Caspians were dressed in coats of leather and armed with local reed bows and short swords [*akinakes*]. They served under the command of Ariomardus brother of Artyphius. The Sarangians stood out among the rest for their brightly dyed clothes; they wore knee-length boots and carried bows and Median-style spears. The Sarangians were commanded by Pherendates son of Megabazus. The Pactyans too wore leather coats and carried local bows and short swords. They acknowledged Artayntes son of Ithamitres as their commander. (68) The Utians and Mycans and Paricanians were equipped in the same way as the Pactyans, and were commanded thus, the Utians and Mycans by Arsamenes son of Darius, the Paricanians by Siromitres son of Oeobazus. (69) The Arabians wore a loose mantle [*zeira*] caught up by a belt, and at their right side they carried a long, double-curved bow. The Ethiopians wore leopard-skins and lion-skins and carried bows made of strips of palm wood not less than four cubits long, and small reed arrows with points of sharp stone instead of iron (this is the stone they also use to make incised seals). They additionally carried spears, with points of sharpened antelope horn, and knobbed clubs. Half of their body was smeared with gypsum as they went into battle, half with ruddle. The Arabians and the Ethiopians who live beyond Egypt were commanded by Arsames son of Darius and of Artystonê daughter of Cyrus (her Darius loved the most of all his wives and had a statue of beaten gold sheets made of her). The Ethiopians beyond Egypt, then, and the Arabians were commanded by Arsames, but (70) the Ethiopians living in the direction of the sunrise (for two groups of

Ethiopians were serving) were arrayed together with the Indians. They differed in appearance in no way from the other Ethiopian group apart from their speech and hair. Whereas the Ethiopians from the east have dead-straight hair, the hair of the Ethiopians from Libya is the thickest and curliest of all mankind. These Ethiopians from Asia were equipped for the most part like the Indians, except that they wore on their heads the skin of a horse's forehead together with its ears and mane; they made the ears stand erect and the mane served as a crest. Instead of shields they held out in front of them the skins of cranes as a form of defence. (71) The Libyans wore leather gear and carried javelins with points hardened in the fire. They acknowledged Massages son of Oarizus as commander. (72) The Paphlagonians served with plaited helmets on their heads, small shields and moderately sized spears, light javelins and daggers; on their feet they wore native boots reaching to mid-calf. Equipped in the same way were the Ligyans, Matienians, Mariandynians and Syrians. These latter the Persians call 'Cappadocians'. The Paphlagonians and Matienians were commanded by Dotus son of Megasidrus, the Mariandynians, Ligyans and Syrians by Gobryes son of Darius and Artystonê. (73) The Phrygians wore equipment very like the Paphlagonians', with just small differences. According to the Macedonians, the Phrygians were called 'Bryges' for as long as they lived next door to the Macedonians in Europe, but when they crossed over to Asia, they changed their name at the same time as their location. The Armenians, as colonists of the Phrygians, were armed just like them. The commander of these two together was Artochmes, a son-in-law of Darius. (74) The Lydians bore arms and armour very like the Greeks'. Of old the Lydians were called 'Meionians' but acquired their new, present name in the time of Lydus son of Atys. The Mysians wore local helmets on their heads, and carried small shields, and javelins with points hardened in the fire. These are colonists of the Lydians, and are called 'Olympienians' after Mount Olympus. Of the Lydians and the Mysians the commander was Artaphrenes son of Artaphrenes, who had jointly with Datis invaded

Marathon. (75) The Thracians served wearing fox-skin caps on their head and tunics about their body, with embroidered mantles thrown over them, and on their feet and lower legs they wore deerskin boots; they carried javelins, light wicker shields and small daggers. Once these had crossed over to live in Asia they were known as 'Bithynians', but before, as they themselves tell, they were called 'Strymonians', since they lived on the River Strymon. They claim they were uprooted from their original home by the Teucrians and Mysians. The Thracians of Asia were commanded by Bassaces son of Artabanus. (76) [The Pisidians?] had small raw ox-hide shields and each carried a pair of hunting spears of Lycian make, and wore on his head a helmet of bronze with a crest on top and with the ears and horns of an ox attached. For greaves they used wrap-around strips of red-coloured cloth. These people possess an oracular shrine of Ares. (77) The Meionian Cabelians, who are called 'Lasonians', wore the same equipment as the Cilicians – which I shall detail when I come to the Cilicians in order of array. The Milyans carried short spears and wore clothes fastened with brooches. Some of them carried Lycian bows, and wore helmets made of dog-skin on their heads. These Badres son of Hystanes commanded. (78) The Moschians wore wooden helmets on their heads, and carried shields and small spears but with long points. The Tibarenians, Macronians and Mossynoecians were equipped like the Moschians. In order of line the Moschians and Tibarenians were commanded by Ariomardus son of Darius, the Macrones and Mossynoecians by Artayctes son of Cherasmis who was governor of Sestus on the Hellespont. (79) The Marians wore on their heads local, woven helmets and carried small hide shields and javelins. The Colchians wore wooden helmets on their heads, and carried small raw ox-hide shields and short spears, as well as knives. Of the Marians and the Colchians the commander was Pharandates son of Teaspis. The Alarodians and Saspeirians served wearing the same equipment as the Colchians. These Masistius son of Siromitres commanded. (80) The island peoples from the Erythraean Sea followed, inhabiting the islands where the Great King settles those labelled the 'Uprooted', who had clothing, arms and armour very like those of the Medes. These islanders were commanded by Mardontes son of Bagaeus, who in the year next after this was a general at the Battle of Mycale and died therein.

(81) These were the peoples which served in the campaign by land and were arrayed in the infantry. These men whom I have mentioned were the commanders of it, and these were the men who set in order and enumerated the divisions and appointed the commanders of thousands and of tens of thousands. The commanders of ten thousand appointed the commanders of hundreds and of tens. There were others who were leaders of contingents and of peoples. These whom I have mentioned were commanders, (82) but in overall command of both them and the entire army as generalissimos were Mardonius son of Gobryas, and Tritantaechmes son of Artabanus (that Artabanus who had expressed the view that they should not conduct an expedition against Hellas) and Smerdomenes son of Otanes (both these being sons of brothers of Darius and so cousins of Xerxes), and Masistes son of Darius and Atossa and Gergis son of Ariazus and Megabyzus son of Zopyrus. (83) These were generals of the entire infantry force – apart from the Ten Thousand: of that specially selected force of Persians the general was Hydarnes son of Hydarnes. And the reason why they were called the 'Immortals' was as follows: if ever anyone caused the number to fall short of Ten Thousand by dying violently or from disease, another man would be chosen, so that they were never either more than or fewer than Ten Thousand. Of all the peoples [of the Empire] it was the Persians who created order to the greatest degree and who were themselves the best. They were equipped in the manner already stated, and apart from this were distinguished by the unstinted amount of gold they wore. Besides that, they took with them covered wagons and concubines, and a huge entourage of servants all elaborately accoutred. Special extra provisions for them, separate from the other soldiers', were borne by camels and yoked beasts of burden.

(84) These peoples all serve as cavalry, but for the expedition only the following provided cavalrymen. First, the Persians, equipped in the same way as their infantry except that on their heads some of them had beaten metalwork both of bronze and of iron. (85) Then, there are nomads called 'Sagartians' who are Persian by ethnicity and in speech but wear equipment that is somewhere between that of the Persians and that of the Pactyans. These furnished eight thousand horse, but they are not in the habit of carrying either bronze or iron weapons apart from daggers. Instead, they use ropes of twisted leather thongs and place their faith in these as they go into battle. The manner of fighting of these men is as follows: when they engage with the enemy, they throw their ropes with nooses at the end of them; whatever they lasso, whether horse or man, they drag towards themselves, and the entangled catch is destroyed. Such is their manner of fighting, and they were arrayed alongside the Persians. (86) The Medes' cavalrymen wore the same equipment as their infantrymen, as too did the Cissians. The Indians' cavalrymen were equipped like their infantrymen, and they rode both racehorses and chariots pulled by horses or asses. The Bactrians and Caspians alike were equipped in the same manner as their infantry. The Libyans also – and these all drove chariots too. Likewise the [?] and Paricanians were equipped in the same manner as their infantry. The Arabians had the same equipment as their infantry, but they all rode racing camels that were no whit slower than horses. (87) These were the only peoples that served as cavalry, to a total number of eighty thousand horse, apart from the camels and the chariots. The rest of the cavalry forces were drawn up by divisions, but the Arabians were placed last and behind them so as not to frighten the horse troops, inasmuch as horses cannot endure camels. (88) The cavalry commanders were Harmamithres and Tithaeus, both sons of Datis. The third co-commander of them was Pharnouches, but he had been left behind at Sardis sick. For as they were departing from Sardis, an unwished-for disaster struck him. A dog ran under his horse's feet as he was riding out, and the horse failed to see it in advance and was

startled and reared up, throwing Pharnouches, who fell and began to vomit up blood. The disease turned into consumption. Pharnouches's servants immediately carried out his orders and led the horse away to the place where it had thrown him down and there cut off its legs at the knees. In this way was Pharnouches deprived of his command.

THE NAVY (7.89–99)

(89) Of the trireme warships the number in total was 1,207, constituted as follows. The Phoenicians together with the Syrians of Palestine furnished 300, and the men were equipped in this manner: about their heads they wore leather caps very like the Hellenic style, they wore linen corslets, and they carried rimless shields and javelins. In ancient times these Phoenicians lived, as they themselves say, by the Erythraean Sea, but they crossed over from there and now dwell in Syria beside the sea. This part of Syria and all up to Egypt is called 'Palestine'. The Egyptians furnished 200 ships. These men wore about their heads reticulated helmets, carried convex shields with large rims, and spears made for fighting at sea and large axes. The great majority of them wore breastplates and carried large knives. (90) Thus were these men equipped. The Cypriots, who furnished 150 ships, were equipped as follows. Their kings wound turbans around their heads, the rest wore tunics, but in other respects they were accoutred like Greeks. The peoples of Cyprus are of diverse ethnic origin: some are from [the island of] Salamis and from Athens, some are from Arcadia, some from [the island of] Cythnos, some from Phoenicia, and some from Ethiopia, as the Cypriots themselves say. The Cilicians furnished 100 ships. (91) They again wore local helmets on their heads, but for shields they carried targes of raw oxhide and they wore woollen tunics. Each man had two javelins and a sword, the latter fashioned very like the Egyptians' knives. Of old they were called 'Hypachaeans' but from the time of Cilix son of

Agenor the Phoenician they have had their present name. The Pamphylians furnished 30 ships and were armed in the Greek manner. These Pamphylians are descended from those dispersed from Troy together with Amphilochus and Calchas. (92) The Lycians furnished 50 ships; they wore both breastplate and greaves and carried cornel-wood bows, featherless reed arrows, and javelins. They had goatskins hanging down around their shoulders, and on their heads wore felt caps crowned with feathers; they bore daggers and sickles. The Lycians were formerly called 'Termilae' as they originated from Crete, but took their present name from Lycus son of Pandion, an Athenian. (93) The Dorians from Asia, who are of Peloponnesian origin, furnished 30 ships and were accoutred in the Greek manner. The Carians furnished 70 ships, in all other respects outfitted like the Greeks but also carrying sickles and daggers. What these were formerly called has been related in the first part of my narrative [*Leleges*, 1.171]. (94) The Ionians furnished 100 ships, and they were accoutred as other Greeks. As long as they lived in the Peloponnese in the area now known as 'Achaea' and before the coming of Danaus and Xouthus, they were called 'Coastal Pelasgians', as the Greeks relate, but 'Ionians' after the time of Ion son of Xouthus. (95) The offshore islanders furnished 17, also wearing Greek armour. Originally they were Pelasgian by ethnicity but later were called 'Ionians' according to the same rationale, like the cities of the Ionian Dodecapolis founded from Athens. The Aeolians furnished 60 ships, and these were equipped like Greeks; anciently they were called 'Pelasgians', as the Greeks report. The Hellespontians, apart from the men of Abydus and the rest of the men who served from the Black Sea, furnished 100 ships and were equipped in the Greek manner. (The Abydenes had been tasked by the Great King to remain on their home soil and guard the bridges.) These are colonists of the Ionians and Dorians. (96) As marines in all the ships, there served Persians and Medes and Sacae. The best sailers among the ships were furnished by the Phoenicians and – of the Phoenicians – the

Sidonians. Over these, as over those serving in the infantry, were placed local commanders for each people – since I am not compelled to do so, I make no account of these in my History. For neither were the commanders of each people men of note nor were there as many commanders appointed as there were cities. They followed moreover not in the capacity of generals but rather as slaves, like all the other combatants, since it was those who were Persians as I have already mentioned who had the absolute power of command over each of the national groups. (97) Of the fleet the following were supreme commanders: Ariabignes son of Darius and Prexaspes son of Aspathines and Megabazus son of Megabates and Achaemenes son of Darius. Specifically, Ariabignes son of Darius and of the daughter of Gobryas commanded the Ionians and Carians, Achaemenes (brother of Xerxes by both parents) the Egyptians; and the other two, the remainder. In addition, it transpired that 30-oared and 50-oared galleys and light vessels and small horse-transports had been gathered to the total number of 3,000. (98) Of those who sailed on board those of most note, after the overall commanders, were the Sidonian Tetramnestus son of Anysus, and the Tyrian Mattên son of Siromus, and the Aradian Merbalus son of Agbalus, and the Cilician Syennesis son of Oromedon, and the Lycian Cyberniscus son of Sicas, and the Cypriots Gorgus son of Chersis and Timonax son of Timagores, and the Carians Histiaeus son of Tymnes and Pigres son of Hysseldomus and Damasithymus son of Candaules. (99) Of the other divisional commanders I make no mention since I am not compelled to, with the sole exception of Artemisia, a source of greatest wonder to me as a woman campaigning against Hellas. After her husband died, she obtained the tyranny although she had a son who was a young man, and she went on the expedition impelled only by her spirit of adventure and manly courage [*andreia*], though there was no necessity for her to do so. Her name was Artemisia daughter of Lygdamis, and she was by birth on her father's side Halicarnassian, on her mother's side Cretan. She led the forces of Halicarnassus, Cos, Nisyros and

Calydna, furnishing five ships. And of the entire fleet, after those of the Sidonians, she furnished the best reputed ships. Of all the allies it was she who revealed to the Great King the most shrewd counsels. Of the cities which I have stated she commanded, I declare all to be Dorian by ethnicity, the Halicarnassians originally from Troezen, the remainder from Epidaurus.

Appendix 3
Herodotus – Antidote
to Fundamentalism*

*I believe that imagining the other is a powerful antidote to
fanaticism and hatred.*

Amos Oz, from his Goethe Prize speech of 28 August 2005

Contemporary Iran is associated with two of the issues that most powerfully concern and alarm the world on a truly global basis: uranium
conversion with a potential for the fashioning of nuclear weapons of
mass destruction; and, second, international terrorism motivated by a
revolutionary, religiously inspired ideology. We have come a very long
way indeed from 1971, when the then Shah-an-Shah ('King of Kings'),
Mohammed Reza Pahlavi, celebrated with near-obscene grandilo-
quence the supposed 2,500th anniversary of Cyrus the Great's death
('supposed' because he died in 529 BCE, so the anniversary in fact fell
in 1972). How were the not so mighty to be fallen. Just eight years
later, in 1979, the Peacock Throne was no more, and a very specifically
post-ancient, Islamic regime was in place. That was not, however, the
end of the reach of ancient Persia, not by any manner of means. At

---

* The original version of this Appendix was delivered as a lecture at the Museum of
the University of Athens in May 2005, to launch the collective volume on Herodotus
published by the En Kuklôi ('In a Circle') group of the University of Athens directed
by Dr Mairi Yossi (Faculty of Classics). I am indebted to Dr Yossi and her collabora-
tors for their kind invitation and matchless *philoxenia*.

least, not in terms of the ongoing tradition of literary imagination and fictional construction in the West.

First, in 1996 a new Xerxes was born, a minor character admittedly, in Rohinton Mistry's marvellous novel set in the mid-1970s 'emergency' regime of Indira Gandhi, *A Fine Balance*. More precisely, this Xerxes is born into a Parsi family, the nephew of one of the novel's four protagonists, in what is clearly meant to be Bombay (now Mumbai). Mistry is himself a Parsi, and originally from Bombay/Mumbai, but had relocated to Canada before writing the novel – which process clearly demanded just such a physical as well as temporal distancing for the author to achieve his remarkably powerful effects of reconstruction and retrospective analysis. Xerxes's father still practises, as his sister does not, the Parsi religion to the full, with above all its distinctive approach to burial – or rather non-burial – in 'towers of silence'. At a stroke we are taken back some three thousand years, to the world of Zoroaster and the Magi, the original practitioners of a Zoroastrianism of which present-day Parsis – whose very name betrays their Persian origin though they live scattered to the four winds – are the living legatees and perpetuators.

Then, in 2004, a new Leonidas was born, not in Greece, but in modern-day Fethiye in Turkey, anciently Greek Telmissos (the home, for example, of Alexander the Great's pet diviner and guru, Aristander). This new Leonidas was Daskalos Leonidas, 'Master' (Teacher) Leonidas, or alternatively Leonidas Effendi, who – whether or not his creator, Louis de Bernières, was quite aware of it – bore more than a passing resemblance to the ancient namesake of his who was one of Alexander the Great's two principal tutors in his boyhood, Leonidas of Epirus, a kinsman of Alexander's formidable mother Olympias. De Bernières's *Birds without Wings* is a splendid novel of another huge politico-ethnic upheaval, the Greek–Turkish stand-off of the early 1920s with its attendant massacres and consequent population exchanges and uprootings. Leonidas is seen, unsympathetically, through the eyes of two Turkish inhabitants of Fethiye (meaning 'Conquest'), Iskander (Turkish for

Alexander) the Potter and Karatavuk the Letter-Writer, the latter a pupil of Mehmetçik who in turn has been taught his – Greek – letters by Master Leonidas. For Leonidas is what the ancient Greeks would have called a *grammatistes*, a grammar teacher with a primary responsibility for teaching writing, using the immensely brilliant, originally ancient Greek invention of a simple alphabetic script of a mere twenty-five letters or so, as modified from a Phoenician (north-west Semitic) base model in the eighth century BCE. This Leonidas – and here he bears a more than passing resemblance not just to Epirote Leonidas but to the standard-issue central-casting Spartan teacher of our period – favours what we might delicately call the direct method of instruction, sometimes not quite falling short of a resort to outright physical violence in order to inculcate his pedagogy.

Mistry the Canada-based, Bombay-originating Parsi. De Bernières the Englishman of Huguenot descent with a fascination for exotic and powerfully political scenarios (apart from his signature *Captain Corelli's Mandolin*, he is the author of a series of quasi-magic-realism novels set in unnamed Latin American countries languishing under severe right-wing dictatorships). A third, major fiction-writer of our times has recently added his quotient to our story of active Greek and Persian heritage: the Brazilian Paulo Coelho, best known probably for *The Alchemist*. In his author's note to *The Devil and Miss Prym* (2000, English translation, 2001), a morality fable set somewhere in remote and mountainous contemporary Spain, Coelho begins by remarking: 'The first story about division comes from ancient Persia.' He is referring to the division – in both senses, of partition and of antagonism – between Ormuzd, the symbol of Light and Truth, and Ahriman, the symbol of Darkness and Evil. De Bernières, too, focused his novel on a bipolar division, between Christian Greek and Muslim Turk. Mistry's polarity was, rather, the balance – a 'fine' one indeed – between hope and despair. Division and balance were also at the heart of Herodotus's project, but his master-trope or metaphor, if we may call it that, was limit.

He had concluded his preface with the sobering observation that entropy (to use a modern scientific metaphor) was endemic to the life-cycles of states: small cities of men in his day had, most of them, once been great; and, vice versa, cities or states that in his day were great would, for sure, in the fullness of time become small. For, as he puts it sententiously, 'human prosperity never [note: not just 'rarely'] abides long in the same place'. Which sentiment – using the technique of ring-composition – anticipates and looks forward to his very-long-postponed conclusion, at the end of what we think of as Book 9.* There we find Cyrus – Cyrus II the Great of Persia, the original founder of the Persian Empire and so the First Mover of the whole mechanism of give and take, loss and gain, injury and requital that Herodotus had chronicled so marvellously – giving his people some advice. Advice that Herodotus clearly regarded as sage and which boiled down, essentially, to this, thoroughly Greek, lesson: know your proper limits, and stick to them. In the case of Cyrus's Persians, this meant deciding to remain living in a rugged land, the mother of fine soldiers who would come to rule many other people and peoples rather than be slaves to others.

Or so they rightly should have done, but in fact, and with evil consequences, did not – from as early as the reign of the founder Cyrus himself. Cyrus died, not in his bed in Pasargadae, his original capital, but far away in central Asia, fighting the Massagetae tribesmen of the Caspian. Cambyses his son won Egypt for the Empire, but in effect went mad in the process and as a result was either murdered or committed suicide. Even Darius, the cautious and canny 'local retail tradesman' who rebuilt the Empire on remarkably durable foundations, failed militarily first in Scythia, and then in Greece, where his forces lost the Battle of Marathon; and he died before achieving the

---

* This is actually a later division of his work, by learned scholars working in the library attached to the Museum (Shrine of the Muses) at post-Classical Alexandria in Egypt, who amused themselves by inscribing each of the 'books' under the sign of one of the nine Muses.

vengeance he was – allegedly – reminded every day to seek. As for his son and successor Xerxes, he came to a very bad end, the victim of an in-house, harem-based assassination in 465. Herodotus will have known this, but did not choose to include it among the mere score of post-Graeco-Persian Wars events that he did record. It was enough for him to have detailed the total failure of Xerxes's manifestly overambitious, overweening, and – fatally – sacrilegious attempt to add mainland Greece to his empire's possessions. The ultimate paradox, though, was that the Greece Xerxes sought to conquer was not a rich, soft land of luxuries. It was a land where poverty was naturalized, a land best suited to the austerity of the Persians' ultimate anti-type and nemesis, the Spartans, the true heroes of our tale – though not entirely, it has to be admitted, of Herodotus's.

So we too return, in a *kuklos* (circle) of our own making, to our starting point, the historiography of Thermopylae, and above all the historiography of Herodotus. Earlier I have been concerned chiefly with technical questions to do with Herodotus's reliability and credibility. Here I shall attempt something broader, and perhaps rasher, an assessment of his relevance as a guide to living in the early twenty-first century. The responsibility of trying to do anything like proper justice to a thinker and writer who was one of the great innovating geniuses of the fifth century BCE is a heavy one. But the responsibility is heavier even than that. For Herodotus was also the founder of an entire intellectual discipline and practice, or craft, the one that I am honoured to try my hand at myself, namely the eponymous *historia*.

So I begin with a paradox – a suitably Herodotean one. On the one hand, Herodotus was himself conventionally pious in the normal and normative ancient Greek terms of his time. He was a believer, as we have seen, in the existence of the gods (or what he sometimes called 'the divine', *to theion*) and in their ability to act powerfully and decisively in the world of men as and when they saw fit. Above all, he seems to have believed implicitly in the power and truth of divinely inspired and authenticated prophecy. Today, this sort of religious outlook might well be considered utterly consistent and compatible with what is normally referred to as religious fundamentalism – except that, unlike pious Jews, Muslims and Christians today, pious ancient Greeks did not have authoritative sacred texts to appeal to, let alone one over-arching sacred text (a Bible, a Qur'an) to guide them. And of course, they believed not in just One All-Mighty God but in a plethora of divinities – because in their view, as the world's first intellectual, Thales of Miletus (*c.* 600 BCE), is said to have said, 'the world is full of gods'.

On the other hand, although Herodotus was conventionally pious in these ancient Greek terms – indeed, I am tempted to say precisely *because* he was pious in this way – he was both intellectually able and morally prepared to see that Others (non-Greeks) did otherwise in the sphere of religion: they believed and they practised no less fervently very different, indeed incompatibly and incommensurably different, religious things. Nor did he apply this perception only to religious beliefs and practice. He saw – both literally and metaphorically – that Others were no less committed to the unimpeachable truth and worth of their customs (*nomoi*) in general, not only religious customs, than the Greeks were. In other words, Herodotus was not only the first his-torian in the West. He was also the first comparative cultural anthro-pologist. It is this Herodotus – Herodotus the relativist in method and pluralist in ethical stance – that I should like to end by presenting. As an antidote, I hope, to what I see as the poison of most contemporary forms of religious fundamentalism, the dominant feature of which appears to be a radical intolerance.

Let me first put my own cards on the table. I am not opposed to all religious belief and practice as such, though I do not happen to have any or do any myself. What matters to me, as an intellectual, is the place of any and all such religious activity and belief within a philo-sophical worldview. To declare my hand: I am firmly with the fifth-century BCE Greek pluralist intellectual Protagoras (from Abdera in northern Greece), who is credited with having written that the subject of the gods was obscure, and that human life is too short fully to come to terms with understanding it; and equally firmly I am with Socrates (on this point anyhow . . .), according to whom, as reported by his most brilliant disciple Plato, 'the unexamined life is not worth living for a human being'. Intellectual examination or enquiry, whether of a Socratic or of a Protagorean sort, is in my view incompatible with any brand of religious fundamentalism – indeed, if the pun may be pardoned, fundamentally so.

With the intellectual ground cleared, so to speak, let's explore in some detail just four passages of Herodotus's *Histories*.

The first (**8.3.1**) reads as follows: 'Violent discord within people of the same ethnicity [just two words in Greek, *stasis* (literally 'standing apart') *emphulos*] is as much worse than war [*polemos*] fought with unanimity [against a *foreign* enemy] as war is worse than peace.' Herodotus, I think, though I cannot prove it, was essentially a man of peace. He at any rate almost certainly never exercised a military or naval command. This does not mean that he did not fight when he felt he had to – and it is significant that he is recorded as having taken part precisely in a violent kind of *stasis* within his own home city of Halicarnassus. What I mean is that he was not one who took delight in war for war's sake. As he put it very vividly elsewhere, in peace sons bury their fathers, but in war fathers bury their sons – a reversal of the natural order of things. This attitude might possibly have made him an untypical Greek. Surely untypical, too, was his belief – as expressed so starkly in this passage – that it was wrong for Greeks to fight other Greeks. That, at any rate, is what I think he meant by *stasis emphulos*: not – or not only – the kind of *stasis* that occurred within individual cities, civil war as we call it. For that, just *stasis* would have been enough. This hostile attitude of his towards inter- or intra-Greek warfare was reinforced by his unusually broad and vehement version of panhellenism.

For most Greeks, their *patris* was their *polis*. So patriotism in ancient Greece was typically local patriotism or civic patriotism, not 'national' patriotism, as it were. In fact, as we have seen, the ancient

Greeks actually did not have, or did not form, a 'nation' in any strong sense. This was an absence, indeed a failing, that Herodotus, I would argue, bitterly regretted. The evidence is in my second passage of choice, also from Book 8 (**144.2**).

We are in winter 480/479. The few and not very firmly united Greeks who are resisting the massive Persian invasion led in person by Great King Xerxes have been defeated at Thermopylae but have won a great naval victory at Salamis. This victory was not, however, decisive. Xerxes, it is true, has returned to Persia, his tail between his legs, but he has left behind in Greece Mardonius, son of his father Darius's bosom pal Gobryas, with a huge army and a still useful navy to finish off the job of conquest that he had begun. Mardonius – unlike his master perhaps – is a man of some guile, a bit of an Odysseus. In order to make his task of final victory in a decisive land battle that much easier, he attempts to bribe the Athenians to desert the loyalist Greek coalition. (It is interesting that he apparently did not consider bribing the Spartans, who – at any rate later – acquired the reputation of being easily bribable . . .) As his intermediary with the Athenians, Mardonius uses the Macedonian King Alexander I, a vassal king of Persia. When the Spartans get to hear of Mardonius's underhand initiative, they – also apparently suspecting that the Athenians were indeed bribable . . . – immediately send a delegation to Athens to persuade the Athenians to stay loyal to the 'Greek' cause.

Was Alexander a Greek? Well, yes, technically. But only technically. He did not always behave like one, or like a good one, anyhow, in Herodotus's eyes. In sharp contrast, that is, to the behaviour of the Spartans and – especially – the Athenians in 481–479. I put it this way because Herodotus uses this episode to bring out what he considers to be its most important aspect of all, its widest possible significance – namely, what it was to be Greek. Hence Herodotus's putting into the mouths of 'the Athenians' a famous declaration of what has been called 'Hellenicity', or Greekness. Here in full is the relevant quotation from the speech delivered by 'the Athenians' to the Spartans, as recorded – or rather invented – by Herodotus:

> *Many and great are the reasons preventing us from doing this [taking the Persians' money and 'enslaving Hellas by taking the side of the Medes']: first, and greatest, the statues and shrines of the gods set on fire or reduced to ruin [by the Medes] – these we must of necessity avenge to the very utmost rather than make an agreement with those who did those deeds; second, to Hellênikon, the fact of our Greekness – being of the same blood and same speech, having in common sanctuaries of the gods and animal blood-sacrifices, and manners of life that are the same for all. If we were to betray all these, it would not be well.*

We notice once again the key importance he attributes to religion – another reason, one might well have thought, why the conventionally pious Herodotus was likely to have been hostile to and intolerant of the religious practices and beliefs of non-Greek, 'barbarian' peoples. Yet, actually, he was neither. In two different, but complementary and mutually reinforcing, ways he acknowledged that the Greeks had no unique or exclusive claim to religious virtue or wisdom. On the one hand, he was the first to acknowledge, in fact to proclaim, that, despite all sorts of other things that they did either differently or precisely oppositely, the barbarians – and especially the Egyptians – had invented and given to the Greeks some key aspects of Greek religion. On the other hand, even where the barbarian religious customs in question were as far removed from, as alien to, indeed as opposite to Greek ones as it was possible to imagine, even – or especially – then Herodotus was prepared to perform an immense act of interpretative charity, almost one of empathetic understanding.

This brings me to my third selected passage (**3.38**). There can presumably be no more revealing feature of human societies' customary religious outlooks and practices than their attitudes to death and burial. This is at the same time an intimately revealing marker and constituent of both personal and group identity. Tell me how you die – that is to say, how you treat the process of death and burial – and I'll tell you who you are. Hence the magnum force of Herodotus's prime illustrative anecdote, or parable. Here we notice at once a feature of his manner of exposition that is going to recur in my fourth passage, and indeed elsewhere at key moments in his work (most relevantly, in the so-called Persian Debate on the theory of political constitutions, also in Book 3). Namely, his choice of a non-Greek, more specifically a Persian, setting in order to provide the focus for a moral or ethical discussion that is really about – and intended solely for – his Greek audience.

This is the parable. At some unspecified date Great King Darius I, father of Xerxes, summoned to his presence at Susa, one of the major administrative capitals of his empire, representatives of two non-Persian ethnic groups – just two out of the many such groups who we know were employed as a vast multinational army by this greatest of Persian builders. The first to be summoned were Greeks, the second Indians called Callatians. To the former he put the following question: how much would he have to bribe them to persuade them to go against their customary funeral practice and eat – as opposed to cremate – their kindred dead? The Greeks replied that they would never do so, at any price. Darius then asked the Callatian Indians how much he would have to bribe them to persuade them to go against their customary funeral practice and cremate – as opposed to eat – their kindred dead. They were reportedly even more outraged at the very suggestion than the Greeks – and asked Darius not so much as to breathe it aloud. Whereupon Herodotus comments that he agrees with Pindar that 'custom [*nomos*] is king [*basileus*] of all'.

This anecdote, in other words, had been retold by Herodotus precisely in order to exemplify and to bring home to his audience a general rule of all human social groups: that every people believes its own customs to be the best absolutely – the best against all competition. This in itself is a pretty sobering thought to reflect on: you may fondly think that your customs are absolutely the best but, let me tell you, actually that is only your opinion, and other people do things very differently from you, and they too think exactly the same about their way of doing things as you do about yours . . . This is Herodotus the relativist speaking. But it is also Herodotus the pluralist, as – unlike a true ethical relativist – he does not in fact judge all people's customs to be equal. For example, eating people – that is, people they have deliberately killed in order to eat – as is customarily done by the *androphagoi* ('man-eating') Scythians (from the area to north and east of the Black Sea), is for Herodotus absolutely wrong. So it is quite remarkable that, in introducing and commenting on the anecdote, he does not pass negative moral judgement on the cannibalistic funerary practice of the Indians. That, surely, is to display an extreme tolerance – and also to point the way towards a proper respect for the sincere beliefs and practices of Others, no matter how 'other' those beliefs and practices may seem (to Us) to be.

I end with another deservedly famous passage of our author (1.207). Like a couple of the examples already cited, it is set in a Persian context – though not in Susa, this time, but far away to the north and east, in the territory of the barbarous Massagetae of central Asia, to east of what is left today of the Aral Sea. In 529 Great King Cyrus II is conducting yet another punitive expedition of conquest, against a people who are ruled by a ferocious queen. He calls a conclave (if I may borrow that term from the Roman Catholic Church) of his leading Persians and also some non-Persian special advisers, including a certain Croesus. This is once vastly rich, ex-King Croesus of Lydia, who had allegedly been spared by Cyrus despite his classic act of *hubris* (insolent breaching of established boundaries) in fatally misreading an ambiguous Delphic oracle in about 545. Encouraged by the Delphic prophecy that if he crossed the Halys River he would destroy a great empire, he crossed in the firm expectation of destroying Cyrus's empire – only to end up by destroying his own.

Herodotus too is happy to keep Croesus alive, but for a different reason: so that Croesus can serve in his narrative as a wise adviser, or warner figure, to the Great King of Persia, his conqueror and magnanimous sparer; as he does in the scene from Book 1 in which I am especially interested now. Croesus begins his homily to Cyrus, piously, by saying that it was Zeus who had surrendered him and his life to Cyrus. (How Cyrus – as opposed to Herodotus himself or his audience – would have read such a claim is of course another matter.) Croesus then proceeds to mention his own great and bitter sufferings – not simply to lament them, but in order to make a wider point. He insists that he personally has learned a powerful lesson from them, but also that the same lesson can be learned by Cyrus too – provided only that he does not make the mistake of equating himself with the immortal gods. Cyrus, that is, must remember that he is mortal – as Simonides was to remind Regent Pausanias of Sparta in a later generation and context. The lesson Croesus has learned is this: that the affairs of humans are configured like the motion of a revolving wheel, a *kuklos* (whence our 'cycle'). By this Croesus means that the same persons are not allowed always to continue in a state of good fortune.

We can ignore the rest of Croesus's speech; he goes on to give spectacularly bad advice to Cyrus, who then gets himself killed precisely in this rash campaign against the Massagetae. What interests me, rather, is the notion of the circle itself. For this is a metaphor that catches very well one major difference between ancient Greek patterns of thinking and our own. The ancient Greeks were by no means unfamiliar with a notion of Progress – technological, cultural, even sometimes moral progress. But it was hardly a dominant idea, let alone the driving force, of their culture. For them, the blessed Golden Age was typically thought of as in the past, as having happened once upon a time long ago. So this blissfully desirable state was seen as an ideal to be at best retrieved and possibly emulated, but not necessarily surpassed. One version of this essentially static worldview took the form of eternal recurrence, precisely Croesus's *kuklos*: the wheel of fortune which deposited people back where they started, or brought them low after they had been riding high.

This too is how Herodotus chooses to end his *Histories*, with a hint that excess always presages a disastrous fall for a people, and that moderation in relative poverty is the preferable state to be in. If we too are to be properly mindful of the need for Herodotean balance and objectivity, the last, sobering word should probably go to the great modern poet, Constantine Cavafy (in the translation of Edmund Keeley and Philip Sherrard):

> *Honor to those who in the life they lead*
> *define and guard a Thermopylae . . .*
> *And even more honor is due to them*
> *when they foresee (as many do foresee)*
> *that in the end Ephialtis will make his appearance,*
> *that the Medes will break through after all.*

The victory in the Persian Wars was indeed won by Greeks, or even by 'the Greeks' – those of them, that is, who at the critical moment united under Sparta to resist the Persian invader. But Cavafy's traitorous Ephialtis was also a Greek and human, all too human. By suffering one learns. This is the lesson that Greek tragic drama also enduringly teaches, outside the theatre as well as inside, off as well as on the literal, formal stage.

Pericles, Thucydides's Pericles, in the last speech put into his mouth by the historian opines sententiously that all good things must come to an end, all greatness must decline. This is not the only Herodotean touch to be found in his successor's work, and it is one instance among many of the sureness of Pericles's *pronoia*, or foresight. For an observer of Spartan history with a long-sighted eye would know that not much more than a century after Thermopylae the inexorable *kuklos* of human fortune had brought the Spartans low, very low indeed. They would rise again, somewhat, but never again to scale the heights of greatness in their golden century from about 550 to 450.

The memory of them, however, would continue, as we have seen in the Epilogue, down from antiquity right through the medieval and early modern worlds to our own contemporary era. And perhaps we may be permitted, at the finish, to overlook the darker patches, some very dark indeed, and look, rather, on the bright side – to hold in our admiring gaze the heroic Spartans, both men and women, of 480, the year of Thermopylae.

Glossary

Achaemenid – Dynasty founded by Cyrus II the Great *c*. 550, named after legendary king Achaemenes, lasted till 330 BCE.

acropolis – High city or citadel, common to many Greek cities, including Sparta (a modest affair compared to that of Athens).

Agiads and Eurypontids – The two hereditary Spartan royal families, descended notionally from Agis and Eurypon (tenth century BCE?), each provided one of the two reigning kings; lineal father–son succession often broke down, as in the case of Eurypontid King Leotychidas (r. 490–478), who was a distant relative of his predecessor Demaratus, and regencies were sometimes necessary to cover minorities, as in the case of Agiad Regent Pausanias who led the Greeks to victory at Plataea in 479.

agôgê – Sparta's unique state education, compulsory for all males from age 7 to 17 inclusive; a less formal counterpart existed for girls at the same ages, leading to their marriage at age 18.

agôn – The ancient Greek word for 'contest' or 'competition', both peaceful (e.g. the Olympic Games) and not (war was an *agôn*); the concept was central to ancient Greek culture, which has therefore been characterized as 'agonal' or 'agonistic'; the English word 'agony' comes from the Greek word for 'competitiveness'.

agora – Originally any place of gathering; with the rise of the *polis* became specialized political-cum-commercial space, the civic centre.

Ahura Mazda – Single supreme god of the **Zoroastrians**, who created all things and stood for truth and light as symbolized by fire.

alphabet, Greek – Graphic sign-system borrowed, probably in 8th century BCE, from the Phoenician (north-west Semitic) language, with addition of signs for vowels; local variants ran from 24 to 28 signs; in Greek *alpha* (from Phoenician *aleph*) and *beta* (*beit*) were the names for the first two letters, hence 'alphabet'.

Amphictyonic League – Representatives of mainly central Greek communities formed Council of League to oversee the sanctuary of Delphi and the holding of the Pythian Games every four years (first in 582).

andreia – Literally 'maleness', but by extension 'masculinity' as a moral value, and also by further extension 'courage', the prime quality of pugnacity required in Greek warfare.

aristocracy – Power (*kratos*) of the 'best' men (*aristoi*), i.e. the richest and those with the most imposing family pedigrees, normally involving claims to linear descent from a founding hero and/or god.

Asia Minor – That part of the continent of Asia that is now formed by the western half of Turkey (sometimes also called 'Anatolia'); it includes **Ionia** among much else.

Assembly (*Ecclesia*) – All Greek **poleis** (cities) were composed of citizens, who were entitled to attend the regular meetings of its Assembly; the Assembly of both Sparta and Athens met at least once a month, Sparta's on a feast-day of Apollo, hence Assembly meetings were also called Apellai (after Apellon, the Doric form of Apollo). See also *dêmos*.

Atheno-Peloponnesian War – Hugely destructive war between Athens and Sparta and their respective allies, 431–404 BCE, with intervals.

Attica – Home territory of Athens, *c.* 2,400 sq. km.

daric – Gold coin of the realm of the Persian Empire named after Darius I (r. 522–486), who is represented as an archer, the first ruler in known history to be imaged on a coin.

Delian League – Anti-Persian alliance founded and dominated by Athens, 478–404; oaths of eternal alliance, symbolized by dropping lumps of iron into the sea (the alliance would last until the lumps floated to the surface . . .), were first sworn on Apollo's sacred isle of Delos in winter 478/7; peace was probably made with Persia *c.* 449, but the Empire posed a constant threat to Greek liberty; the alliance was eventually dissolved by Sparta, then in alliance with Persia, in 404.

democracy – Literally, power (*kratos*) of the *dêmos* (people), first instituted at Athens 508/7 BCE through the reforms attributed to Cleisthenes, and further developed in 462/1 through the reforms of Ephialtes and Pericles; the word *dêmokratia* is first attested in the 420s but certainly existed much earlier.

dêmos – People, the entire citizen body, the municipality, *or* the masses, the majority, the common people.

Dorians – Ethnic division of Greeks, based – as **Ionians** – on dialect of spoken and written Greek (Doric) and on some distinctive customs, e.g. the annual religious festival of the Carneia in honour of Apollo was common to all Dorians.

ephor – Literally 'supervisor' or 'overseer', title of the five chief popularly elected officials of Sparta; any Spartan might apply for election, but the office, though powerful, was annual and could be held only once in a lifetime.

Eurypontids – see **Agiads**.

Gerousia – Literally 'Senate', or Council of Elders, the supreme council of Sparta, thirty in number, including the two reigning kings ex officio; admission was by popular election, open only to members of certain aristocratic families aged sixty or over, and membership was for life.

Greekness (*to hellênikon*) – Famously (or notoriously) the ancient Greeks could rarely be persuaded to bury their ethnic or national differences, preferring to give their primary allegiance to their own individual *polis*; but they usually agreed on who was a Greek and who was not ('barbarian'), based on shared concepts of *nomos*; see also **Hellas**.

hêgemôn – Literally 'leader', especially of a multistate military alliance, such as Sparta of the **Peloponnesian League**.

Hellas – The name for the combined totality of Greeks settled all round the Mediterranean and Black Seas, with a focus on the southern Balkan peninsula and the Aegean; Hellas never became the single state of 'Greece', and Greeks found it very difficult to maintain permanently any other than local religious associations, such as the **Amphictyonic League**.

Hellenistic age – Conventionally dated from death of Alexander the Great of Macedon, 323 BCE, to death of Cleopatra of Egypt, the last of the Ptolemy dynasty, in 30 BCE.

Helots – Indentured serf-like populations of Laconia and Messenia, perhaps 50–100,000 in all; subjugated native Greeks unlike the vast majority of the Greeks' slaves, e.g. at Athens (where there may have been as many as 100,000 chattel-type slaves).

Herodotus – 'Father of history' (according to Cicero), born Halicarnassus *c.* 484, published *c.* 425 his *Histories*, or 'research' (*historiê*, whence our 'history'), on Graeco-barbarian relations *c.* 550–479 in both oral and written form; later the work was subdivided into 9 books, each named after one of the Muses.

historiê – Literally 'enquiry'; by extension applied to the results of enquiry into the human past and so 'history' in our sense (the ending in -ê is in the Ionic dialect used by Herodotus; in Attic – Athenian – Greek, the form used was *historia*).

homoioi – Literally 'same-ish', so alike or equal in some, but not in all, respects; a technical term for the full citizens of Sparta, who distinguished themselves from various categories of 'Inferiors' (sub-*homoioi*), including degraded ex-Spartans, demoted for economic or other reasons.

hoplite – Heavily armed Greek infantryman; probably took his name from heavy, basically wooden two-handled shield (*hoplon*); fought in interlocked phalanx formation usually 8 or more ranks deep.

hubris – Technical Greek term for stepping over the fixed boundary line dividing men from gods, or criminally violating another human's status, especially with accompanying violence; English 'hubris' has a looser meaning of any behaviour or attitude deemed excessively ambitious or overweening.

Immortals – The 10,000-strong elite Persian infantry body that served both as the Great King's bodyguard and as a crack commando force, as at Thermopylae; the Greeks erroneously called them 'Immortals' as they supposed that, in order to keep the number constant, the Great King always had available with him reserves who could be substituted whenever one of the 10,000 fell.

Ionia/Ionians – Ionia in the geographical sense was the central area of western Asia Minor, including such cities as Miletus and Ephesus; Ionians in the wider sense were an ethnic division of Greeks, sharing – as **Dorians** – a dialect of spoken and written Greek and some distinctive customs (*nomoi*, q.v.), e.g. the annual religious festival of the Apaturia.

Lacedaemon – (1) Official name of the *polis* of Sparta; (2) territory of Spartan *polis*, including Messenia as well as Laconia (Laconia is the Roman and modern name for the area of south-east Peloponnese east of Mt Taygetus), measuring 8,000 sq. km., easily the largest in the Greek world. From Lacedaemon, Spartans and *Perioeci* were called Lacedaemonians. Non-Spartan devotees of Sparta and all things Spartan were known as laconizers.

Magi – Iranian, originally Median, priests, whence our 'magic'.

Medes – Indo-European-speaking people of northern Iran related to and regularly confused (by Greeks) with **Persians** (hence **medizing**), with capital city at Ecbatana (Hamadan).

medizing/medism – Taking the Persian side politically and so betraying some notion of **Hellas**; notorious medizers include Spartan ex-King Demaratus.

nemesis – Divinely inspired vengeance, righteous anger.

nomos – From a root verb 'to distribute', used to mean either 'custom' or 'law'; *nomoi* (pl.) were what Greeks had in common and made them Greek (see **Greekness, Ionia/Ionians**).

oikos – Household, comprising property and livestock as well as family members, both free and unfree.

oligarchy – Rule (*archê*) of the wealthy few (*oligoi*), a variant of **aristocracy**.

Olympia – Sanctuary in north-west **Peloponnese** dedicated to Zeus Olympios (of Mt Olympus in southern Macedonia, the highest mountain in Greece, on the summit of which the gods were supposed to live) and site of quadrennial Olympic Games, both managed by the city of Elis.

Olympiad – Method of time-reckoning according to four-year periods from one Olympic Games to the next, the first conventionally dated to what we call 776 BCE; 480, an Olympic year, was thus the first of the 75th Olympiad.

ostracism – Enforced exile from Athens for ten years, applied to leading political figures (such as Themistocles, in *c.* 471) and decided by counting names of 'candidates' on inscribed or incised potsherds (*ostraka*) submitted by a minimum of 6,000 citizen voters whenever the Athenian **Assembly** voted to exercise the procedure (as they regularly did in the 480s).

Peloponnese – 'Island of Pelops', landmass linked to central Greece by Isthmus of Corinth; the Isthmus's central and key position explains why it was the site of the meeting in 481 at which the few Greek loyalists led by Sparta swore to resist Xerxes.

Peloponnesian League – A multi-ethnic grouping of Peloponnesian and central Greek states brought into alliance by and under the leadership of their *hêgemôn* (military leader) Sparta, to whom each ally swore to have the same friends and enemies and to follow Sparta wherever she might lead them.

Peloponnesian War – see **Atheno-Peloponnesian War**.

Perioeci – 'Outdwellers' or 'dwellers around', the formal description of the inhabitants of 80 or so small towns and villages around Sparta in Laconia and Messenia who were not unfree (like the **Helots**) but were not full citizens of the Spartan state either; they were required or might volunteer to serve in war, when they were called generically 'Lacedaemonians'.

Persians – Indo-European-speaking people of central and southern Iran related to and regularly confused (by Greeks) with **Medes**, with capital cities at Pasargadae, Susa and Persepolis.

Plataea – Small town on border of Boeotia with **Attica**, allied with Athens since 519 and site of decisive land battle of the Graeco-Persian Wars, 479.

polis (pl. *poleis*) – City (both political entity of state and urban centre of state, sometimes also its **acropolis** – 'high city'), best translated as 'citizen-state'; there were well over 1,000 *poleis* stretching from Spain to Georgia, which collectively constituted **Hellas**.

politeia – Citizenship, constitution (e.g. **democracy**).

proskunêsis – Obeisance, the kowtow, a gesture that Greeks thought appropriate only towards gods but which all **Persians** were socially obliged to perform in the presence of the Great King (who was not deemed by the Persians to be a living god).

Pythia – Vatic priestess, an elderly lady in our period, of Apollo's oracular shrine at Delphi in central Greece.

Sacred Band – Elite Theban infantry force of 300, consisting of 150 homosexual pairs, founded 378.

satrap – Persian viceroy, governor of a **satrapy**, often a member of the **Achaemenid** royal family, directly appointed by and responsible to the Great King.

satrapy – Administrative province of Persian Empire, one of 20 or more, such as Hellespontine Phrygia (satrapal capital, Dascyleum) and Lydia (capital, Sardis) in western Asia Minor.

Sparta – see **Lacedaemon**.

stasis – A process or state of 'standing apart', so faction, civil strife, civil war.

Thebes – Chief *polis* of the Boeotians and head of the Boeotian federal state (447–386, 378–338), notorious for **medizing** in 480–479.

Thirty Tyrants – Self-appointed junta of extreme oligarchs that ruled Athens with Spartan backing 404–403 after defeat of Athens in the **Atheno-Peloponnesian War**.

trireme – Oared warship, the ship of the line, borrowed in plan by Greeks from Phoenicians but turned against them to deadly effect at the Battle of Salamis; it was so called (*triêrês* in Greek) because it was a three-banker, rowed by some 170 oarsman disposed in three superimposed banks.

tyrant – Non-legitimate, absolute monarch ruling by usurpation and/or force; Persia tended to support Greek tyrants as a method of indirectly ruling the Greek cities within the **satrapies** of Hellespontine Phrygia and Lydia.

xenia/xenos – **Xenia** was a form of ritualized friendship between usually aristocratic or socially prominent men from different cities and/or cultures, which imposed strict, hereditary obligations, such as reciprocal hospitality, on the partner *xenoi* (pl. of *xenos*).

Zoroastrianism – Religion believing in **Ahura Mazda** as one supreme god, derived from teachings of prophet Zoroaster (Greek form of Zarathustra), who may have lived as early as 1000 BCE and come from Bactria (Balkh).

Bibliography

The following bibliography is selective, and reflects chiefly works in English that I have drawn upon directly and have sometimes cited in the text or notes. The topics I have been dealing with – Sparta, the Graeco-Persian Wars, Herodotus – are among those most heavily researched by specialist historians of ancient Greece and the Near and Middle East, and the Achaemenid Empire is coming up hard on the rails for a number of different, mutually reinforcing reasons: prominently among them, the increasing availability of primary written and archaeological data, and the subject's extreme topical interest. But I have tried to make the selection helpful also for those who wish to pursue their enquiries further and more deeply in a scholarly way. Some works, of course, apply to more than one chapter, but I have normally listed them only where I have found them to be most helpful and relevant.

One – The Ancient World in 500 BCE: From India to the Aegean

Several useful **general works** on ancient Greek history cover the period of the Graeco-Persian Wars: see esp. Bengtson et al. 1969 (mainly written by Bengtson himself with the addition of chapters by specialists on particular topics or areas); Cartledge 2001a (biographical) and Cartledge (ed.) 1998 (a richly illustrated history by divers hands, mainly that of the editor); Fornara 1983 (translated 'documents'); Freeman 1999; Grote 1846–56: chs 39–40 (outdated, clearly, but pioneering and still consultable with profit); Kebric 1997: ch. 5 ('The Problem with Persia', a prosopographical/biographical approach via the lives of Polygnotus, Ephialtes, Artemisia and Timarete); Osborne 1996 (expert up-to-date problematizing synthesis) and 2002 (special reference to Herodotus). For interactions between Greeks and non-Greeks, with special emphasis on the archaeological evidence, see Boardman 1999; for a selection of archaeological artefacts with illustrations, see Boardman 1988.

On the wars specifically, see Balcer 1989 and 1995; Burn 1984 (admirably written, originally published 1962, with updated addenda by D. Lewis); Cawkwell 2004 (masterly but argumentative and controversial); Green 1970/1996 (the best single relevant work, to be returned to often); Hignett 1963 (excessively nitpicking but indispensable for scholars). On Spartan history in particular, see Cartledge 1979/2001 and other general works cited under Chapter Four.

The relationship between, and antithesis of, Greeks and non-Greek 'barbarians', especially Persians, are explored in any number of publications, beginning with the landmark lectures of Momigliano 1975. See generally Coleman & Walz (eds) 1997; Georges 1994; Hall, J. M. 1997, 2002; Harrison 2000b; Harrison (ed.) 2002; Khan (ed.) 1993; Malkin (ed.) 2001; and Walser 1984. And for specific angles, see, e.g., Cartledge 2002 (an attempt to reconstruct the Greeks' worldview through negative self-definition); Drews 1973 (Greek historiography); Ehrenberg 1974a (East v. West), 1974b (freedom); Hall, E. 1989 and Hall, E. (ed.) 1996 (tragic drama, esp. Aeschylus's *Persians* of 472); Hornblower 2001 (war); Konstan 1987 (empire); Malkin 2004 (religion – e.g., p. 350 'So what [Herodotus] means is, "Ammon is how you say 'Zeus' in Egyptian"'); Miller 1997 (stressing Athenian cultural borrowings from Persia); Pelling 1997 (de-emphasizing the 'East v. West' dichotomy); Stronk 1990–1 (Sparta and Persia); and West 1997 (Greek cultural borrowings).

Two The Dynamics of Empire: Persia of the Achaemenids, 485

Anything written by distinguished Collège de France professor Pierre Briant may safely be recommended with great enthusiasm: Briant 2002 is a behemoth, in English translation; 1999 is a snappier version, also in English; cf. 1989/2002, 1997–2001.

There are many good **general histories** of ancient Persia and the Persian

Empire: e.g., Cook 1983; Curtis 2000 (expert guide by British Museum curator); Frye 1963 and 1984; Gershevitch (ed.) 1985; Ghirshman 1971 (excellent pictures from the official commemorative volume of the then Shah's 2,500th anniversary celebrations of the ancient Persian monarchy); Herzfeld 1968 (by the excavator of Persepolis); Laroche 1971/1974: pp. 84–116 (pictures better even than Ghirshman); Lockhart & Boyle 1978; Olmstead 1948 (e.g., ch. XX 'New Year's Day at Persepolis'); Wheeler 1968; and Wiesehöfer 1994/2001. The most recent, Allen 2005, deserves special praise: it is intelligently written, not loaded with prejudice, beautifully illustrated throughout, and includes an exemplary bibliography. It incidentally casts a strange light on the title (*Forgotten Empire*) of Curtis & Tallis (eds) 2005, the worthy catalogue of an intriguing small exhibition including artefacts never before seen outside Iran, also published by the British Museum Press.

On **archaeology and iconography**, see Boardman 1999 and 2000; Loukonine & Ivanov 1996/2003; Moorey 1988; Nylander 1970 (Ionians in Pasargadae); Pope 1975/1999: ch. 4 (decipherment of Persian cuneiform); Root 1979; Root 1985; Schmandt-Bessarat (ed.) 1980; Stronach 1978 (Pasargadae, Cyrus's original capital).

On **administration**, see Abraham 2004 (Egibi business house); Briant & Herrenschmidt (eds) 1989 (tribute); Brosius (ed. and trans.) 2000 (documents) and 2003 (Persepolis archives); Cameron 1948 (Persepolis Treasury Texts); Cardascia 1951 (Murashu banking house); French 1998 (Royal Road); Graf 1994 (roads); Hallock 1969, 1972 (Persepolis archives); Herrenschmidt 1996/2000 (Old Persian); Kent 1953 (Old Persian); Lewis 1994 and 1997: pp. 325–31 (Persepolis fortification texts); Petit 1990 (satraps); Stolper 1985 (Murashu banking house); Tuplin 1987 (general) and 1998 (seasonal migration of kings).

On **military matters**, see Sekunda & Chew 1992.

On **historiography**, see Burkert 2004; Drews 1973; Robinson 1995; Sancisi-Weerdenburg 1983, 1989/2002, 1999; Sancisi-Weerdenburg & Kuhrt (eds) 1987–91 (6 vols); and Sancisi-Weerdenburg, Kuhrt & Root (eds) 1991.

On the **Medes**, see Cuyler Young 1988; Flusin 1999; Lewis 1980 and 1997 (Datis).

On **Zoroastrian religion**, see Boyce 1975/1982/1991; and Godrej & Punthakey Mistree (eds) 2002.

On **women** and **society**, see Brosius 1996.

For **other particular aspects**, see Badian 1998 (Indians in royal service); Balcer 1993 (prosopography); Cook 1985 (rise of Achaemenids); Curtis (ed.) 1997 (Mesopotamia and Iran); Dandamaev 1994 (Media and Iran); Dusinberre 2003 (Sardis); Frye 1964 (kingship); Harmatta (ed.) 1994 (central Asia); Kuhrt 1995 (within the context of Near Eastern history generally); Kuhrt 1988 and Sealey 1976 ('earth and water'); Lewis 1977 (Sparta); Llewellyn-Jones 2002 (eunuchs); Pope 1975/1999 and Robinson 1995 (decipherment of Persian cuneiform); Potts 1999 (Elam, of which Susa was the principal city); Romey & Rose 2001 (an archaeological 'fake', purporting to be the tomb and corpse of an Achaemenid princess); Root 1985 (kingship); Sancisi-Weerdenburg 1999 (Kings and historiography); Sekunda & Warry 1998 (Alexander the Great's campaign against Darius III); Sherwin-White 1978 (diplomacy).

Three Hellas: The Hellenic World in 485

See suggestions for Chapter One. Also Austin 1990 (tyrants); Badian 1994 (Macedonians); Brunt 1953/1993 ('Hellenic League'); Ellinger 2002 (Pan); Evans 1976, Georges 2000, and Murray 1988 (Ionian Revolt).

Four Sparta 485: A Unique Culture and Society

Among **general works** see Cartledge 1979/2001(based originally on 1975 archaeological–historical doctoral dissertation, updated in new edition); Cartledge 1987 (mainly on the period 445–360 but with earlier relevance); Cartledge 2001b (selected essays, both reprinted in updated form and original); Cartledge 2003 (history aimed at the general reader covering esp. the last seven centuries BCE); Cartledge 2004 (the basis of the Epilogue, p. 119–213); Christ 1986/1996 (admirable introductory essay to Christ (ed.) 1986, a fine collection of reprinted essays in German or German translation with excellent bibliography); Clauss 1983 (useful mainly for bibliography); Ducat 1999b (Spartan society and war, one of a series of articles by a leading French expert on ancient Sparta); Ehrenberg 1946: ch. 4 (essay controversially debates whether Sparta was 'totalitarian' or merely authoritarian, still relevant despite heavy overdetermination by original context of publication and miserable personal experience); Fitzhardinge 1980 (a useful and handsomely illustrated survey of Spartan archaeology in the 'Archaic' period, c. 700–500); Forrest 1968/1980 ('This account of Spartan history has not shown much sympathy with Sparta; sympathy is killed by the narrow-minded jealousy she showed for so long to anyone whose power looked like becoming greater than her own and by the utter inhumanity of her behaviour when her own power was supreme [after 404]', p. 152, written in 1967/8); Hooker 1980 (thematically organized, very good on religion); Lazenby 1985 (army, ch. 4 on Thermopylae, an essential preliminary to Lazenby 1993); Lendon 2005: p. 352 n. 20 (Spartan drill); Lewis 1977 (esp. relations with Persia); Ollier 1933–43, Powell & Hodkinson (eds) 1994, Rawson 1969/1991 and Tigerstedt 1965, 1974 (all variously addressed to the Spartan 'myth'); Powell (ed.) 1989 and Powell & Hodkinson (eds) 2002 (two excellent collections of essays, edited by two of the leading British scholars of Sparta); Welwei 2004 (the latest general survey of Spartan history by a well respected senior scholar); and Whitby (ed.) 2001 (imaginatively edited selection of reprinted essays, sometimes abridged and/or translated into English).

Three of the major **Spartan personalities** are the half-brothers King Cleomenes I and his successor Leonidas, and Pausanias the Regent, all from the Agiad royal house: on **Cleomenes,** see Ste Croix 2004 (pp. 438–40 are an editorial Afterword, with bibliography); on **Leonidas,** Baltrusch 1999; Connor 1979 (reburial of remains decades after 480); Grant 1961: pp. 20–4; and Harvey 1979 (was L. somehow implicated in the death of Cleomenes?); on **Pausanias,** there is a huge and growing literature, most recently Ellinger 2005 (the 'other' Pausanias is the 2nd-century CE religious travel writer); see also above, Appendix 1 (Simonides). For possible visual representations, see Krumeich 1997: pp.151–78.

No proper history of Sparta can be written without due attention to the troublesome economic basis of Spartan society and power, the **Helots:** see esp. Ducat 1990 (the first modern general study); Hunt 1997 (part of an immensely original and persuasive attack on the failure of the major Greek historians to give due attention to the role of the unfree in warfare) and 1998 (more controversial attempt to find a major role for Helots at the Battle of Plataea); and Luraghi & Alcock (eds) 2003 (published version of the first major international conference ever dedicated specifically to Helot issues).

No proper history of Sparta can be written, either, without due attention to Spartan **religion**: Parker 1989 is an exemplary account.

Various aspects of **Spartan society and mores** are expertly addressed in the following: David 1992 (hair-dressing and maintenance) and 2004 (suicide, two essays by the leading Israeli scholar of Sparta); Figueira (ed.) 2004 (an admirable collection edited by the leading American scholar of Sparta); Hammond, M. 1980 ('with your shield – or on it!' explained); Hodkinson 2000 (major study of property power); Hornblower 2000 (violence) and Rankin 1993: p. 187 (Sparta a 'society dedicated to the infliction of terror and violence'); Kennell 1995 (history of the timing of introduction of the full-blown educational system, dated rather too late to my mind); Loraux 1995: esp. pp. 70–3, and Piccirilli 1995 (attitudes to death); Miller, W. I. 2000: ch. 2 (the behaviour and fate of Aristodamus, who though one of the 300 did not die at Thermopylae); Richer 1994 and Toher 1999 (burial of kings).

One of the great peculiarities of Sparta was the high status and profile of Spartan **women**, variously accounted for or elaborated on in Blundell 1995: pp. 150–8; Cartledge 1981/2001; Ducat 1998 and 1999a; Hodkinson 2000; Millender 2002 (brilliant study of role played by Athenian ideology); Powell 1999 (political role) and 2004.

Five Thermopylae I: Mobilization

Six Thermopylae II: Preparations for Battle

Seven Thermopylae III: The Battle

I have run together here reading suggestions relating to all stages of the evolution of the Thermopylae scenario. (See also Chapter One, pp. 15–28, for the Graeco-Persian Wars in general.)

For military aspects of the **Graeco-Persian Wars** generally, see De Souza 2003: pp. 54–8; Grundy 1901; Hammond, N. 1988; Hanson 1998 (perhaps our best military historian of Greek antiquity, claims to identify a specifically 'Western' way of warfare, brilliantly exemplified by the Greeks in 480–479),

1999 and 2001 (the first of his nine 'landmark' battles is Salamis); Hignett 1963; Holland 2005 (imaginatively conceived and brilliantly written account by an amateur historian of genius); Lazenby 1993 (with Green 1970/1996, the indispensable basic account); Ober 1990 and Starr 1962/1979 (why did Persia lose?); Pritchett 1971–91 (essays of immense learning and range); Sekunda & Hook 1998 (sound narrative with interestingly colourful artistic recreations); Strauss 2004a (Salamis).

For the **Thermopylae campaign** specifically, see Burn 1968: pp. 88–92, with fig. on p. 89 (eastern arrowheads); Cawkwell 2004; Clarke 2003 (claims unpersuasively that Sparta pushed the warrior ethos beyond the limits of sanity); Dascalakis 1956; Dillery 1996, Flower 1998, Hammond, N. 1996 and Van Wees 2004: pp. 180–3 (historiography – see also Appendix I); Evans 1964 and 1969; Grant 1961; Hodkinson 2000: pp. 157, 158 (Dieneces); Hope Simpson 1972; Strauss 2004b; Thomson 1921; Tuplin 2003 (Xerxes's march from Doriscus to Therme); Whatley 1964 (focused on Marathon but of immensely wider historiographical application, emphasizing just how much – or rather how little – we can ever hope to know about *any* ancient battle).

One of the major issues of scholarly debate concerns the **topography**: Burn 1977: pp. 98–103; Grundy 1929; Kraft et al. 1987 and Szemler, Cherf & Kraft 1996 (sufficiently refuted by Cawkwell 2004: Appendix 5; compare Lazenby *Classical Review* n.s. 48 (1998), 522: 'it will take far better arguments than these to convince me that Leonidas died fighting in a pass that did not exist'); Marinatos 1951 (pp. 61–9, results of 1939 excavation); Pritchett 1958, 1965 (on the battle of 191 BCE; 'It is quite apparent that most of those who write about the battles have never left the carriage roads', p. 71) and 1982 (summation); Wallace 1980 (Anopaea pass). Another major issue is whether Leonidas dismissed the allies before the final battle or they dismissed themselves (i.e. fled or melted away): see, e.g., Dascalakis 1957; Grant 1961 (one of the few to take account of Leonidas's personal and familial situation, though far from entirely persuasively).

A side issue but an engaging one is the alleged medism of **Caryae**, a Perioecic city on the northern border of Laconia: Huxley 1967. 'Caryatids', support columns in the form of women, most famously used in the Erechtheum temple on the Athenian Acropolis, are named after the women of Caryae.

Eight The Thermopylae Legend I: Antiquity

On the Spartan legend (etc.) in antiquity generally, see Ollier 1933–43, the earlier chapters of Rawson 1969, and Tigerstedt 1965, 1974, 1978; in brief, Christ 1986/1996. Also Ehrenberg 1974a (West v. East) and 1974b (freedom). Hölkeskamp 2001 is a comparable study of the legend of Marathon.

Nine The Thermopylae Legend II: From Antiquity to Modernity

The post-Antique reception of ancient Sparta, and of the Thermopylae legend in particular, is richly varied. Barzano et al. (eds) 2003 is a collection of essays looking at the transmission of heroic models from antiquity to modernity; Clough 2004 is a useful overview of the legend from a Western perspective; Rebenich 2004 is an acute account specifically of the German reception, especially historiographical. The later chapters of Rawson 1969 are the best attempt yet at covering the entire post-Antique reception of Sparta within the European, and by extension North American, cultural tradition.

What follows are just some illustrations that I have been able to use in this book: de Botton 2004: pp. 187–8 (brief discussion of Sparta in a chapter entitled 'Ideal Human Types'); Buchan 1912 (short fictional story about a man from the island of Lemnos who gets caught up in the Thermopylae –Artemisium conflict); Byron 1981 (1937) (not Lord Byron, but the twentieth-century Robert Byron, debunker of classicizing pieties and champion of Iranian and Islamic art and culture: 'There are still things to be said about Persepolis', p. 165); Golding 1965 (an occasional piece prompted by a visit to the 'Hot Gates'); Hall & Macintosh (eds) 2005 (Persians and Greeks on the British stage); Hughes (ed.) 1944 (a brave tribute to the brave Greeks of the Second World War, published while Greece was still occupied); Keeley 1999 (reminiscences of literary Greece during the 1930s and 40s, much talk of C. P. Cavafy); Losemann 1977 (Nazi misappropriations); Macgregor Morris 2000a, 2000b, 2004 (eighteenth-century handling of the Thermopylae tradition, especially by Richard Glover); Manfredi 2002 (historical novel by a professional classical archaeologist and historian set in the early fifth century BCE world of Sparta; starts badly, from the manifestly unhistorical premise that the apparently deformed infant son of a noble Spartan family would be exposed in such a manner as to be rescuable by an extreme nationalist Helot family that raises him as a nationalist Helot – to fight, eventually, against his own brother, in the manner of Polynices and Eteocles of ancient Greek myth, and more recently the brothers in Theo Angelopoulos's tragic film *The Weeping Meadow*); Miller, Frank 1998, 1999 (the 'graphic novels' that will be the basis of the movie *300*; cf. Winkler 2000 for a discussion of the Hollywood war-movie genre in its relation to Classical models and inspirations); Montaigne 1991 (his late-sixteenth-century *essais* include 'On the Cannibals' in which, rather surprisingly perhaps, his acute judgement of Thermopylae is to be found, pp. 238–9 of Screech's Penguin Classics edition: 'True victory lies in your role in the conflict, not in coming safely through'); Pinelli 2005 (David's *Léonidas*); and, last but by no means least, Pressfield 1999 (an 'epic' novel is just right; the author has done extensive homework, writes boldly and evocatively, and his imaginative supplements are usually soundly based).

Epilogue Thermopylae: Turning-point in World History

Cartledge 2004 provides full annotation. Most references are of course to be found elsewhere in this book anyway.

Those who wish to pursue the analogy I have tried to develop between the Spartan way of death at Thermopylae and Japanese patriotic suicides at the end of the Second World War may wish to consult a remarkable collection of testimonies by students enlisted in the various Special Attack Units which came to be labelled kamikaze ('divine wind'): *Listen to the Voices from the Sea: Writings of the Fallen Japanese Students* (*Kike Wadatsumi no Koe*), compiled by Nihon Senbotsu Gakusei Kinen-Kai; trans. Midori Yamanouchi and Joseph L. Quinn SJ (Scranton: University of Scranton Press, 2000). For example, Hachiro Sasaki writes on 11 June 1943: 'I wish to die beautifully as a person in the midst of a supreme effort' (cf. Loraux 1995 on the Spartans' 'beautiful death'); but whereas the Spartan 300 were elite soldiers, Sasaki continues, 'As an unknown member of society, my only option is to live and die while remaining faithful to my duties and responsibilities' (both quotations, p. 122). He was killed in action on 14 April 1945 over the Okinawa Sea.

Appendix 1 *and* Appendix 3 – Herodotus

The most accessible and usable **English translation** for non-specialists is probably Herodotus 1996, as corrected and updated by John Marincola. See also Herodotus 2004, revised throughout by Donald Lateiner. Romm ed. 2003 is a good selection in translation with the editor's running commentary. In their excellent recent scholarly commentary on Herodotus Book 9 Flower and Marincola (eds) 2002 deal fully with his account of Plataea, which sealed the Greeks' victory over the invading Persians; see also their Introduction, 20ff., and Appendixes A and D. A commentary of similar quality on Book 7, the Thermopylae book, would be well received.

It is a good index of Herodotus's current 'popularity' among scholars that he has been the subject of no fewer than five major **collective volumes** within the past five years alone: Bakker et al. (eds) 2002; Derow & Parker (eds) 2003; Karageorghis & Taifacos (eds) 2004; Luraghi (ed.) 2001; and Greenwood & Irwin (eds) forthcoming. Major **general works** to be highly recommended include: Gould 1989; Hartog 1988; Lateiner 1989; Munson 2001; and Thomas 2000. Other smaller general studies include: Marincola 2001; Momigliano 1966; Osborne 2002; and Romm 1998. Fehling 1989 should be read only as the curiosity that it is.

The following analyse in close detail, from the point of view of source criticism among others, Herodotus's account of **Thermopylae**: Dillery 1996; Flower 1998; Flower & Marincola (eds) 2002; and Van Wees 2004: p. 180–3.

The following selection will also give some small inkling of the immense range of Herodotus's interests and of the topics on which he has something eminently worth reading: Boedeker 1987a (invention of history) and 1987b (Demaratus); Cartledge 1995 (Greek identity); Dewald 1981 (women); Forrest 1979 (Ionian Revolt); Forsdyke 2001: pp. 341–54, and 2002 (Spartan despotism); Georges 1986 (oracles and credibility); Harrison 2000a (religion); Lévy 1999 (Sparta); Lewis 1997: pp. 345–61 (Persians); Mikalson 2003 (religion); Millender 2002a and 2002b (Spartan despotism); Moles 2002 (H. and Athens); Moyer 2002 (reliability of H. on Egypt defended); Munson 1988 (Artemisia) and 1993 (Spartan kingship); Murray 1987 (oral historiography); Raaflaub 1987 (historiography) and 2002 (H. as intellectual); Redfield 1985 (H. as ethnographer); Stahl, H.-P. 1975 (Croesus's conversations); Waters 1971 (tyrants and despots).

Simonides, the texts are easily accessible in D. A. Campbell's excellent Loeb Classical Library edition and translation. The major event in Simonides studies recently has been the partial recovery on papyrus of his post-epic poem on Plataea, apparently commissioned by the Spartans and for performance at Sparta: Boedeker 1995, 1998a, 1998b: p.190, 2001a, 2001b; Boedeker & Sider (eds) 2001. For a fine pre-discovery account, see Davies, A. 1981 (in a chapter on 'Lyric and Other Poetry'); compare Davies, M. 2004: p. 278 (the story of Simonides's remembering where all the guests had been sitting at a banquet in Thessaly, after the banqueting hall was wrecked by an earthquake and all the guests killed – while Simonides himself was said to have escaped through divine intervention). On the 480 Spartan poems specifically, see Molyneux 1992: pp. 186–7; and Podlecki 1968.

On **Ctesias**, see Auberger 1991; Lenfant 2004 (texts, translation); and Bigwood 1978.

On **Diodorus** (Book XI), see Green 2006 (translation and commentary).

Other sources are Bowen ed. 1992 (Plutarch on the malice of Herodotus); Rood 1999 (Thucydides on the Greco-Persian Wars; cf. Cawkwell 2004); Talbert (ed. and trans.) 2005 (Plutarch and Xenophon on Spartan lives, sayings and society).

Books, Articles, Commentaries, Editions

Abraham, K. 2004 *Business and Politics under the Persian Empire: The Financial Dealings of Marduk-nasir-apli of the House of Egibi (521–487 BCE)* (Bethesda, Md.: Occasional Publications of the Department of Near Eastern Studies and the Program of Jewish Studies, Cornell University)

Allen, L. 2005 *The Persian Empire. A History* (London: British Museum Press)

Auberger, J. 1991 *Ctésias. Histoires de l'Orient* (Paris: Les Belles Lettres)

Austin, M. M. 1990 'Greek tyrants and the Persians, 546–479 BCE' *Classical Quarterly* n.s. 40: 289–306

Badian, E. 1994 'Herodotus on Alexander I of Macedon: a study in some subtle silences' in S. Hornblower (ed.) *Greek Historiography* (Oxford: Oxford University Press) 107–30

1998 'The King's Indians' in W. Will (ed.) *Alexander der Grosse. Eine Welteroberung und ihr Hintergrund* (Bonn: Habelt) 205–24

Bakker, E. J., de Jong, I. J. F. & van Wees, H. 2002 (eds) *Brill's Companion to Herodotus* (Leiden: Brill)

Balcer, J. M. 1989 'The Persian Wars against Greece: a reassessment' *Historia* 38: 127–43

——1993 *A Prosopographical Study of the Ancient Persians Royal and Noble c. 550–450 BC* (Lewiston, New York)

—— 1995 *The Persian Conquest of the Greeks 545–450 BC* (Konstanz: Universitäts-Verlag)

Baltrusch, E. 1999 'Leonidas und Pausanias' in K. Brodersen (ed.) *Grosse Gestalten der griechischen Antike* (Munich: Beck) 310–18

Barzano, A. et al. 2003 (eds) *Modelli eroici dell' antichità alla cultura europea* (Rome: L'Erma di Bretschneider)

Bengtson, H. et al. 1969 *The Greeks and the Persians. From the Sixth to the Fourth Centuries* (London: Weidenfeld & Nicolson) (German original 1965)

Bigwood, J. M. 1978 'Ctesias as historian of the Persian Wars' *Phoenix* 32: 19–41

Blundell, S. 1995 *Women in Ancient Greece* (London: British Museum Press)

Boardman, J. 1988 'The Greek World' *Cambridge Ancient History* plates to vol. IV: 95–178 (Cambridge: Cambridge U.P.)

——1999 *The Greeks Overseas*, 4th edn (London: Thames & Hudson)

—— 2000. *Persia and the West. An Archaeological Investigation of the Genesis of Achaemenid Art* (London: Thames & Hudson)

Boedeker, D. 1987a 'Herodotus and the invention of history' *Arethusa* 20: 5–8

1987b 'The two faces of Demaratus' *Arethusa* 20: 185–201

1995 'Simonides on Plataea: narrative elegy, mythodic history' *Zeitschrift für Papyrologie und Epigraphik* 107: 217–29

—— 1998a 'The New Simonides and heroization at Plataea' in N. Fisher & H. Van Wees (eds) *Archaic Greece: New Approaches and New Evidence* (London: Duckworth) 231–49

—— 1998b 'Presenting the past in fifth-century Athens' in D. Boedeker & K. A. Raaflaub (eds) *Democracy, Empire, and the Arts in Fifth-Century Athens* (Cambridge, Mass., & London: Harvard U.P.) 185–202

—— 2001a 'Heroic historiography: Simonides and Herodotus on Plataea' in Boedeker & Sider (eds) 2001: 120–34

—— 2001b 'Paths to heroization at Plataea' in Boedeker & Sider (eds) 2001: 148–63

—— & Sider, D. 2001 (eds) *The New Simonides: Contexts of Praise and Desire* (Oxford: Oxford U.P.)

de Botton, A. 2004 *Status Anxiety* (London: Hamish Hamilton)

Bowen, A. J. 1992 (ed.) *Plutarch: The Malice of Herodotus* (Warminster: Aris & Phillips)

Boyce, M. 1975/1982/1991 *A History of Zoroastrianism*, 3 vols (Leiden: Brill)

Briant, P. 1989/2002 'History and ideology: the Greeks and Persian "decadence"' in Harrison (ed.) 2002: 193–210

—— 1997–2001 *Bulletin d'histoire achéménide* (I–II) (*TOPOI* suppls 1, 2)

—— 1999 'The Achaemenid Empire' in K. Raaflaub & N. Rosenstein (eds) *War and Society in the Ancient and Medieval Worlds. Asia, the Mediterranean, Europe, and Mesoamerica* (Washington, DC: Center for Hellenic Studies) 105–28

—— 2002 *From Cyrus to Alexander. A History of the Persian Empire* (Eisenbrauns: Winona Lake) (French original 1996)

—— & Herrenschmidt, C. 1989 (eds) *Le Tribut dans l'empire perse* (Paris & Louvain: Peeters)

Brosius, M. 1996. *Women in Ancient Persia (559–331 BCE)* (Oxford: Oxford U.P.)

—— 2000 (ed. and trans.) *The Persian Empire from Cyrus II to Artaxerxes I* (LACTOR 16) (London: London Association of Classical Teachers)

—— 2003 'Reconstructing an archive: account and journal texts from Persepolis' in Brosius (ed.) *Ancient Archives and Archival Traditions. Concepts of Record-Keeping in the Ancient World* (Oxford: Oxford U.P.) 264–83

Brunt, P. A. 1953/1993 'The Hellenic League against Persia', repr. in *Studies in Greek History and Thought* (Oxford: Oxford U.P.) 47–74, with addenda 75–83

Buchan, John 1912 'The Lemnian' in *The Moon Endureth* (London: Hodder & Stoughton) ch. III

Burkert, W. 2004 *Babylon, Memphis, Persepolis: Eastern Contexts of Greek Culture* (Cambridge, Mass.: Harvard U.P.)

Burn, A. R. 1968 *The Warring States of Greece* (London: Thames & Hudson) 88–92

—— 1977 'Thermopylai revisited and some topographical notes on Marathon and Plataiai' in K. H. Kinzl (ed.) *Greece and the Eastern Mediterranean in Ancient History and Prehistory. Studies Presented to Fritz Schachermeyr on his Eightieth Birthday* (Berlin & New York: W. de Gruyter) 89–105, at 98–103

—— 1984 *Persia and the Greeks. The Defence of the West 546–478 BC*, rev. edn (London: Duckworth) (original edn 1962)

Byron, R. 1981 *The Road to Oxiana* (repr. London: Picador) (original edn 1937)

Cambridge Ancient History [*CAH*] 1988 vol. IV, 2nd edn *Persia, Greece and the Western Mediterranean c. 525–479 BC* (Cambridge: Cambridge U.P.) esp. pt I 'The Persian Empire'

Cameron, G. G. 1948 *Persepolis Treasury Tablets* (Chicago: Oriental Institute)

Cardascia, G. 1951 *Les archives de Murashu* (Paris: ??)

Cartledge, P. A. 1979/2001 *Sparta and Lakonia. A Regional History 1300–362 BC*, 2nd edn (Routledge: London & New York)

—— 1981/2001 'Spartan wives: liberation or licence?' *Classical Quarterly* 31: 84–105, updated repr. in Cartledge 2001b: ch. 9

—— 1987 *Agesilaos and the Crisis of Sparta* (London: Duckworth, & Baltimore: Johns Hopkins University Press) (pb repr. 2000)

—— 1995 "We are all Greeks"? Ancient (especially Herodotean) and modern contestations of Hellenism' *Bulletin of the Institute of Classical Studies* 40: 75–82

—— 1998 (ed.) *The Cambridge Illustrated History of Ancient Greece* (Cambridge: Cambridge U.P.) (corrected pb repr. 2002)

—— 2001a *The Greeks. Crucible of Civilization* (London: BBC Books)

—— 2001b *Spartan Reflections* (London: Duckworth, & Berkeley & Los Angeles: University of California Press)

—— 2002 *The Greeks. A Portrait of Self and Others*, 2nd edn (Oxford: Oxford U.P.)

—— 2003 *The Spartans. An Epic History*, 2nd edn London: Pan Macmillan, & New York: Overlook Press)

—— 2004 'What have the Spartans done for us? Sparta's contribution to Western civilization' *Greece & Rome* 2nd ser., 52.2: 164–79

Cawkwell, G. L. 2004 *The Greek Wars. The Failure of Persia* (Oxford: Oxford U.P.)

Christ, K. 1986/1996 'Sparta Forschung und Spartabild. Eine Einleitung' in Christ (ed.) 1986: 1–72, repr. in Christ 1996: 9–57, with addenda 219–21

—— 1996 *Griechische Geschichte und deutsche Geschichtswissenschaft* (Munich: Beck)

—— 1986 (ed.) *Sparta* (Darmstadt: Wissenschaftliches Buchgesellschaft)

Clarke, M. 2003 'Spartan Atê at Thermopylae? Semantics and Ideology at Herodotus, *Histories* 7.223.4' in Powell & Hodkinson (eds) 2002: 63–84

Clauss, M. 1983 *Sparta. Eine Einführung in seine Geschichte und Zivilisation* (Munich: Beck)

Clough, E. 2004 'Loyalty and liberty: Thermopylae in the Western imagination' in Figueira (ed.) 2004: 363–81

Coleman, J. E. & Walz, C. A. 1997 (eds) *Greeks and Barbarians. Essays on the Interactions between Greeks and Non-Greeks in Antiquity and the Consequences for Eurocentrism* (Bethesda, Md.: Occasional Publications of the Department of Near Eastern Studies and the Program of Jewish Studies, Cornell University)

Connor, W. R. 1979 'Pausanias 3.14.1: a sidelight on Spartan history' *Transactions and Proceedings of the American Philological Association* 109: 21–8

Cook, J. M. 1983 *The Persian Empire* (London: Dent)

—— 1985 'The rise of the Achaemenids and establishment of their empire' in *Cambridge History of Iran* vol. 2 (Cambridge: Cambridge U.P.) 200–91

Curtis, J. 2000 *Ancient Persia*, 2nd edn (London: British Museum Press)

—— 1997 (ed.) *Mesopotamia and Iran in the Persian Period: Conquest and Imperialism* (London: British Museum Press)

—— and N. Tallis 2005 (eds) *Forgotten Empire: The World of Ancient Persia* (London: British Museum Press)

Cuyler Young, T., Jr 1980 '480/79 BC – a Persian perspective' *Iranica Antiqua* 15: 213–39

—— 1988 'The early history of the Medes and the Persians and the Achaemenid Empire to the death of Cambyses' and 'The consolidation of the Empire and its limits of growth under Darius and Xerxes' in *Cambridge Ancient History* vol. IV, 2nd edn (Cambridge: Cambridge U.P.) 1–52, 53–111

Dandamaev, M. A. 1989 *A Political History of the Achaemenid Empire* (Leiden: Brill)

—— 1994 'Media and Achaemenid Iran' in Harmatta (ed.) 1994: ch. 2

Dascalakis, A. V. 1956 'Ho agôn tôn Thermopulôn: Hai Dunameis tôn Hellênôn kai hê efthunê tês Spartês' *Athena* 60: 17–68

—— 1957 'Peri ton agôna tôn Thermopylôn. Hê apokhôrêsis tôn summakhôn kai hê thusia tou Leônida' *Platon* 9: 7–46

David, E. 1992 'Sparta's social hair' *Eranos* 90: 11–21

—— 2004 'Suicide in Spartan society' in Figueira (ed.) 2004: 25–46

Davies, Anna 1981 'Lyric and Other Poetry' in M. I. Finley (ed.) *The Legacy of Greece. A New Appraisal* (Oxford: Oxford U.P.) 93–119

Davies, M. 2004 'Simonides and the "Grateful Dead" *Prometheus* 30.3: 275–81

De Souza, P. 2003 *The Greek and Persian Wars 499–386 BC* (Wellingborough: Osprey)

Derow, P. & Parker, R. 2003 (eds) *Herodotus and his World* (Oxford: Oxford U.P.)

Dewald, C. 1981 'Women and culture in Herodotus' *Histories*' in H. Foley (ed.) *Reflections of Women in Antiquity* (New York: Gordon & Breach) 91–125

Dillery, J. 1996 'Reconfiguring the past: Thyrea, Thermopylae and narrative patterns in Herodotus' *American Journal of Philology* 117: 17–54

Drews, R. 1973 *The Greek Accounts of Eastern History* (Washington, DC: Center for Hellenic Studies)

Ducat, J. 1990 *Les hilotes* (*Bulletin de Correspondance Hellénique* suppl. XX) (Paris: Les Belles Lettres)

—— 1998 'La femme de Sparte et la cité' *Ktema* 23: 385–406

—— 1999a 'La femme de Sparte et la guerre' *Pallas* 51: 159–71

—— 1999b 'La société spartiate et la guerre' in F. Prost (ed.) *Armées et sociétés de la Grèce antique. Aspects sociaux et politiques de la guerre aux Ve et IVe siècles avant J.-C.*, 35–50 (Paris: Errance)

Dusinberre, E. R. M. 2003 *Aspects of Empire in Achaemenid Sardis* (Cambridge & New York: Cambridge U.P.)

Ehrenberg, V. 1946 *Aspects of Antiquity* (Oxford: Oxford U.P.)

—— 1974a 'East and West in Antiquity' in Ehrenberg *Man, State and Deity. Essays in Ancient History* (London: Methuen) 1–18

—— 1974b 'Freedom – ideal and reality' in Ehrenberg *Man, State and Deity. Essays in Ancient History* (London: Methuen) 19–34

Ellinger, P. 2002 'Artémis, Pan et Marathon. Mythe, polythéisme et événement historique' in S. des Bouvrie (ed.) *Myth and Symbol* I. *Symbolic Phenomena in Ancient Greek Culture* (Bergen: Norwegian Institute at Athens) 313–32

—— 2005 *La Fin des Maux d'un Pausanias à l'Autre. Essai de mythologie et d'histoire* (Paris: Les Belles Lettres)

Evans, J. A. S. 1964 'The "final problem" at Thermopylae' *Greek, Roman and Byzantine Studies* 5: 231–7

—— 1969 'Notes on Thermopylae and Artemision' *Historia* 18: 389–406

—— 1976 'Herodotus and the Ionian Revolt' *Historia* 25: 31–7

Fehling, D. 1989 *Herodotus and His 'Sources'. Citation, Invention and*

Narrative Art, ed. and trans. J. G. Howie (Leeds: Leeds Latin Seminar) (German original 1971)

Figueira, T. J. 2004 (ed.) *Spartan Society* (Swansea: Classical Press of Wales)

Fisher, N. R. E. 1992 *Hybris. A study in the Values of Honour and Shame* (Warminster: Aris & Phillips)

Fitzhardinge, L. F. 1980 *The Spartans* (London: Thames & Hudson)

Flower, M. A. 1998 'Simonides, Ephorus and Herodotus on the Battle of Thermopylae' *Classical Quarterly* 48: 365–79

—— & Marincola, J. (eds) 2002 *Herodotus Histories: Book IX* (Cambridge: Cambridge U.P.)

Flusin, M. 1999 'Comment les Mèdes ont raconté leur histoire: l'épopée d'Arbacès et le Medikos Logos d'Hérodote' *Ktema* 24: 135–46

Fornara, C. W. 1983 *Archaic Times to the End of the Peloponnesian War*, 2nd edn (Cambridge: Cambridge U.P.)

Forrest, W. G. 1968 *A History of Sparta 950–192 BC* (London: Hutchinson) (repr. Duckworth, 1980, with a new introduction)

—— 1979 'Motivation in Herodotus: the case of the Ionian Revolt' *International History Review* 1: 311–22

Forsdyke, S. 2001 'Athenian democratic ideology and Herodotus' Histories' *American Journal of Philology* 122: 333–62

—— 2002 'Herodotus on Greek history, c. 525–480 BC' in *Brill's Companion to Herodotus*, ed. E. J. Bakker et al. (Leiden) 521–49

Frankfort, H. 1970 'The art of Ancient Persia' in *The Art and Architecture of the Ancient Orient*, 4th impr. (Harmondsworth: Penguin) ch. 12

Freeman, C. 1999 *The Greek Achievement* (Oxford: Oxford U.P.)

French, D. H. 1998 'Pre- and early-Roman roads of Asia Minor' *Iran* 36: 15–43

Frye, R. N. 1963 *The Heritage of Persia* (New York: World Publishing Co.)

—— 1964 'The charisma of kingship in ancient Iran' *Iranica Antiqua* 4: 36–54

—— 1984 *History of Ancient Iran* (Munich: Beck)

Georges, P. 1986 'Saving Herodotus's phenomena. The oracles and events of 480 BC' *Classical Antiquity* 5: 14–59

—— 1994 *Barbarian Asia and the Greek Experience. From the Archaic Period to the Age of Xenophon* (Baltimore & London: Johns Hopkins U.P.)

—— 2000 'Persian Ionia under Darius: the Revolt reconsidered' *Historia* 49: 1–39

Gershevitch, I. 1985 (ed.) *The Cambridge History of Iran: The Median and Achaemenian Periods* (Cambridge: Cambridge U.P.)

Ghirshman, R. 1971 'The classical age' in Ghirshman, R., Minorsky, V. & Sanghvi, W. *Persia. The Immortal Kingdom* (London: Orient Commerce Establishment) 20–97

Godrej, P. J. & Punthakey Mistree, F. 2002 (eds) *A Zoroastrian Tapestry* (Ahmedabad: Mapin)

Golding, William 1965 'The Hot Gates' in *The Hot Gates and Other Occasional Pieces* (New York: Harcourt Brace Jovanovich) 13–20

Gould, J. 1989 *Herodotus* (London: Weidenfeld & Nicolson)

Graf, D. F. 1994 'The Persian Royal Road system' *Achaemenid History* 8: 167–89

Grant, J. R. 1961 'Leonidas' last stand' *Phoenix* 15: 14–27

Green, P. 1970/1996 *The Greco-Persian Wars*, new edn (California & London: University of California Press)

—— 1970/1996 *The Year of Salamis 480–479* BC (London: Weidenfeld & Nicolson) = *The Greco-Persian Wars* (Berkeley, Los Angeles & London: University of California Press)

—— 2006 *Diodorus Siculus, Book 11–12.37.1 Greek History, 480–431* BC – *the Alternative Version* (Austin, Tex.: University of Texas P.)

Greenwood, E. & Irwin, E. forthcoming (eds) *Reading Herodotus: The Logoi of Book V* (Cambridge: Cambridge U.P.)

Grote, G. 1846–56 *History of Greece*, 12 vols (London: John Murray)

Grundy, G. B. 1901 *The Great Persian War and Its Preliminaries: A Study* of the Evidence, Literary and Topographical (London: John Murray)

—— 1929 'Thermopylae' (lecture, 12 April 1912) in H. Lunn (ed.) *Aegean Civilizations* (London: Epworth Press) 201–17

Hall, E. 1989 *Inventing the Barbarian. Greek Self-definition Through Tragedy* (Oxford: Oxford U.P.)

—— 1996 (ed.) *Aeschylus: Persians* (Warminster: Aris & Phillips)

—— & Macintosh, F. 2005 *Greek Tragedy and the British Theatre 1660–1914* (Oxford: Oxford U.P.)

Hall, J. M. 1997 *Ethnic Identity in Greek Antiquity* (Cambridge: Cambridge U.P.)

—— 2002 *Hellenicity: Between Ethnicity and Culture* (Chicago: University of Chicago Press)

Hallock, R. T. 1969 *Persepolis Fortification Tablets* (Chicago: University of Chicago Press)

—— 1972 *The Evidence of the Persepolis Tablets* (Cambridge: Cambridge U.P.)

Hammond, M. 1980 'A famous exemplum of Spartan toughness' *Classical Journal* 75: 97–109

Hammond, N. 1988 'The Expedition of Xerxes' *Cambridge Ancient History* [*CAH*] vol. IV, 2nd edn, *Persia, Greece and the Western Mediterranean c. 525–479 BC* (Cambridge: Cambridge U.P.) ch. 10, at 546–63, with map at 556, fig. 46

—— 1996 'Sparta at Thermopylae' *Historia* 45: 1–20

Hanson, V. D. 1998 *The Western Way of War. Infantry Battle in Classical Greece*, new edn (California & London: University of California Press)

—— 1999 *The Wars of the Ancient Greeks and Their Invention of Western Military Culture* (London: Cassell)

—— 2001 *Carnage and Culture. Landmark Battles in the Rise of Western Power* (New York: Doubleday)

Harmatta, J. (ed.) 1994 *History of Civilizations of Central Asia* II. *The Development of Sedentary and Nomadic Civilizations: 700 BC to AD 250* (Paris: UNESCO)

Harrison, T. 2000a *Divinity and History: The Religion of Herodotus* (Oxford: Oxford U.P.)

—— 2000b *The Emptiness of Asia. Aeschylus' Persians and the History of the Fifth Century* (London: Duckworth)

—— 2002 'The Persian Invasions' in *Brill's Companion to Herodotus*, ed. E. J. Bakker et al. (eds) (Leiden) 551–78

—— 2002 (ed.) *Greeks and Barbarians* (Edinburgh: Edinburgh U.P.)

Hartog, F. 1988 *The Mirror of Herodotus. An Essay on the Interpretation of the Other* (Berkeley: University of California Press) (original French edn 1980, rev. 1991)

Harvey, F. D. 1979 'Leonidas the regicide? Speculations on the death of Kleomenes I' in *Arktouros. Fest. B.M.W. Knox* (Berlin & New York: W. de Gruyter) 253–60

Herodotus 1996 *The Histories*, trans. A. de Sélincourt, rev. edn J. Marincola (London: Penguin)

—— 2004 *The Histories*, trans. G. C. Macaulay, rev. edn by D. Lateiner (New York: Barnes & Noble)

Herrenschmidt, C. 1996/2000 'Old Persian cuneiform: writing as cosmological ritual and text' in J. Bottéro, C. Herrenschmidt, & J.-P. Vernant *Ancestor of the West: Writing, Reasoning and Religion in Mesopotamia, Elam and Greece* (Chicago & London: University of Chicago Press) 108–25

Herzfeld, E. 1968 *The Persian Empire. Studies in Geography and Ethnography of the Ancient Near East* (Wiesbaden: Franz Steiner)

Hignett, C. 1963 *Xerxes' Invasion of Greece* (Oxford: Oxford U.P.)

Hodkinson, S. 2000 *Property and Wealth in Classical Sparta* (London: Duckworth & Classical Press of Wales)

Hölkeskamp, K.-J. 2001 'Marathon – vom Monument zum Mythos' in D. Papenfuss and V. M. Strocka (eds) *Gab es das Griechischer Wunder? Griechenland zwischen dem Ende des 6. und der mitte des 5. Jahrhunderts v. Chr.* (Mainz: Philipp von Zabern) 329–53

Holland, Tom 2005 *Persian Fire. The First World Empire and the Battle for the West* (London: Little, Brown)

Hooker, J. T. 1980 *The Ancient Spartans* (London: Dent)

Hope Simpson, R. 1972 'Leonidas' decision' *Phoenix* 26: 1–11

Hornblower, S. 2000 'Sticks, stones and Spartans: the sociology of Spartan violence' in H. van Wees (ed.) *War and Violence in Ancient Greece* (London: Duckworth & Classical Press of Wales) 57–82

—— 2001 'Greeks and Persians. West against East' in A. V. Hartmann & B. Heuser (eds) *War, Peace and World Orders in European History* (London & New York: Routledge) 48–61

Hughes B. 2005 *Helen of Troy: Goddess, Princess, Whore* (London: Cape)

Hughes, H. 1944 (ed.) *The Glory That Is Greece* (London: Hutchinson)

Hunt, P. 1997 'Helots at the battle of Plataea' *Historia* 46: 129–44

—— 1998 *Slaves, Warfare and Ideology in the Greek Historians* (Cambridge: Cambridge U.P.)

Huxley, G. L. 1967 'The medism of Caryae' *Greek, Roman and Byzantine Studies* 8: 29–32

Karageorghis, V. & Taifacos, I. 2004 (eds) *The World of Herodotus* (Nicosia: A. G. Leventis Foundation)

Kebric, R. B. 1997 *Greek People*, 2nd edn (Mountainview, Calif.: Mayfield)

Keeley, E. 1999 *Inventing Paradise. The Greek Journey 1937–1947* (Farrar, Straus, Giroux: New York)

Kennell, N. M. 1995 *The Gymnasium of Virtue. Education and Culture in Ancient Sparta* (Chapel Hill & London: University of North Carolina Press)

Kent, R. G. 1953 *Old Persian. Grammar, Texts, Lexicon, 2nd edn* (New Haven: Yale U.P.)

Khan, H. A. 1993 (ed.) *The Birth of the European Identity* (Nottingham: Nottingham Classical Literature Studies 2)

Konstan, D. 1987 'Persians, Greeks and empire' *Arethusa* 20: 59–73

Kraft, J. C., Rapp, G. R., Szemler, G. J., Tziavos, C., and Kase, E. W. 1987 'The pass at Thermopylae' *Journal of Field Archaeology* 14: 181–98

Krumeich, R. 1997 *Bildnisse Griechischer Herrscher und Staatsmänner im 5. Jahrhundert v. Chr.* (Munich: Biering & Brinkmann)

Kuhrt, A. 1988 'Earth and Water' *Achaemenid History* 3: 87–99

—— 1995 *The Ancient Near East, c. 3000–330 BC*, 2 vols (London & New York: Routledge)

Laroche, L. 1971/1974 *Monuments of Civilization. The Middle East* (London: Cassell)

Lateiner, D. 1989 *The Historical Method of Herodotus* (Toronto: University of Toronto Press)

Lazenby, J. F. 1985 *The Spartan Army* (Warminster: Aris & Phillips)

— 1993 *The Defence of Greece, 490–479 BC* (Warminster: Aris & Phillips) 130–48

Lendon, J. E. 2005 *Soldiers and Ghosts. A History of Battle in Classical Antiquity* (New Haven & London: Yale U.P.)

Lenfant, D. 2004 Ctésias de Cnide, La Perse, L'Inde, Autres Fragments (Paris: Les Belles Lettres)

Lévy, E. 1999 'La Sparte d'Hérodote' *Ktema* 24: 125–34

Lewis, D. M. 1977 *Sparta and Persia* (Leiden: Brill)

— 1980 'Datis the Mede' *Journal of Hellenic Studies* 100: 194–5 (repr. in Lewis 1997: 342–4)

— 1994 'The Persepolis tablets: speech, seal and script' in A. K. Bowman & G. Woolf (eds) *Literacy and Power in the Ancient World* (Cambridge: Cambridge U.P.) 17–32

— 1997 *Selected Papers in Greek and Near Eastern History*, ed. P. J. Rhodes (Cambridge: Cambridge U.P.) chs 31 'The Persepolis Fortification Texts' (325–31) and 34 'Persians in Herodotus' (345–61)

Llewellyn-Jones, L. 2002 'Eunuchs and the royal harem in Achaemenid Persia' in S. Tougher (ed.) *Eunuchs in Antiquity and Beyond* (London: Duckworth) 19–49

Lockhart, L. & Boyle, J. A. 1978 'The beginnings: the Achaemenids' in Boyle (ed.) *Persia: History and Heritage* (London: Henry Melland) 17–23

Loraux, N. 1995 'The Spartans' "beautiful death"' (1977) in *The Experiences of Tiresias. The Feminine and the Greek Man* (Princeton & Chichester: Princeton University Press) 63–74

Losemann, V. 1977 *Nationalsozialismus und Antike. Studien zur Entwicklung des Faches Alte Geschichte 1933–1945* (Hamburg: Hoffmann & Campe)

Loukonine, V. and Ivanov, A. 1996/2003 *Persian Art* (Sirocco: London)

Luraghi, N. 2001 (ed.) *The Historian's Craft in the Age of Herodotus* (Oxford: Oxford U.P.)

—— & Alcock, S.E. 2003 (eds) *Helots and Their Masters in Laconia and Messenia* (Cambridge, Mass.: Harvard U.P.)

Macgregor Morris, I. 2000a 'The Age of Leonidas' (unpublished PhD dissertation, University of Manchester)

—— 2000b '"To make a new Thermopylae": Hellenism, Greek liberation and the Battle of Thermopylae' *Greece & Rome* 47.2: 211–30

—— 2004 'The paradigm of democracy: Sparta in Enlightenment thought' in Figueira (ed.) 2004: 339–62

Malkin, I. 2004 'Postcolonial concepts and ancient Greek colonization' *Modern Language Quarterly* 65.3: 341–64

—— 2001 (ed.) *Ancient Perceptions of Greek Ethnicity* (Cambridge, Mass.: Harvard U.P.)

Manfredi, V. M. 2002 *Spartan* (London: Macmillan) (Italian original 1988)

Marinatos, Sp. 1951 *Thermopylae. An Historical and Archaeological Guide* (Athens: Greek Archaeological Service)

Marincola, J. 2001 'Herodotus' in *Greek Historians* (*Greece & Rome* New Surveys in the Classics 31: Oxford) 19–60

Mikalson, J. D. 2003 *Herodotus and Religion in the Persian Wars* (Durham, NC: University of North Carolina Press)

Millender, E. G. 2002 'Athenian ideology and the empowered Spartan woman' in S. Hodkinson & A. Powell (eds) *Sparta. New Perspectives* (London: Duckworth & Classical Press of Wales) 355–91

—— 2002a 'Herodotus and Spartan despotism' in A. Powell and S. Hodkinson (eds) *Sparta beyond the Mirage* (London: Duckworth & Classical Press of Wales 1–62

—— 2002b 'Nomos Despotes: Spartan obedience and Athenian lawfulness in fifth-century Greek thought', in E. Robinson and V. Gorman (eds) *Oikistes: Studies in Constitutions, Colonies, and Military Power in the Ancient World Offered in Honor of A. J. Graham* (Leiden: Brill) 33–59

Miller, Frank with Lynn Varley 1998, 1999 *300* (Milwaukie, Ore.: Dark Horse Books)

Miller, M. C. 1997 *Athens and Persia in the Fifth Century* BC. *A Study in Receptivity* (Cambridge: Cambridge U.P.)

Miller, W. I. 2000 *The Mystery of Courage* (Cambridge, Mass.: Harvard U.P.)

Moles, J. L. 2002 'Herodotus and Athens' in *Brill's Companion to Herodotus*, ed. E. J. Bakker et al. (Leiden: Brill) 33–52

Molyneux, J. H. 1992 *Simonides. A Historical Study* (Wauconda, Ill.: Bolchazy-Carducci)

Momigliano, A. D. 1966 'The place of Herodotus in the history of historiography' (1958) repr. in his *Studies in Historiography* (London: Weidenfeld & Nicolson) 127–42

—— 1975. *Alien Wisdom. The Limits of Hellenization* (Cambridge: Cambridge U.P.)

Montaigne, M. de 1991 *The Complete Essays*, ed. M. A. Screech (Harmondsworth: Penguin)

Moorey, P. R. S. 1988 'The Persian Empire' *Cambridge Ancient History* plates to vol. IV: 1–94 (Cambridge: Cambridge U.P.)

Moyer, I. S. 2002 'Herodotus and an Egyptian mirage: the genealogies of the Theban priests' *Journal of Hellenic Studies* 122: 70–90

Munson, R. V. 1988 'Artemisia in Herodotus' *Classical Antiquity* 7: 91–106

—— 1993 'Three aspects of Spartan kingship in Herodotus' in R. Rosen & J. Farrell (eds) *NOMODEIKTES. Fest. M. Ostwald* (Ann Arbor: University of Michigan Press) 39–54

—— 2001 *Telling Wonders. Ethnographic and Political Discourse in the Work of Herodotus* (Ann Arbor: University of Michigan Press)

Murray, O. 1987 'Herodotus and oral history' in Sancisi-Weerdenburg & Kuhrt (eds) vol. 2: 93–115 (repr. in Luraghi ed. 2001: 314–25)

—— 1988 'The Ionian Revolt' in *Cambridge Ancient History* vol. IV, 2nd edn: 461–90

Nylander, C. 1970 *Ionians in Pasargadae. Studies in Old Persian Architecture* (Uppsala: Acta Universitatis Upsaliensis)

Ober, J. 1990 'Xerxes of Persia and the Greek Wars: why the big battalions lost' in B. S. Strauss & J. Ober *The Anatomy of Error. Ancient Military Disasters and Their Lessons for Modern Strategists* (New York: St Martin's) 17–43

Ollier, F. 1933–43 *Le mirage spartiate. étude sur l'idéalisation de Sparte dans l'antiquité grecque*, 2 vols (Paris: de Boccard) (repr. in 1 vol., Chicago: Ares Press, 1973)

Olmstead, A. T. 1948 *History of the Persian Empire* (Chicago: University of Chicago Press)

Osborne, R. G. 1996 *Greece in the Making 1200–479 BCE* (London: Methuen)

—— 2002 'Archaic Greek history' in *Brill's Companion to Herodotus*, E. J. Bakker et al. (eds) (Leiden:Brill) 497–509

Parker, R. 1989 'Spartan religion' in A. Powell (ed.) *Classical Sparta: Techniques behind Her Success* (London: Routledge) 142–72

Pelling, C. B. R. 1997 'East is east and west is west – or are they? National stereotypes in Herodotus' *Histos* 1 (March) http://www.dur.ac.uk /Classics/histos/1997/pelling.html

Petit, T. 1990 S*atrapes et satrapies dans l'empire Achéménide de Cyrus le Grand à Xerxès Ier* (Paris: Les Belles Lettres)

Piccirilli, L. 1995 'L'ideale Spartano della morte eroica: crisi e trasformazione' *Annali della Scuola Normale di Pisa* 115: 525–41

Pinelli, A. 2005 *David* (Milan: 5 Continents Editions)

Podlecki, A. J. 1968 'Simonides: 480' *Historia* 17: 257–75

Pope, M. 1975/1999 *The Story of Decipherment. From Egyptian Hieroglyphic to Linear B*, rev. edn (London: Thames & Hudson)

Potts, D. T. 1999 *The Archaeology of Elam. Formation and Transformation of an Ancient Iranian State* (Cambridge: Cambridge U.P.)

Powell, A. 1999 'Spartan women assertive in politics? Plutarch's Lives of Agis and Kleomenes' in S. Hodkinson & A. Powell (eds) *Sparta. New Perspectives* (London: Duckworth & Classical Press of Wales) 393–419

—— 2004 'The women of Sparta – and of other Greek cities – at war' in Figueira (ed.) 2004: 137–50

—— 1989 (ed.) *Classical Sparta: Techniques behind Her Success* (London: Routledge)

—— & Hodkinson, S. 1994 (eds) *The Shadow of Sparta* (Swansea: Classical Press of Wales)

—— & Hodkinson, S. 2002 (eds) *Sparta: Beyond the Mirage* (Swansea: Classical Press of Wales)

Pressfield, Steven 1999 *Gates of Fire. An Epic Novel on the Battle of Thermopylae* (London: Doubleday) (original US edn 1998)

Pritchett, W. K. 1958 'New light on Thermopylae' *American Journal of Archaeology* 62: 203–13

—— 1965 'The Battle of Thermopylae in 191 BC' *Studies in Ancient Greek Topography* vol. 1 (Berkeley, Los Angeles & London: University of California Press) 71–82

—— 1971–91 *The Greek State at War*, 5 vols (California & London: University of California Press)

—— 1982 'Herodotos and his critics on Thermopylae' *Studies in Ancient Greek Topography* vol. 4 (Berkeley, Los Angeles & London: University of California Press) 176–210

Raaflaub, K. A. 1987 'Herodotus, political thought, and the meaning of history' *Arethusa* 20: 221–48

—— 2002 'Philosophy, science, politics: Herodotus and the intellectual trends of his time' in Bakker et al. (eds) 2002: 149–86

Rankin, H. D. 1993 'Achilles and the Terrorist' *Multarum Artium Scientia. Fest. R. Godfrey Tanner* (*Prudentia* suppl. vol.) 182–9

Rawson, E. 1969 *The Spartan Tradition in European Thought* (Oxford: Oxford U.P.) (pb repr. with preface by K. Thomas 1991)

Ray, J. D. 2001 *Reflections of Osiris* (London: Profile)

Rebenich, S. 2004 'From Thermopylae to Stalingrad: the myth of Leonidas in German historiography' in Figueira (ed.) 2004: 323–49

Redfield, J. M. 1985 'Herodotus the tourist' *Classical Philology* 80: 97–118

Richer, N. 1994 'Aspects des funérailles à Sparte' *Cahiers du Centre Glotz* 5: 51–96

Robinson, A. 1995 *The Story of Writing* (London: Thames & Hudson)

Romey, K. M. & Rose, M. 2001 'Saga of the Persian Princess' *Archaeology* (Jan.–Feb.): 24–5

Romm, J. S. 1998 *Herodotus* (New Haven: Yale U.P.)

—— 2003 (ed.) *Herodotus on the War for Greek Freedom. Selections from the Histories*, trans. S. Shirley (Indianapolis, Ind.: Hackett)

Rood, T. 1999 'Thucydides' Persian Wars' in C. S. Kraus (ed.) *The Limits of Historiography. Genre and Narrative in Ancient Historical Texts* (Leiden: Brill) 141–68

Root, M. C. 1979 *The King and Kingship in Achaemenid Art. Essays on the Creation of an Iconography of Empire* (Leiden: Brill)

—— 1985 'The Parthenon frieze and the Apadana reliefs at Persepolis: reassessing a programmatic relationship' *American Journal of Archaeology* 89: 103–20

Ste Croix, G. E. M. de 2004 'Herodotus and King Cleomenes I of Sparta' in his *Athenian Democratic Origins and Other Essays*, ed. D. Harvey & R. Parker (Oxford: Oxford U.P.) 421–40

Sancisi-Weerdenburg, H. 1983 'Exit Atossa: images of women in Greek historiography on Persia' in A. Cameron & A. Kuhrt (eds) *Images of Women in Antiquity* (Routledge: London & New York) 20–33 (new edn 1993)

—— 1989/2002 'The personality of Xerxes, King of Kings' 1989 repr. in E. J. Bakker et al. (eds) *Brill's Companion to Herodotus* (Brill: Leiden) 579–90

—— 1999 'The Persian kings and history' in C. S. Kraus (ed.) *The Limits of Historiography. Genre and Narrative in Ancient Historical Texts* (Leiden: Brill) 91–112

—— & Kuhrt, A. 1987–91 (eds) *Achaemenid History*, 6 vols (Brill: Leiden)

—— Kuhrt, A. & Root, M. C. 1991 (eds) *Achaemenid History*, vol. 8 (Leiden: Brill)

Schmandt-Bessarat, D. 1980 (ed.) *Ancient Persia. The Art of an Empire* (Malibu, Calif.: Getty Center)

Sealey, R. 1976 'The pit and the well: the Persian heralds of 491 BC' *Classical Journal* 72: 13–20

Sekunda, N. & Chew, S. 1992 *The Persian Army 560–330 BC* (Wellingborough: Osprey)

—— & Hook, R. 1998 *The Spartan Army* (Wellingborough: Osprey)

—— & Warry, J. 1998 *Alexander the Great. His Armies and Campaigns 334–323 BC* (Wellingborough: Osprey)

Sherwin-White, S. M. 1978 'Hand-tokens and Achaemenid practice' *Iran* 16: 183

Stahl, H.-P. 1975 'Learning through suffering? Croesus' conversations in the History of Herodotus' *Yale Classical Studies* 24: 1–36

Starr, C. G. 1962/1979 'Why did the Greeks defeat the Persians?' repr. in *Essays on Ancient History*, ed. A. Ferrill and T. Kelly (Leiden: Brill) 193–204

Stolper, M. W. 1985 *Entrepreneurs and Empire: the Murashu Archive, the Murashu Firm and Persian Rule in Babylonia* (Istanbul: Netherlands Historical-Archaeological Institute)

Strauss, B. S. 2004a *Salamis. The Greatest Naval Battle of the Ancient World, 480 BC* (New York: Simon & Schuster)

—— 2004b 'Thermopylae. Death of a king, birth of a legend' *Military History Quarterly* (autumn): 17–25

Stronach, D. 1978 *Pasargadae* (Oxford: Oxford U.P.)

Stronk, J. 1990–1 'Sparta and Persia' *Talanta* 22–3: 117–36

Szemler, G., Cherf, W. & Kraft, J. 1996 *Thermopylai. Myth and Reality in 480 BC* (Chicago: Ares)

Talbert, R. 2005 (ed. and trans.) *Plutarch on Sparta*, 2nd edn (London: Penguin)

Thomas, R. 2000 *Herodotus in Context. Ethnography, Science and the Art of Persuasion* (Cambridge: Cambridge U.P.)

Thomson, J. A. K. 1921 'Keeping the pass' in *Greeks and Barbarians* (London: Allen & Unwin) 32–44

Tigerstedt, E. N. 1965, 1974, 1978 *The Legend of Sparta in Classical Antiquity*, 2 vols + index vol. (Stockholm etc: Almqvist & Wiksell)

Tod, M. N. 1944 'Retrospect' in H. Hughes (ed.) *The Glory That Is Greece* (London: Hutchinson) 146–50

Toher, M. 1999 'On the *Eidolon* of a Spartan king' *Rheinisches Museum für Philologie* 142: 113–27

Tuplin, C. J. 1987 'The administration of the Achaemenid Empire' in I. Carradice (ed.) *Coinage and Administration in the Athenian and Persian Empires* (Oxford: British Archaeological Reports 334) 109–66

—— 1998 'The seasonal migration of Achaemenid kings: a report on old and new evidence' in M. Brosius and A. Kuhrt (eds) *Achaemenid History* XI. *Studies in Persian History. Essays in Memory of David M. Lewis* (Leiden: Brill) 63–114

—— 2003 'Xerxes' march from Doriscus to Therme' *Historia* 52: 385–409

Van Wees H. 2004 *Greek Warfare. Myths and Realities* (London: Duckworth)

Wallace, P. W. 1980 'The Anopaia path at Thermopylae' *American Journal of Archaeology* 84: 115–23

Walser, G. 1984 *Hellas und Iran: Studien zu den griechisch-persischen Beziehungen vor Alexander* (Darmstadt: Wissenschaftliches Buchgesellschaft)

Waters, K. H. 1971 *Herodotus on Tyrants and Despots: A Study in Objectivity* (Wiesbaden: Steiner)

Welwei, K.-W. 2004 *Sparta. Aufstieg und Niedergang einer antiken Grossmacht* (Stuttgart: Klett-Cotta)

West, M. L. 1997 *The East Face of Helicon* (Oxford: Oxford U.P.)

Whatley, N. 1964 'On the possibility of reconstructing Marathon and other ancient battles' *Journal of Hellenic Studies* 84: 119–39

Wheeler, Mortimer 1968 *Flames over Persepolis. Turning-point in History* (New York: Reynal & Co.)

Whitby, M. 2001 (ed.) *Sparta* (Edinburgh: Edinburgh U.P.)

Wiesehöfer, J. 1994/2001 *Das antike Persien. Von 550 v. Chr. bis 650 n. Chr.* (Munich & Zurich: Artemis), Eng. trans. *Ancient Persia from 550 BC to AD 650* (London & New York: I. B. Tauris)

Winkler, M. 2000 '*Dulce et decorum est pro patria mori?* Classical literature in the war film' *International Journal of the Classical Tradition* 7.2: 177–214

Videos and Websites

The Greek and Persian Wars, Cromwell Productions Ltd,
www.cromwelledu.com

'Decisive Battles' – *Thermopylae,* Paradine Productions

http://uts.cc.utexas.edu/sparta/topics/300.htm

http://www.aint-it-cool.com/display.cgi?id=4969

http://www.night-flight.com/fmiller300.html (comic strip version of the battle)

http://www.encyclopedia.com/html/T/Thermopy.asp

http://www.rhul.ac.uk/Classics/NJL/novels.html (Dr N. J. Lowe's listing of 'Ancient Greece in Fiction') pp. 6–7 for novels and short stories on the Graeco-Persian Wars

http://www.csun.edu/hcfll004/sparta.html (Prof. J. P. Adams)

http://playlab.uconn.edu/pylae22k.htm (Prof. A. Yiannakis's expedition to determine Anopaea route)

References

Prologue
1 Pindar fragment 110.

Chapter One
1 Herodotus 1.152–3.

Chapter Two
1 Herodotus 8.126.
2 Herodotus 7.66.
3 Chs 89ff.
4 Brosius 2000: no. 46.
5 Esther 1:5–7.
6 Herodotus 3.89.
7 Herodotus 5.52.
8 Herodotus 8.98.
9 Brosius 2000: no. 198, after Fornara 1983: no. 35, slightly modified.
10 Brosius 2000: no. 91.

Chapter Three
1 Herodotus 5.97.
2 Herodotus 6.89.
3 Herodotus 6.43.
4 Herodotus 8.30.
5 Herodotus 8.144.2.
6 Herodotus 3.38.

Chapter Four
1 Herodotus 5.49.
2 Herodotus 6.82.
3 Herodotus 9.7; compare 5.63.
4 Tyrtaeus fragment 12.11–14.

Chapter Five
1 Herodotus 7.102.
2 Herodotus 7.133.
3 Herodotus 1.151.
4 Herodotus 7.61.
5 Herodotus 7.74.
6 Herodotus 8.3.3.
7 Herodotus 7.49.

Chapter Seven
1 Trans. A. de Sélincourt.

Chapter Eight
1 Herodotus 7.139.
2 *Tusculan Disputations* 1.01.
3 *Odes* 3.2.13.
4 Lines 97–8.

Chapter Nine
1 Trans. M. A. Screech.
2 From *Dialogue* XL, in my translation.
3 Trans. Rebenich.
4 Trans. Rebenich.

Epilogue
1 Herodotus 8.27.1.

Index

```
             IHOP #1553
          7500 Menaul Blvd , NE
            ATbuquerque, NM
            (505) 830 - 4467
           Have a GREAT Day!
Date:          Jul01'08·02·08AM
Card Type:     Visa/M.C.
Acct #:        XXXXXXXXXXXX8402
Trans Key:     EIF600667828339
Exp Date:      XX/XX
Auth Code:     760564
Check:         479
Table:         27/1
Server:        169 RON G

Subtotal:              4.47

Tip:

Total:


_____
                      Signature
      I agree to pay above total
    according to my card agreement.
       ***GUEST COPY***
```

ALSO BY PAUL CARTLEDGE

ALEXANDER THE GREAT

Alexander the Great is the towering hero of the classical world: a fearless general, the conqueror of the Persians, and the visionary ruler of a vast empire. In this seminal biography, Paul Cartledge gives us the most reliable and intimate portrait of the man himself. Cartledge brilliantly evokes Alexander's remarkable political and military accomplishments, cutting through the myths to show why he was such a great leader. He explores our endless fascination with Alexander and gives us insight into his charismatic leadership, his capacity for brutality, and his sophisticated grasp of international politics. As he brings Alexander vividly to life, Cartledge also captures his enduring impact on world history and culture.

History/Biography/978-1-4000-7919-3

THE SPARTANS
The World of the Warrior-Heroes of Ancient Greece

The Spartans were a society of warrior-heroes who were the living exemplars of such core values as duty, discipline, self-sacrifice, and extreme toughness. This book, written by one of the world's leading experts on Sparta, traces the rise and fall of Spartan society and explores the tremendous influence the Spartans had on their world and even on ours. Paul Cartledge brings to life figures like legendary founding father Lycurgus and King Leonidas, who embodied the heroism so closely identified with this unique culture, and he shows how Spartan women enjoyed an unusually dominant and powerful role in this hyper-masculine society. Based firmly on original sources, *The Spartans* is the definitive book about one of the most fascinating cultures of ancient Greece.

History/Ancient Greece/978-1-4000-7885-1

VINTAGE BOOKS
Available at your local bookstore, or visit www.randomhouse.com.